THE ARCHITECTURAL HISTORY OF
KING'S COLLEGE CHAPEL

1 King's College Chapel
from the south-west

FRANCIS WOODMAN

THE ARCHITECTURAL HISTORY OF
KING'S COLLEGE CHAPEL

AND ITS PLACE IN THE DEVELOPMENT OF LATE GOTHIC ARCHITECTURE
IN ENGLAND AND FRANCE

ROUTLEDGE & KEGAN PAUL

LONDON, BOSTON AND HENLEY

To M. H. J.

First published in 1986
by Routledge & Kegan Paul plc

14 Leicester Square, London WC2H 7PH, England

9 Park Street, Boston, Mass. 02108, USA and

Broadway House, Newtown Road,
Henley on Thames, Oxon RG9 1EN, England

Set in Monophoto Imprint
and printed in Great Britain
by BAS Printers Limited,
Over Wallop, Hampshire

Library of Congress Cataloging in Publication Data

Woodman, Francis, 1948–

The architectural history of King's College Chapel
and its place in the development of late Gothic
architecture in England and France.
Bibliography : p.
Includes index.
1. Kings College (University of Cambridge). Chapel.
2. Architecture, Gothic—England—Cambridge
(Cambridgeshire) 3. Cambridge (Cambridgeshire)—
Buildings, structures, etc. I. Title.
NA5471.C15W6   1986   726'.5'0942659   85-19322

ISBN 0-7100-9871-5

By the same author
The Architectural History of Canterbury Cathedral

CONTENTS

Appendixes

FIGURES

PREFACE

When I first began the architectural history of King's College Chapel I was asked how I could possibly write a book about a building that did exactly the same thing, twelve times in a row. I knew even then that the problem would be quite the reverse. Considering that we still know comparatively little about the actual process of design and construction in the Middle Ages, King's College Chapel presents us, quite simply, with the most complete, the most fascinating and the most rewarding exposition that we could ask for. That it is also one of the most magnificent buildings in the world is a mere bonus. The fabric of King's College Chapel can be read like a book, though admittedly many of the early pages are missing. The building is like a rediscovered manuscript, with gaps in the early sections, the middle part complete enough for us to fill in what went before, while the final chapters are entire and unequivocal. The rarity of the surviving building accounts from the last, sixteenth-century campaign, alone justify a study of the Chapel in great depth. Similarly, the personalities involved in its construction and patronage range from brief pencil sketches to fully painted portraits. The cast list includes Henry VI, Edward IV, Richard III, and the Tudor Henrys VII and VIII. The longest run of all was made by William Waynflete, Bishop of Winchester, who joined the project in the 1440s and whose energy and driving force kept the construction more or less moving through three difficult reigns.

Architecturally, the main interest comes at the beginning and the end, Reginald Ely, the first master mason and John Wastell, the last. There can be no doubt that Wastell is one of England's greatest but least appreciated architectural talents, and one who deserves the kind of recognition that has been awarded to Jones, Wren, Soane and the like. His work at King's was something of a rescue mission. Wastell was brought in after three master masons had worked on the fabric, each with his own ideas and each making his own alterations, additions and eliminations to the design. By 1508, the work had been in abeyance for nearly a quarter of a century, and Wastell was asked not only to complete the great unfinished and half-built shell but also to design a vault for the whole building that would suit both his design and those of his predecessors.

The result is a remarkable architectural *Tour de Force*, famous the world over.

King's College Chapel is one of the most extraordinary buildings in the whole repertoire of English medieval architecture. It encompasses the Perpendicular style of the mid fifteenth century, the exuberance of the Tudor period and some of the earliest manifestations of the English Renaissance. The history of the Chapel is that of the English Crown over eight decades, and the combination of royal patronage and the frequent revision and embellishment of the original plan makes King's College Chapel *the* English building of the late Middle Ages, every element capturing the artistic and political revolution of its time.

The purpose of this book is to examine the architectural history of the Chapel and to place it within the context of its stylistic and historic background. The progress of the building work was dogged by political intrigue and the rise and fall of dynasties. Therefore, some historical background is essential and will form one of the introductory sections. Similarly, King's College Chapel was intended to function as part of a university college and its design and planning must also be examined in that light. The greatest attention, however, must be paid to the architecture of the Chapel, in a national and international context, and this theme will recur throughout the book. The prolonged period of construction of this magnificent building, and its association with the patronage and taste of Lancaster, York and Tudor, renders King's College Chapel a particularly suitable subject as the central theme for a study of the closing stages of English Gothic architecture and the dawn of the English Renaissance.

ACKNOWLEDGMENTS

I should like to thank the Provost, the Dean and Governing Body of King's College for their permission to work on the Chapel and for access to the Muniments and Library. My special thanks to Mr Mundell and the Chapel staff for their constant help and consideration and to Michael Roberts for providing me with time and space to work on the papers of the late John Saltmarsh. My great thanks go to Arthur Owen, Archivist of King's College, for his assistance and expertise, and to Patrick Strong of Eton College, and to the Clerk of the Council of the Duchy of Lancaster, for answering my queries and providing such interesting and useful information. I am very grateful for the interest that Professor Sir John Plumb has taken in my work and for assisting me in Cambridge. I also wish to thank Peter Braude for his great technical help and for allowing me to utilise his specialist equipment. My thanks also go to Christ's College and to the Leverhulme Trust whose Fellowship enabled most of the research work to be carried out in Cambridge and to Professor John White of University College London for his unflagging support.

I have had many useful discussions over the years with friends and colleagues, especially Eric Fernie, Stephen Gardner, Robert Smith and Christopher Wilson. This book would not have been written without the encouragement and support of Martin Johnson, and I am very grateful to him for reading the text and for his many helpful suggestions.

On the technical side, my thanks to the staff of Routledge & Kegan Paul, to Stella Shackle of the Sainsbury Centre, University of East Anglia, for her excellent processing and printing of the great majority of the photographs and to Robert Smith for the preparation of figures 31, 35, 43, 53, 145 and 146.

I am very grateful to the British Academy for their generous financial support towards the research costs of this book.

INTRODUCTION

King's College Chapel was begun in 1448 in the dying fall of an era. Europe was still inward-looking, still obsessed with its own increasingly anachronistic struggles. The ideals and aspirations of the High Middle Ages were decaying. The romantic and chivalrous notions of kings and princes fell short of the realities of a new, hard-faced age. Henry VI struggled vainly to hold the English Empire in France, the Byzantines were clinging desperately to Constantinople, the Holy Roman Empire continued through sheer inertia and the Moors still lingered in their fabulous caliphates of southern Spain. European architecture reached stupendous heights of glorious decadence – the Alhambra in Granada and the dizzy monuments of late gothic in France and Germany.

Yet, as the foundations of King's College Chapel were being laid, Brunelleschi's great Florentine dome was nearing completion. When Reginald Ely, master mason, sat down to design King's College Chapel, Michelozzi was already at work on the Palazzo Ricardi in Florence, and Alberti on S. Francesco in Rimini. Italy hovered on the brink of an irresistible tide that would soon sweep through western Christendom and carry the High Middle Ages in its wake.

Like many of Europe's great monuments, the progress of the building at King's was halting and haphazard. The structure was not completed until 1515, some seventy years of construction, by which time the world had changed radically. The eyes that beheld the finished Chapel were those of the sixteenth century. They saw it, not as its founder had, as *2* an act of piety and of deep religious conviction, but as an object of artistic splendour and dynastic propaganda. Religious sentiment for such devotional works had been replaced by the connoisseurship of an altogether more secular age. The attitudes of the early Tudor period towards the Chapel are well illustrated by its fittings, which took another thirty years to complete. The glass, with its enormous scenes that sprawl across the mullions, transformed the Chapel interior from a single and harmonious space into a spectacular picture gallery – it became for stained glass what Nonsuch was to be for sculpture. The great pulpitum of Henry VIII and Anne Boleyn is a splendid piece of domestic woodwork, deliberately solid and far removed from the filagreed panelling of the traditional med-

2 King's College Chapel: interior looking west

ieval rood screen. The most modern addition to the Chapel interior, the Rubens *Adoration*, completes the Tudor vision – that the focal point of the building should be a great work of art.

The Tudor fittings took so long to complete that the Chapel was hardly ever used for the purpose for which it was built, a private college chapel for the performance of mass and the other offices of the medieval church. By the time the Chapel was ready, Fisher and More had gone to the block, Henry VIII was Head of the Church of England and the monasteries had been dissolved. The high altar was not set up until 1544, only to be torn down within a few years by the Protestant reformers. That the Chapel survived the reform and revolutions of the next century, and survived so well, is due in part to its peculiar ownership. Although the building and fitting out of the Chapel had been the personal project of every monarch from Henry VI to Henry VIII, the building actually belongs to King's College. As its private property, the Chapel was not as susceptible to the kind of destruction that was tragically so common to most other English churches during the Civil War. Apart from the glass, which must have sent the Puritans into paroxysms of horror, the Chapel contained little religious iconography to cause offence – the multitude of figure niches had never received their statues, while the screen and other fittings were the products of an age when heraldry, comfort and the 'Antik' had taken over from the purely devotional. How the glass survived poses a more difficult problem, though the very cost of its removal and the replacement of its acreage with more modest

3 King's College Chapel: exterior from the south

designs may have restrained the hands of even the most ardent of saints.

The original design of King's, as detailed by its founder Henry VI in 1448, saw the Chapel as one element of an elaborate architectural scheme, with integrated college buildings to the west, south and east of a huge principal court. The Chapel was intended to fuse with these ranges and form the northern wing of a magnificent, almost palatial, ensemble. Hopes of completing the first grand design appear to have evaporated soon after the overthrow of Henry VI in 1461. The failure to implement the other buildings of the court and the subsequent piecemeal developments of the eighteenth and nineteenth centuries have left the Chapel stranded on a sea of grass like some enormous monument in a park. The completion of the Chapel fabric in the late fifteenth and early sixteenth centuries was undertaken without reference to the college buildings as originally proposed to the south, and while the former plan and overall design of the Chapel was adhered to, nothing could then be done to prevent the inevitable isolation of the great building. It was too late for the addition of a transept, central tower or any other unifying feature that might have altered the external appearance of the Chapel with its uncompromising silhouette – long and repetitive and with abrubt cliff-like ends. The profile has been likened to an upturned table or, rather less kindly, to a dead sow. The principal responsibility for the odd appearance of the isolated Chapel lies with the four corner towers. Whilst clearly intended from the outset, they were not to be so high, nor were they to be alone. The projected college complex to the south was to be ringed by a series of towers and turrets, of which those of the Chapel would have formed but a part.

At first sight, King's College Chapel appears to be all of a piece and gives the impression of having been built to a single design. This is not so. Between the commencement of the building in 1448 and its completion in 1515, the design underwent considerable changes, most especially to the interior elevations.

Furthermore, the design of the high vault, the form of the towers and many of the external features were only settled during the last few years of the work. Four architects were responsible for the Chapel at various times: Reginald Ely, the first master mason and designer of the plan and sections of the elevation; John Wolryche, master mason for an unknown period before the summer of 1477 and responsible for the design of the main lateral tracery and for the level of the vault springing; Simon Clerk, master mason between 1477 and 1485, who completed the five eastern bays of the Chapel; and John Wastell who built the antechapel, the vaults, towers and battlements between 1508 and 1515. One must not give the impression, however, that the plans and designs were thrown away and replaced by new ones every few decades. Rather, the initial design of 1448 evolved and developed, responding to changing fashions in architectural taste and to the finance available. The early work was hampered

4 King's College Chapel: the
north porch and Bays 11
and 12 N

seriously by lack of funds, and by the fall of the founder, Henry VI, in 1461. It has long been believed that the layout of the Chapel, together with considerable sections of the eastern bays, had already been completed by then, and that no further work was undertaken until 1476. The surviving evidence, however, suggests that work did continue after Henry's fall, though at a much reduced level, picking up considerably in the late 1470s. The assumption that nothing was achieved between 1461 and 1476 has led to a schematised architectural history of the Chapel into 'campaigns', i.e. the first, up to 1461, the second 1476–85 and the last between 1508 and 1515. The division of the first two campaigns *4* would not now appear to be so clear-cut. Richard III's attempt to complete the whole Chapel ended in 1485 with his downfall and the accession of the Tudors. The five eastern bays were roofed but not vaulted, and sections of the antechapel merely projected. No further building occurred before 1508, when work began again on the antechapel. The high vault was commenced in 1512, while all the structural work ceased in 1515. The glass and other fitting occupied another thirty years.

King's College Chapel was one of the last great buildings of the Perpendicular age, the style of architecture current in most of England from about 1330 to the end of the Middle Ages. The study of 'Perp.' has now progressed sufficiently for a number of established assumptions to be challenged, the most important being that England created some sort of 'National Style' sitting in splendid isolation off the cultural coast of Europe and free from any alien contamination. In reality, the Perp. of the fourteenth century was the outcome of a re-evaluation by English masons of their own style in the light of French Rayonnant, whilst after 1420, some of the most important workshops, notably Canterbury, Oxford and the royal shops, underwent a series of violent and energetic transformations as a result of renewed contact with France during the various stages in the development of 'Flamboyant'. The fruit borne of this relationship was very important to the development of English architecture, though the number of workshops so influenced was small, and mostly situated in the south and east. The great majority of the other English workshops went on much as before, hardly affected by the growing 'Fantastic' nature of the few, though from time to time some proffered faint provincial imitations of things cosmopolitan. Hence, the two buildings that are invariably presented as being the epitome of late Gothic in England, St George's Windsor and the Henry VII Chapel at Westminster, are, it will be shown, the exceptions rather than the rule. As the fifteenth century wore on, the difference between the royal workshops and its several offshoots, on the one hand, and the great bulk of the provincial shops, on the other, grew increasingly more obvious. King's College Chapel illustrates perfectly the nature of this struggle. The first master mason was infected early in his career by the heady influence of France, the second and third came from different and more sober backgrounds, while the last, and arguably the finest, found himself obliged to complete the Chapel in a style far richer, heavier and more exotic than his own, partly to please his Royal patron but mostly in order to return to the first ideas of the original designer.

The background to English architecture in the reign of Henry VI

Gothic architecture evolved as an engineering solution to aesthetic and technical problems. For the first century of its development the style was dictated to a great extent by structure and it was only in the second quarter of the thirteenth century that the Gothic architects felt sufficient confidence in their constructional devices to devote more of their attention to visual effects. This is not to say that early Gothic buildings such as Laon and St Rémi were devoid of aesthetic considerations, but there is always the feeling that the architects of the twelfth century have made a virtue out of necessity, with their hands tied by so many practical problems. The answers lay eventually with the Chartres elevational system, the flying buttress, and perhaps most signficant of all, with tracery. The introduction of window tracery in the early thirteenth century gave

5 Beauvais Cathedral: interior showing great height of French Gothic in the thirteenth century
6 Paris, the Ste Chapelle: exterior from the south

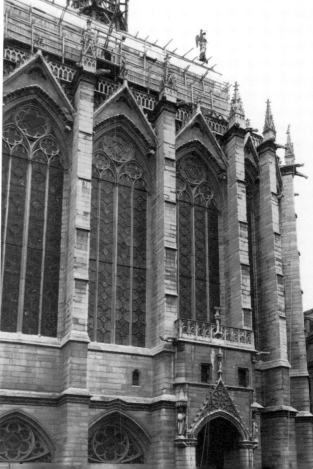

builders their first real opportunity to add to their buildings extensive decoration that could be both attractive and varied, yet integral and essential to the structure. The result was a blossoming of French Gothic with such buildings as Reims, Amiens and Beauvais. For three-quarters of 5 a century, Gothic knew no limits – it soared higher, grew thinner, and glittered with acres of glass. Yet the building that was arguably to have the widest international influence was tiny, the Ste Chapelle in Paris. 6 St Louis created this gem of early Rayonnant to be a reliquary for the Crown of Thorns. Indeed, the very building has been likened to a shrine turned 'outside-in'. The insubstantial architecture has that thin quality of metalwork, in fact the windows are so large and the structural support so meagre that the chapel has to be sustained by a system of metal rods threaded around it. The prestige of the Ste Chapelle, its sparkling interior, transparency and structural fragility, made it a source of wonder, and across Europe architects strove to emulate its qualities. Westminster Abbey is often quoted as an attempt by Henry III to outbid his French rival, and the influence of the Ste Chapelle continued to be felt through several generations of English architects. The elements of the Ste Chapelle most loved by the English were those that were the least French. They loved its decorative richness, the admix of sculpture, enamels and fittings, and the dominant role played by tracery. They also loved its 7 insubstantial structure, seeing it not as a triumph of Gothic thinness but as an opportunity to indulge themselves in yet further architectural conjuring tricks. The English were always more interested in the decorative possibilities afforded by Gothic than in its structural neatness and economy. Few English architects showed any interest in how French

7 Paris, the Ste Chapelle: interior of crypt

Gothic buildings stood up. Rather, they were attracted to those elements of structure that could be elaborated for decorative purposes – shafts *en délit*, carved capitals, tracery and rib vaults. Their inability or unwillingness to grasp the tenets of French structure dictated that English Gothic churches would be low, overbuilt and overblown.

In the second half of the thirteenth century, the English further developed and exploited the plastic and ornamental aspects of Gothic, indeed the movement has been dubbed the 'Decorated Style'. Buildings such as Exeter Cathedral and the Angel Choir at Lincoln mark the high point 8 of this extravagance with their excess of vault ribs, richness of tone and misuse of window tracery. Some reaction to this lavish style was inevitable and, as early as the 1290s, new ideas were developing in southern England and in York, that led ultimately to the creation of a new English style, the Perpendicular. The transition from 'Dec.' to 'Perp.' in the early fourteenth century came as a result of a reassessment of French Gothic, and in particular of the aesthetic advances of the Rayonnant style that had grown up around Paris nearly a century earlier. Rayonnant was 9 characterised by the refinement of the architectural elements, a reduction in the number and variety of parts, the uniformity of the basic units, the linking of horizontal elements by an overlay of vertical tracery either glazed or blinded, monochrome stonework, a general upward progression

8 Lincoln Cathedral: interior of the Angel choir

9 Paris, St Denis: interior of the nave, an early example of the Rayonnant style

10 Westminster, St Stephen's
Chapel: exterior (Carter)

1 For example, the first Rayonnant
product, the nave of St Denis from
the 1230s. For the development of
Rayonnant see R. Branner, Paris
and the origins of Rayonnant
Gothic Architecture to 1240. *Art
Bulletin* 44, 1962, and R. Branner,
St Louis and the Court Style,
London 1965.

2 The consistency of style and the
advanced nature of the
architecture of the Kent School
seen in these works argues that the
development of the style took place
during the 1280s in works now
lost.

3 For Stephen's Chapel Westminster
see: J. Bony, *The English
Decorated Style*, Oxford 1979;
H. M. Colvin *et al.*, *The History of
the King's Works*, vol. 1. *The
Middle Ages*, London 1963;
J. Harvey, The Origins of the
Perpendicular Style, in *Studies in
Building History*, ed. E. M. Jope,
London 1961; M. Hastings, *St
Stephen's Chapel Westminster*,
Cambridge 1956; F. Mackenzie,
*The Architectural Antiquities of the
Collegiate Chapel of St Stephen's,
Westminster*, London 1844;
G. Webb, *Architecture in Britain,
The Middle Ages*,
Harmondsworth, 1956;
C. Wilson, The Origins of the
Perpendicular Style and its
Development to *c.* 1360, PhD.
thesis, Courtauld Institute,
University of London, 1980, soon
to be joined by a book.

of the elevation unimpeded by unnecessary architectural highlights,
transparency where possible or an emphasis on steely metallic surfaces
where not.[1] The masters of Perpendicular took these principles to an
extreme with structure thin to the point of starvation, tracery so regular
and all-embracing as to smother the whole building and a refinement
and diminution of the architectural members to such a degree that great
clusters of bases, capitals, etc. had to be employed where previously a
single larger one would have sufficed.

The Kent School of masons was vital to the early development of Perpendicular. Their interest in French Rayonnant is revealed in many of
their buildings, and the patronage of the Crown that they enjoyed from
the early 1290s ensured that their particular style would flourish and be
seen.[2] From 1292, Kent School masons were involved in the design of
St Stephen's Chapel, Westminster, the most important building in the
early stages of the development of Perpendicular. The chapel, which *10*
served as the House of Commons for many centuries, was all but lost
in the fire of 1834, though a great deal is known of its architecture and
decoration from prints and drawings.[3] The style and details of the first
work upon St Stephen's illustrate the variety of influences present within
the Kent School. Their interest in French building was not restricted
to those in the Paris basin – some of the favourite motifs such as split-
cusped quatrefoils, ogee arches and overlaid tracery cages, are best paral-
leled in Burgundy,[4] while the lierne vault of the chapel crypt was drawn
from a purely English repertoire.[5] St Stephen's was, of course, another
version of the Ste Chapelle, with a vaulted lower church on which stood
a tall, brilliantly lit upper chapel. But unlike the French original, the
upper chapel at Westminster was divided into two horizontal tiers, with
great windows below the vault springing and high clerestories within the

4 Split-cusped quatrefoils can be seen on the west front of Auxerre Cathedral; see Bony, fig. 163.

5 There are some early 'liernes' in France, see Bony, p. 50. Liernes in England may have originated at Pershore, vaulted in the 1280s, though a Kent School or London origin would seem more likely.

6 The clerestory of St Stephen's was removed by Wren in 1692.

7 Built c. 1290.

8 See the Bradfield tomb, Rochester 1283; the Pecham tomb, Canterbury, before 1292; the Crouchback tomb, Westminster, 1297; the Luda tomb, Ely, 1297.

vault lunettes. This horizontal stress was further emphasised on the interior at the level of the clerestory cill by a strong castillated cornice that added to the squareness of the main elevation as opposed to the verticality of the Ste Chapelle.[6] This interest in box shapes was shared by the master carpenters of the early fourteenth century and produced a rash of low profile, almost invisible, roofs set behind castillated parapets: e.g. the choir of Bristol Cathedral. Square and oblong shapes were to dominate both the interior and exterior of St Stephen's and were to become a vital influence on the development of the Perpendicular style that developed from its workshop. Another important design feature of St Stephen's was the miniature quality of much of its architecture. Many of the component parts of the structure were executed in a precious scale that was doubtless intended to convey the shrine-like quality of the Ste Chapelle. A similar interest in the miniature had already found expression in the north of England with the vestibule of the York Minster chapterhouse, which has several stylistic points in common with St Stephen's, *11* especially the curious form of the buttresses.[7] The other principal work at York was the rebuilding of the nave, begun in 1291. It is the most conspicuously French product built in England after Westminster Abbey. The design is a variant of the naves of either St Denis or Strasbourg rather than the sheer and elegant lines of the choir of Clermont Ferrand. The architect of the York nave looked long and hard at his Rayonnant models, and, had the project ever been completed in its original form, it could have taken its rightful place as one of the last pure manifestations of that style. Thus by the 1290s, three great building centres in England, Canterbury, Westminster and York, were each adapting their own versions of French Rayonnant to their own purposes. The York nave is the only surviving large-scale monument to have emerged from this new mode for things French, but the fashion can also be detected in the enormous tomb output of the Kent School. The late thirteenth century saw a considerable development in the complexity and size of tombs which went from floor slabs or simple standing chests to elaborate architectural ensembles with corner piers, buttresses, gables and umbrella canopies – a format doubtless derived from the architectural frames employed in French miniature paintings. The Kent School tombs *12* all follow the same basic pattern and are conceived as buildings though small in scale and almost entirely non-structural.[8] For example – the vaults are often merely incised on a few blocks while the buttresses are appendages rather than true supports. In effect, the tombs of the Kent School are a truer reflection of the non-structural nature of the Ste Chapelle than were those English buildings that attempted to emulate only the decorative richness of the Parisian chapel. The difference is one between real building and decoration on a monumental scale. These conflicts lie at the heart of the Kent School style; their tombs were dressed up as architecture while their architecture paraded as tombs.

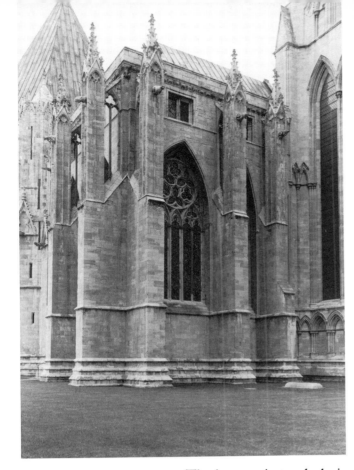

11 York Minster: exterior of the Chapter House vestibule

12 Ely Cathedral: the de Luda Tomb, a Kent School work of *c.* 1297

9 For the most recent research see Wilson.

10 Ibid.

The interest in tomb design which flowered in the late thirteenth and early fourteenth centuries came at a vital stage in the development of the Perpendicular style, for some of its first products were to be tombs, or else such small-scale structures that could assume the proportions of tomb architecture. The first Perpendicular style may have been virtually the sole creation of Thomas of Canterbury, master mason of St Stephen's Westminster between *c.* 1331 and 1335.[9] His successor at Westminster, William Ramsey, designed the new chapter-house for St Paul's Cathedral in 1331. It was the epitome of the new style. A double-storey building in a doll's-house scale, with all the sharp angular quality of a cut crystal set in an ivory casket. Thus, in arrangement and treatment it too belonged to the miniaturist tradition of the Ste Chapelle. The architectural precision of the chapter-house was well suited to the smallness of the building, but its success initiated a fashion for the miniature and the precious that was less suited to larger structures. It might be said that with the remodelling of the south transept arm of Gloucester after 1333 everything started to go wrong.[10] The design, probably again by Ramsey, blew the chapter-house of St Paul's out of all proportion, with a quantity of small units crowded together with such density as to be almost self-defeating. The interior elevation is a mere facade, a lattice of tracery laid over the

13

13 London, Old St Paul's: exterior of Chapter House (Hollar)

earlier structure. It is the surviving Romanesque core that continues to carry out the major supporting role whilst also acting as a pegboard on to which the panelling is applied. The visible architecture has entered a world of unreality where the elements vital to the structure have been disguised rather than exploited for their architectural integrity. The *14* Gloucester work is crucial to the expansion of the Perpendicular style, for not only was it the first large-scale interior to be attempted but it also had important associations with the Crown through the presence of the tomb of Edward II. In addition, it brought the new London taste face to face with the strong Decorated traditions of the West Country. Once again, English masons were presented with an exciting new idea but one whose unique mode of execution offered no solution for reproduction. The reaction of the West Country was mixed – some workshops ignored it altogether whilst others adapted the richness of their own style to a Perp. mould, for example, the choir of Wells and the central tower of Worcester. This blending of the two stylistic traditions even had its effect on Gloucester for by the time that the choir vaults were executed *c.* 1345–50 the relative unity of the south transept vault design had been lost in an orgy of liernes, ribs and bosses. Nevertheless, Gloucester broke the dominance of the West Country Decorated style with a firm rejection of its delight in colour, variety, horizontal lines, receding planes and sculptural richness. Gloucester brought something of the new unified and harmonious London style, full of light and steely cleanliness.

The Perpendicular style continued its close links with the Crown through the considerable works at Windsor of the mid-fourteenth century. It was also taken up by the friars whose churches increased in size and numbers at this time. A style devoid of unnecessary decorative richness and heaviness could easily be adapted for the bare and uncluttered interiors favoured by the mendicants and it could satisfy the rigours of their rule while being entirely suited to their needs. The friars enjoyed considerable royal patronage and they probably played an important role as messengers of London taste in the regional dissemination of the Perpendicular style. The supreme achievement of the first phase of Perp. was the new nave of Canterbury Cathedral, begun in 1377.[11] A 'Friars' church built for Benedictine monks, its interior is sublime, full of air and light. The effect is austere yet elegant, with a richness based on architectural propriety and restraint rather than ostentation. The heat and *15* intensity of Gloucester has been cooled and the anguish of that earlier attempt to assimilate all the architectural elements into a single entity has been soothed away in a triumph of foils and balances. The success of Canterbury lies as much in what is omitted as in what is there.

By the late fourteenth century, Perpendicular was set to go in two different directions. It could travel along the path of Canterbury with large

11 See F. Woodman, *The Architectural History of Canterbury Cathedral*, London 1981.

14 Gloucester Cathedral; interior of the south transept

15 Canterbury Cathedral: interior of the nave

12 Begun 1318.

13 J. Caley and J. Hunter (eds) '*Valor Ecclesiasticus temp. Henry VIII auctoritate regia institutus*, 6 vols, London 1810–34.

scale, uncluttered and visually unified buildings – the equivalent of the transitional Rayonnant/Flamboyant churches in France such as St Ouen at Rouen,[12] or it could develop the small scale and fantastic unreality of tombs, screens and chapels. In fact, it went both ways. The rise of tomb architecture that had been so marked in the late thirteenth century became a dominant feature of the architecture of the fourteenth century. The provision of Chantry masses to be said in perpetuity for the souls of the faithful departed had become very popular by *c.* 1300. Edward I provided for numerous chantries for the soul of his queen, Eleanor of Castile, after her death in 1291, but the real impetus to the growth of chantries was the scourge of the Black Death in 1349. By the Reformation, the *Valor Ecclesiasticus*, Henry VIII's survey of the revenues of the Church, recorded some 1,733 chantries in England and Wales, including some 310 in the small diocese of London alone.[13] During the second half of the fourteenth century it became fashionable not only to provide benefactions for the support of a chantry priest, but also to accommodate a private altar within a purpose-built chapel. Some of these were free standing or additions built on to existing fabrics, but most were cage-like enclosures of wood or stone, placed at convenient and occasionally inconvenient places inside the church – usually within an arch of an arcade or at the termination of an aisle. The importance of such chapels to the development of Perp. was that they were non-structural and hence were a perfect object for the miniature and fantastic trend that had flourished from the earliest decades of the new style. They lent themselves to a display of some of the favourite motifs of Perpendicular: niches, canopies, gables, complex moulding and repeated panelling. Their vaults could be wildly enthusiastic, for they were entirely unreal. Soon, the churches of England, great and small, began to fill with a fragile exuberance of chantry chapels. The architectural development of the chantry chapel was an inevitable extension of the explosion of tomb design – the two element were suited totally to each other and the minuteness of Perp. details provided the exact medium for their execution. Tomb architecture even began to contribute its own stylistic motifs to the general stock, one of the best examples being the trapped buttress, where the offsets and string courses of a 'core' buttress merely peep through the gaps left by clusters of attached pilasters. So complex were some of these buttress designs that often, the additional members being so numerous, the 'core' buttress does not actually have to exist at all.

At the close of the fourteenth century, master masons still managed to keep the two strands of Perpendicular architecture quite separate, so that it might be possible to find the most elaborate of tombs built within an austere yet contemporary interior. But around 1420 things began to change. In some architectural centres the two distinct streams that had produced such diverse designs as the Canterbury nave and the Tewks-

16 Rouen, St Ouen: interior
of choir after 1318
17 Winchester Cathedral: the
Fox Chantry *c.* 1520

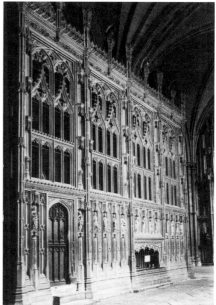

bury Trinity Chapel began to merge into a monumental style with all
the complexity and richness of the miniature. Thus the unreal world of
tombs and fittings became a 'Fantastic' style of Gothic architecture.
While attention still had to be paid to constructional demands, the
emphasis of design shifted from stylistic simplicity and engineering
integrity to an increasingly chaotic overlay of diminutive architectural
motifs. Mouldings became smaller and finer and had to be grouped into
large configurations in order to accommodate structural reality – for while
the individual units could be diminished at will, the amount of built structure required to support a vault of a certain weight at a given height
did not change. The result was an almost manic clustering of bases, shafts
and capitals. The repeated blind panel, the favourite Perpendicular motif,
was used in even greater density so that walls lost their intended surface
clarity under a welter of closely packed undulating mouldings. The high
point of the first phase of Fantastic Perp. came in the reign of Henry
VI with the project for the Oxford Divinity School, *c.* 1430, the *18*
Beauchamp Chantry at Warwick, the choir of Sherbourne, *c.* 1440, and
the Old Court Gate at King's College Cambridge, of 1443. As buildings
became more like fantastic tombs, so tomb architecture grew more and
more exotic, producing whole miniature buildings like the Henry V
Chantry in Westminster Abbey, after 1422, the Beaufort Chantry in Win- *19*
chester, *c.* 1440, the Little Chantry in Warwick, *c.* 1445 and the Pulpitum
of Canterbury Cathedral of *c.* 1452.[14] Thus, the first phase of the Fantastic movement came to fruition just at the time when the design of
King's College Chapel was conceived.

14 See Woodman, pp. 188–96.

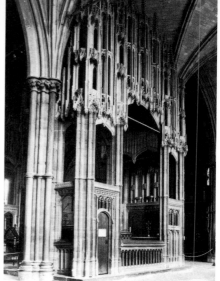

18 Oxford, The Divinity
   School: interior
19 Winchester Cathedral: the
   Beaufort Chantry c. 1440

The architecture of King's College Chapel and its place in Eastern England

King's College Chapel occupies an unusual position in the history of English architecture in the late Middle Ages. It was a royal building from the outset and it enjoyed the patronage of five successive kings. But its design does not stem from any special royal tradition nor was it at any stage under the control of one of the official royal workshops. The four master masons were all of East Anglian, or at least of eastern English, extraction, and the resulting architecture summarises many of the achievements of the region. The first master mason, Reginald Ely, came from Norwich, the second city of England during the fifteenth century, and the rich architectural inheritance of Norwich should be examined for any influence it might have exercised at King's. Of the second master, John Wolryche, little is known, but from the stylistic evidence of his work at King's he too came from East Anglia. The third and fourth master masons, Simon Clerk and John Wastell, have similar backgrounds, Cambridge and Bury St Edmunds. The admix of master masons is matched by the variety of architectural influences exhibited by King's College Chapel, with elements of the Fantastic movement of the first half of the century, tracery patterns that betray a strong Yorkshire influence, combined with mouldings, vaults and other details drawn from other eastern English sources.

Perhaps the notion that there existed an 'Eastern English' style of Perpendicular by the fifteenth century is as yet too novel to win instant recognition, yet many regional variations did exist within the one 'National Style' – after all, the concept of a West Country School of Perp. has been accepted for decades. In the fifteenth century, Perpendicular broke up into several regional schools, less and less dependent upon London.

Local centres of importance prior to the emergence of Perp., such as Oxford and York, reasserted their influence upon their own regions. In the east, a mature and rather subdued style evolved which can be found throughout East Anglia, the northern Home Counties and into the East Midlands. Only Norwich stands out as a persistent proponent of the Fantastic style well into the mid century. For the rest, the 'Eastern' style might be distinguished by its soberness, its uncomplicated and rather flat mouldings, small and finely moulded capitals and bases, a general restraint within the masonry parts complemented by the occasional outburst of frivolous carpentry. The finest examples of this style, such as St Mary's Bury and Burwell, possess an elegant poise, understating their presence yet succeeding through sheer good taste and well tempered design.

Cambridge was in an extremely fortunate position. It was a natural gathering place for the best architectural talent of the region, while its important patronage ensured that it was also able to exercise a strong influence upon the development of style over a wide area.

The late Gothic style in eastern England grew out of a fusion between several workshops that had themselves emerged only at the turn of the fifteenth century, a time when most of the older and established shops were dominated by London trained masters. Apart from Canterbury and York, there was little building activity within the great cathedral and monastic foundations: Norwich tinkered away with its cloister, but Lincoln, Ely, Peterborough and Bury were all silent. Canterbury was in the process of a modernisation that would see the replacement or revamping of almost half the cathedral by *c.* 1455.[15] The work is pure London, indeed if one wishes to study the London style between *c.* 1380 and 1460 one goes to Canterbury. York was still coming to terms with the Perpendicular style. The giant east window of the Minster designed *c.* 1400 displays some attempt to instill Metropolitan order on to native chaos. The favoured tracery forms that grew from the design were bizarre and angular versions of 'Northern Flowing', freeze-dried into an awkward assortment of jagged patterns. Yet the central tower of York Minster is a good example of how one style could be transported over a great distance. The design was by William Colchester, the king's master mason, sent 'on loan' to do the job.[16] Apart from the friction caused between him and the disgruntled local talent, the indigenous workshops of York were to be presented with a pure London product on their doorstep. The barrenness of Northern Perp. was assisted by the smooth, glassy texture of the local white magnesian limestone, a hard material that militates against small fussy detailing and that was principally responsible for the mural and dry quality of much of the fifteenth-century building in Yorkshire. The shiny surface value of Yorkshire magnesian limestone was to have been exploited at King's College Chapel, where the original intention was to face the exterior with finely cut ashlar from

20

21

15 Ibid, Chapters 5 and 6.

16 L. Salzman, *Building in England down to 1540*, Oxford 1952, p. 28.

20 York Minster: exterior, the east window

21 York Minster: the central tower

the Huddleston quarry near Sherburn.

Norwich provides another vital link in the architectural background of King's College Chapel as well as being a textbook illustration of the shift from southern to northern influence during the early part of the fifteenth century. The link with King's is direct – Reginald Ely, the first master mason, came from Coltishall just outside the city. But the early fifteenth century saw the presence in the city of a new workshop, one combining London forms with elements drawns from the north, and particularly from Yorkshire, with the added spice of more than a hint of the Fantastic style. Their two principal works in the city, the church of the Dominican Priory and the church of St Peter Mancroft, are both of national importance. They combine much of the current style of East Anglia with motifs drawn from the north, such as the tracery patterns.[17] The Mancroft workshop may also have been responsible for the pretty Erpingham Gate to Norwich Cathedral which was conceived as a big

17 See p. 103.

front door to the close. It is a perfect example of exploded tomb architecture with all the frills and fussiness of a small-scale, indoor work. It is this architectural tradition that we find reflected in Reginald Ely's work at King's Cambridge. It is ironic that Henry VI personally disliked the Fantastic movement of his day, yet, in selecting Reginald Ely as master mason of his new College at Cambridge, Henry chose one of the most singular exponents of the style. Such extravagance offended Henry's aesectic piety and he specified on at least one occasion that his building projects were to avoid just such 'superfluite and too gret curiouss workes of entaille and besy moldyng'.[18] Yet even the disapprobation of the king could not abate the progress of the new wave that continued to whip up whirlwind creations of stone and glass. But where Henry failed, civil war suceeded. The fighting between the Houses of Lancaster and York that broke out in 1455 soon brought major church building to a grinding halt, and for over a decade, the mason's workshops stood silent across the land.

18 R. Willis and J. Clark, *The Architectural History of the University of Cambridge*, vol. I, Cambridge 1886, p. 354.

An outline of the reign of Henry VI

When Henry VI ascended to the throne of England he was hardly nine months old. He was half-English and half French. His father, Henry V, hero of Agincourt and 'too famous to live long', had died shortly after the resumption of the war with France. The Hundred Years War had already passed the age of eighty and the incessant hostilities were to dominate the first three decades of the new reign. The war had begun back in the 1330s over the claim of Edward III to the French throne through his mother, Isabella Valois, the eldest surviving child of Philip IV. Naturally, the French resisted the English claim and promoted their own candidate, Isabella's cousin, whom they proclaimed as Philip VI. The ensuing war saw considerable English successes, especially during the period under the command of Prince Edward of Woodstock, the so-called Black Prince, who established an extensive English empire in France centred on Calais in the north and Bordeaux in the west. But after the death of the Black Prince, and soon after that of his father Edward III, the French re-established themselves and when the fighting died down late in the fourteenth century, many of the English gains had been recovered.

The war was re-opened by the Lancastrian king, Henry IV, at the beginning of the fifteenth century, and entered a new phase under his dashing son, Henry V. His success was rapid, and in 1416, only a year after the victory of Agincourt, the English launched a full-scale invasion of Normandy, which was taken quickly. The French king, Charles VI, was in a difficult situation with a factious court and the powerful Duke of Burgundy waiting menacingly in the wings. The French made terms

22

22 Canterbury Cathedral: portrait figure of Henry VI from the pulpitum *c.* 1452

with the English, under which Henry V would receive the hand in marriage of Catherine de Valois, daughter of Charles VI. Thus it was that Catherine became Queen of England and mother to Henry VI. The terms of the Anglo-French Treaty of Troyes also included the recognition of Henry V and his children as heirs to the throne of France after the death of Charles, and in the meantime, Henry would act as Regent of the French realm.

On 6 December 1421, Catherine gave birth to a son at Windsor, a place of foreboding to the King who prophesied on hearing the news: 'I, Henry of Monmouth shall small time reign and much get; Henry, born at Windsor, shall long reign and lose all.' On 1 September 1422, Henry V died, soon to be followed by the French King, Charles VI. Under the terms of the Treaty of Troyes the young Henry VI inherited the French kingdom in place of the Dauphin Charles, who nevertheless, proclaimed himself king and was crowned at Poitiers as Charles VII. The young Queen Catherine de Valois, now a widow in England, refused to return to France and instead made off and married her former husband's Clerk of the Wardrobe, Owen Tudor – an unlikely liaison but one that changed the course of English history. Meanwhile, the English regency, led by the infant King's uncles Gloucester and Bedford, and his great-uncle, Henry Beaufort, Bishop of Winchester, pursued the English conquest of the whole French kingdom. The new French king, Charles VII, established his territory in the centre and the south, making Bourges his capital and stronghold. Paris had become untenable following an alliance between England and an enraged Burgundy, still seething after the murder of their Duke, John the Fearless, by the Armagnacs. Thus Paris, together with much of northern and western France fell under the control of the Anglo-Burgundian forces. On 17 December 1430, Henry VI, just nine years old, was crowned King of France in Notre Dame. For a further five years, the English continued to enjoy the possession of Paris, though in reality they held it only at the pleasure of Burgundy. Even before the coronation, things had gone sour for the English. Their failure to capture Orleans in 1429 and thus open the way south into the territory of Charles VII had been compounded by the remarkable relief of that city by Jeanne d'Arc, and despite her subsequent capture and execution, the tide of events had turned in favour of the French. The English suffered further reverses in 1434, with the Pope's recognition of Charles VII as the rightful King of France, and the desertion of the alliance by the Burgundians in the following year. Paris had to be relinquished and over the next few years the French slowly recovered much of their former territory.

By 1444 England was desperately in need of a French alliance in order to improve its position. The solution was a royal marriage for Henry VI. A treaty was arranged with Anjou by which Margaret, daughter of the Count and niece of the late Charles VI, would marry the twenty-two-year-old Henry. Margaret was a forceful and determined fourteen-year-old, but her influence and strong personality were to be felt more on events in England than in assisting her husband's position in France. Margaret's arrival in England coincided with the deaths of some of the King's ablest advisors: in 1443, Cardinal Henry Chichele, Archbishop of Canterbury, in 1447, both the Duke of Gloucester (the 'Good Duke Humphry') and Cardinal Beaufort. Henry VI soon became surrounded by less agreeable and more ambitious supporters, especially Edmund Beaufort, the Duke of Somerset, and increasingly he submitted to the single-minded determination of his wife. He was, in short, weak. But Henry VI was also ill. He was afflicted by a curious malady that led to prolonged periods of insanity. He would not recognise people, even the Queen, and during these lapses considerable struggles ensued for the power of regency. Margaret claimed pre-eminence, but other factions were also in evidence, particularly that surrounding Richard, Duke of York, himself a direct descendant of Edward III. The struggles concealed yet another vexed question – that of an heir. As yet, Henry and Margaret had no children and York clearly saw himself as the strongest candidate for heir presumptive. Others, notably the Beauforts, promoted the interests of Lady Margaret Beaufort, whose complicated claim to the throne could be traced through both her paternal grandparents, Lady Margaret Holland and John Beaufort, Earl of Somerset. The Beauforts strengthened their hand considerably through the marriage of Lady Margaret to Edmund Tudor, half-brother of Henry VI by the second marriage of their mother, Queen Catherine de Valois. But events at home were still overshadowed by the worsening situation in France. Throughout the 1440s the war had proceeded disastrously, the French recapturing Normandy in 1449 and then Bordeaux in 1453, leaving only Calais to the English. At home, Henry's government grew weaker and his court more factious. Yet it was precisely at this time that Henry devoted his attention and finance to the building of Eton and King's College Cambridge. In August 1453, Henry fell into another fit of insanity. In the following October, Queen Margaret gave birth to a son, Edward; 'of whoose birth the peple spake straungely.' The arrival of an heir provoked the Yorkist faction and it was only a matter of time before fighting broke out. The first skirmish in what has become known as the Wars of the Roses was little more than street fighting. The first Battle of St Albans on 22 May 1455, was an attempt by the Yorkists, led by Duke Richard, to remove those supporters of Henry VI who were a particular anathema. Immediately after their victory, the Yorkists professed their loyalty to Henry, yet the situation was clear to everyone – the King now ruled by courtesy of Richard Duke of York, whom Henry was forced to name as Protector. For the next five years, York and Lancaster struggled for power and by 1460 Richard had laid formal claim to the throne. But a few months later Richard was killed at the Battle of Wakefield. The death of the Duke of York left the country in a perplexed state. Henry

VI was still king but in the hands of Warwick and the remaining Yorkist lords. Queen Margaret had inflicted a crushing defeat upon the Yorkist forces and had removed Richard from the scene. But far from improving her own cause, she had strangely improved that of her rivals. Richard, whose haste to secure the Crown had caused such dissention in his own ranks, was dead. The sudden re-emergence of the Queen at the head of an army consisting mostly of Scots, Welsh and Burgundian mercenaries, made Edward, Earl of March and now heir to the title of York, seem an infinitely more attractive proposition, at least as Protector.

Margaret was quick to act. She plundered her way south to St Albans where, on 17 February 1461, she met and defeated Warwick and seized the person of the King. London lay open to her and the Lancastrian cause seemed momentarily triumphant. But then she hesitated. Henry VI pleaded with her not to allow her unruly army to pillage London. The Queen sent negotiators to the city but too late. On 26 February, Edward now Duke of York entered London, where the citizens were quickly persuaded to accept him as King. On 1 March, Edward was formally proclaimed as King Edward IV in Westminster Abbey just two months prior to his nineteenth birthday. The Lancastrians fled north, where they came into the field of battle against the new King at Towton. Their defeat was decisive, and Henry and Margaret were forced to flee to Scotland and thence to France. A new dynasty had been established under the banner of the White Rose of Clifford Castle. Henry VI had lost both the kingdoms of France and England before reaching the age of forty and the prophecy of his father had been borne out.

CHAPTER I

THE LANCASTRIAN CAMPAIGN

The building of King's College Chapel, initiated by Henry VI, continued even after his downfall in 1461 though without the patronage of the new Royal house and consequently at a much reduced rate. Nevertheless, some work was done and, as far as the structure is concerned, this piecemeal progress can be seen as an extension of the first, Lancastrian, campaign rather than as part of the new phase from 1477. This date saw the appointment of Simon Clerk as master mason and within a short time, a major campaign funded directly by the Yorkist kings. We shall therefore speak of the Lancastrian campaign as extending from 1441 to 1476. The early history of the existing Chapel at King's is extremely complex and frustrating. Little documentary evidence has survived that concerns directly the progress of construction while the building itself is at times very difficult to interpret. For the first phase of the work, therefore, it is best to separate the various strands of the evidence that does exist and to consider each of them individually. They are: the documents, the finances, the evidence from building materials, the master masons and secondary references. In this way, a general picture can be presented prior to any attempt at a detailed investigation and interpretation of the structure.

King's College Cambridge was founded by Henry VI on 12 February 1441. Henry was nineteen years old. The College was dedicated to 'the honour of Almighty God, in whose hands are the hearts of Kings: of the most blessed and immaculate Virgin Mary, Mother of Christ: and also of the glorious Confessor and Bishop Nicholas, Patron of my intended College, on whose festival we first saw the light.'[1] The great Chapel that was eventually built for the College is a very special 'combination' building. As a royal chapel, it stands in the tradition of St Stephen's Westminster and the Ste Chapelle in Paris. It has all the slender elegance and brittleness that appear to have been the hallmark of such buildings in the Middle Ages. Yet the Chapel was also designed to function as part of a university college and its architecture cannot be fully comprehended without some idea of collegiate planning in both Oxford and Cambridge prior to the founding of King's in 1441.

The formal establishment of 'Oxbridge' colleges began in the

1 King's College Muniments 4.76.

thirteenth century. Originally they were small, quasi-monastic and theological in outlook. Their early loose association and organisation was reflected in their architecture, or lack of it, for many of the students were lodged in hostels or inns. The first colleges often made use of the nearest parish church and provided for themselves only the most limited purpose-built accommodation. The number of students and fellows in any particular college was not great, perhaps two dozen in total. William of Wykham's two colleges, Winchester and New College Oxford, had been the most important influence upon the development of Collegiate architecture, particularly in Oxford.[2] By the early fifteenth century, the most notable feature of Oxford collegiate planning had become the distribution of the principal buildings around a quad or court, with an emphasis placed on the college's own chapel, if it had one, and an elaboration of the main gate plus the inclusion of a large common hall. In contrast, the college buildings of Cambridge pre 1440 show little affinity with their Oxford counterparts. The early college plans demonstrate a haphazard and additive approach to the accumulation of the sites and the occasional nature of the devlopments.[3] Yet, by the mid fifteenth century, a number of distinct trends can be detected. Two of the earliest Cambridge college layouts, Peterhouse and Corpus Christi, were arranged around a free-standing court, placed to the south of a pre-existing church. In both cases the church doubled as the college chapel, leaving the courts entirely domestic. This parallels the development of purely ecclesiastical college buildings in the late fourteenth century such as Cobham in Kent.[4] The dining halls of the two Cambridge colleges stood opposite the main street gate, a feature common to expensive domestic architecture, particularly in crowded town centres. The link

23

2 See The Royal Commission on Historical Monuments, *City of Oxford*, London 1939, p. 88 plan; G. H. Cook, *English Collegiate Churches*, London 1959, p. 184. The scheme was adapted from Windsor Castle where Wykham had been Clerk of the Works.

3 See The Royal Commission on Historical Monuments, *The City of Cambridge*, 3 vols, London 1959.

4 See G. H. Cook, p. 209.

23 Oxford, New College: Chapel from the south-east

between bourgeois architecture and the first Cambridge colleges is very apt before 1440 as they were small in scale and far less pretentious than those of Oxford. They lacked the grand chapels such as Merton and All Souls, and their principal entrances avoided the elaboration afforded to the Oxford gatehouses.

When Henry VI decided to found a new college in Cambridge, he could have chosen a layout and design from either of the two university traditions. It is notable therefore, that his first, small-scale project, was to be laid out in the more modest Cambridge tradition, while his second and far larger conception for the existing college opted for the grand manner of Oxford. The original buildings for the first, small project were intended to stand on a site to the north of the present Chapel, now completely occupied by the Old Schools. The land for that college site had been transferred to the King on 22 January 1441, by his commissioners John Fray, Chief Baron of the Eschequer, John Somerset, Chancellor of the Eschequer and John Langton, Chancellor of the University of Cambridge.[5] The initial site was very small but well suited to the needs of a college then intended for only twelve scholars. The plan, as far as it was ever carried out, followed the rather vague tradition of Cambridge – no integrated chapel and the hall pushed off to one side. The surviving *24* architectural fragments, however, speak of the highest quality work more in the Oxford tradition. The entrance gate on the west side formed the centrepiece of an elaborate facade broken at regular intervals with stone turrets. The gatehouse was decorated lavishly and the dressed ashlar surfaces spoke of a new and ambitious era of Cambridge building. The pro- *25* jected rectangular court was never completed, for the Old Schools complex already occupied the greater part of its intended site and, before any action could be taken to sweep them away, Henry had decided upon a greatly enlarged scheme that would require a bigger site altogether. The Old Court buildings, as the incomplete court became known, were finished peremptorily, to await the larger and more magnificent accommodation now promised by the King. The primitive college had certainly been provided with a chapel. It stood apart from the Old Court on the grassy site now between the Old Schools and the existing King's College Chapel. The old chapel is referred to many times in the College Muniments: the laying of the foundation stone took place on 17 September 1444; Henry VII kept St George's Day in the old chapel in 1506; it eventually fell down in 1536/7.[6]

However, by the autumn of 1443, the King had changed his mind completely about the scale of his Cambridge project and had decided to increase the numbers of the foundation and to provide it with additional land on which to build. He also now proposed a more formal connection between his new college at Eton and that at Cambridge. To this end Henry VI began the acquisition of a new site to the south of the

5 Calender of Patent Rolls, 1436–41. 522.

6 A *Custus Ecclesie* exists for the old Chapel as early as 1447/8. For the collapse see J. Caius, *Historiiae Cantabrigiensis Academiae*, Book 1, 1574, p. 69. For the foundation stone see letter from A. Oswald in J. Saltmarsh, *King's College*, Cambridge 1959, p. 91.

24 Cambridge, King's
College: Old Court plan as
in 1635

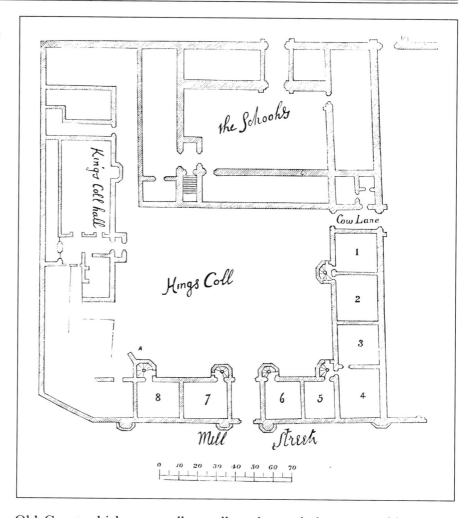

the Schools

Kings Coll hall

Cow Lane

Kings Coll

1

2

3

8   7   6   5   4

Mill   Street

0   10   20   30   40   50   60   70

7 Willis and Clark, vol. 1.
    pp. 334–50.

8 *Rotuli Parliamentorum*. The Rolls
    of Parliament, 7 vols, 1783, vol. V.
    pp. 163–4.

Old Court which eventually swallowed up whole streets of houses, a
church and even another college.[7] The decision to enlarge King's College
and to link it with Eton is often seen as an attempt by Henry to emulate
the twin foundations of William of Wykham at Oxford and Winchester,
but while the King doubtless wished his colleges to be linked intimately
the pressure for a much larger foundation at Cambridge appears to have
come from the Provost and scholars: 'Considering their own numbers,
and those of others daily flocking together to the said College.'[8] By 1445,
the size of the foundation had grown from twelve to seventy scholars,
while the total community exceeded one hundred.

It is not clear at what date the decision to enlarge the foundation dictated that the first college project should be abandoned and an entirely
new building begun. Clearly, this did not happen before the autumn of
1444 when the small college chapel was commenced. Presumably the

25 Cambridge, King's College: Old Court buildings in 1822 (Ackerman)

9 The College is named after both Margaret of Anjou and Elizabeth Woodville.

10 Willis and Clark, vol. II. pp. 11–52. See also A. Oswald, Andrew Doket and his Architect. *Cambridge Antiquarian Society Proceedings*, 1949, XLII, pp. 8–26.

original purpose of acquiring extra land to the south of the first small site was in order to extend the Old Court complex in that direction. But it would seem that as the potential site grew throughout the 1440s, so the architectural vision became larger and grander. The eventual proposal to start all over again on the new site had been taken by March 1448 when the King's Will and Intent was drawn up detailing the new design. Even so, further changes were made to this proposal before the great court and the present Chapel finally came to be laid out.

Henry VI did not envisage the completion of his second and larger scheme for King's College until at least 1468. In the meantime, another Cambridge college had been begun and substantially built, one that was to have a considerable effect upon the final proposals for King's. On 3 December 1446, St Bernard's College was founded. It was to stand on a site immediately to the south of the new site for King's. Within eighteen months the college had gained the patronage of the Queen, Margaret of Anjou, and later in the century it became known as Queens' College.[9] The construction proceeded with great speed; the north, east and south ranges were all in progress in 1448, while the internal timberwork of the hall and all the pertinent fittings of the kitchen were the subject of a contract in March 1449.[10] The plan is extremely simple and is perhaps the finest expression of Cambridge collegiate architecture. The principal

26

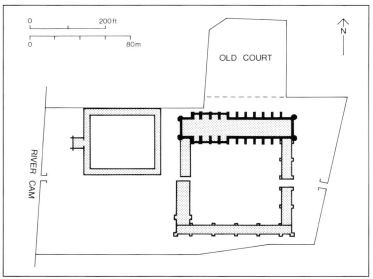

OLD COURT

RIVER CAM

26 Cambridge, Queens'
College
27 Cambridge, King's
College: the plan of 1448
based on the Will and
Intent

11 The notation used throughout this
book numbers the bays of the
Chapel 1 to 12, east to west. The
lateral window bays are called
either north – N or south – S.
Hence the fifth lateral bay on the
north side counting from the east
is called Bay 5 N, the ninth on the
south Bay 9 S, etc. The closets
behind the lateral bays are
numbered according to their
lateral window bay, i.e. side closet
Bay 5 N.

gatehouse stands in the centre of an east range which is treated externally
as a major facade with corner towers and intermediate turrets. The hall
lies directly opposite the entrance so that the screens passage is aligned
axially with the gate. The chapel occupies the eastern half of the north
range with its east gable wall forming part of the main entrance facade.
The plan is that of Pembroke College made formal by its degree of symmetry and architectural massing. The scale, however, is small and the
material, rose-red brick with stone dressings, imbues the buildings with
a domestic charm. Queens' College provides an embryonic plan for the
second and enlarged scheme for King's, while the architectonic nature
of the main facade harks back to the unfinished 1441 project for the Old
Court in the abandoned first phase. It is little wonder that all three
designs, the Old Court, Queens' and the second scheme for King's should
be attributed to the same architect, Reginald Ely.

The first indication that Henry VI intended to supplant the old small
chapel of King's College with a new, larger structure is contained in the
so-called 'Will and Intent' of 12 March 1448. This document details the
plan and arrangement for the new schemes for both King's College and
Eton. The Chapel proposed for King's was to be a long, unaisled building, divided roughly into two halves – a choir or chapel proper and an
antechapel. There was to be a two-storey vestry against the north-eastern
bay, Bay 1 N;[11] otherwise the choir was to be unencumbered by additions. The antechapel was to be flanked by eight small closets to act as
side chapels but not perform any practical function as side aisles. On
the south side, the end bays (Bays 1 S and 12 S) were to be connected
directly to the new college buildings, while a detached cloister and bell
tower were to stand to the west close to the River Cam.   27

The King's Will and Intent.[12]

And as touchying the demensions of the chirche of my said College of oure lady and saint Nicholas of Cambrige,.I. haue deuised and appointed that the same chirch shal conteyne in lengthe CCiij(xx) viij fete of assyse without any yles and alle of the widenesse of xl fete and the lengthe of the same chirch from the West ende vnto the Auters atte the queris dore, shal conteyne Cxx fete, And from the Provostes stalle vnto the grece called the gradus chori .iiij(xx)x fete for xxxvj stalles on either side of the same quere, answeryng vnto .lxx felawes and .x prestes conductes which must be de prima forma; and from the said stalles vnto the Est ende of the said chirch.lxij fete of assise. Also a reredos berying the Rodeloft departyng the quere and the body of the chirch, conteynyng in lengthe.xl fete and in brede .xiiij fete: the walls of the same chirche to be in height .iiij(xx)x fete, embatelled vauted and chare rofed sufficiently boteraced, and euery boterace fined with finailx.[13] And in the Est end of the said chirch shal be a wyndowe of .xj daies,[14] and in the west ende of the same chirch a window of ix daies and betwix euery boterace a wyndowe of .v daies And betwix euery of the same boteraces in the body of the chirche, on bothe sides of the same chirche, a closette with an auter therin, conteynyng in lengthe.xx fete, and in brede.x fete, vauted and finished vnter the soil of the yle wyndowes.[15] and in the pament of the chirch to be enhaunced .iiij fete aboue the groundes without, and the heighte of the pament of the quere, j fote di' aboue the pament of the chirche, and the pament of the high auter .iij fete aboue that. Item, on the north side of the quere a vestiarie conteyning in lengthe .l fete, and in brede .xxij fete, departed in to.ij houses benethe and .ij houses aboue, which shal conteyne in height .xxij(l) fete in all with an entre fro the quere vauted. Item, atte the west ende of the chirche a cloistre square, the Est pane conteynyng in lengthe .Clxxv fete, and the west pane as much;[16] and the north pane .cc fete, and the south pane asmuche, of the which the deambulatorie.xiij fete wide, and in heighte .xx fete to the corbel table, with clerestories and boteraced with finialx, vauted and embatelled, and the grounde therof.iiij fete lower than the chirch grounde; and in the myddel of the west pane of the cloistre a strong toure square, conteynyng.xxiiij fete within the walls, and in height.Cxx fete vnto the corbel table, and .iiij smale tourettis ouer that, fined with pynacles, and a dore in to the said cloistre ward, and outward noon.

And as touchyng the demensions of the housynge of the said College, I haue deuised and appointed in the south side of the said chirche, a quadrant closying unto bothe endes of the said chirche, the Est pane whereof shal conteyne.CCxxx fete in lengthe,and in brede within the walles.xxij fete; in the myddes of the same pane a tour for a yatehous, conteynyng in lengthe .xxx fete, and in brede .xxij fete, and in height .lx fete, with. iij chambres ouer the yate euery aboue other; And on either side of the same yate .iiij chambres, euery conteynyng in lengthe .xxv fete, and in brede .xxij fete: and ouer euery of thoo chambres .ij chambres above, of the same measure or more, with .ij toures outward and .ij toures inward. the south pane shall conteyne in lengthe .CCxxxviij fete and in brede .xxij fete within, in which shal be .vij chambres,euery conteynyng in lengthe .xxix fete, and in brede .xxij.'

12 Willis and Clark, vol. I. pp. 368–9.

13 'Chare rofed' – leaded, a chare being a weight of lead.

14 'Daies' – lights or vertical divisions of a window.

15 'Soil' – window cill.

16 'Pane' – cloister walk.

The great length of the new Chapel was one result of choosing a collegiate plan whereby the chapel filled one whole side of the main quadrangle. Thus the arrangement of King's can be related to All Souls Oxford, though expanded considerably. The inclusion of a detached cloister to the west, with its own bell tower, was a direct quote from New College Oxford. The interior dimensions of the proposed choir, some 168 ft (51·21 m) from the pulpitum door to the east wall, were determined partly by the decision to place the stalls in a single line *in prima forma* and not to double or treble them as at present. Thirty-six stalls with an average width of 3 ft (90 cm) would occupy the 90 ft (24·43 m) allocated to them in the Will, so that the stalls were to fill the entire length of the choir between the Provost's stall at the west end and the first step up to the sanctuary. This step, the *gradus chori*, was to cross the Chapel at the mid point of Bay 3, the position of the present doors into the north and south closets. Thus in the original design of 1448, the position of one half of these doors would have been covered by the stalls, whilst the remaining half would have been one step up. Quite plainly, the present doors were not envisaged in March 1448. The entrance to the proposed two-storey vestry must have been intended for Bay 1 N or 2 N.

The chapel scheme of March 1448 postdates Henry's intention to link his Cambridge college with his foundation at Eton. The chapel in Henry's Buckinghamshire college was also to accommodate the parish church of Eton village, for which he intended the addition of an aisled nave. The choir was to be the college chapel proper and was to be a single unaisled space. Eton College Chapel went through so many vicissitudes and alterations in plan that its history has become one of the most complex of any of England's medieval churches, but, it is worth investigating for any parallels it might have with King's College Chapel.[17] The first choir at Eton measured some 103 by 32 ft (31·39 by 9·75 m). It was built between *c.* 1441 and 1448, only to be demolished in favour of a larger scheme. The Will and Intent of 1448 also includes a plan for Eton which still lists the dimensions of the first chapel, so that its demolition probably occurred after March of that year. Evidently, Henry VI decided upon the present dimensions for Eton after sending his master mason to measure the choirs of Winchester and Salisbury Cathedrals in January 1449. Yet, it is a curious fact that the new choir of Eton begun early in that year reproduces the dimensions given in the Will and Intent for the intended plan of King's College Chapel. The altar area was to be 62 by 40 ft (18·90 by 12·19 m) while the area allocated to the stalls was 88 by 40 ft (26·82 by 12·19 m) with the stalls running from the reredos to the first altar step exactly as in the proposal for King's. Eton College Chapel was recommenced about one year after the Will and Intent of March 1448, by which time the Cambridge Chapel had been begun, but to a different plan. It would almost seem as though the measurements

28

17 Willis and Clark, vol. I. pp. 350–51; H. M. Colvin *et al.*, vol. I. pp. 279–92; M. Lyte, *History of Eton College*, London 1889.

for the 1448 scheme at King's were transferred to the new choir at Eton, while a slightly different proposal was adopted for Cambridge.

The antechapel proposal for King's was entirely different from the intended parochial nave at Eton and it is here that some of the more curious omissions from the Will and Intent become apparent. The most notable is the absence from the design of King's College Chapel of any doors – no means of entry from the outside into either the choir or antechapel is specified in the Will, yet some decision must have been taken over such an important and practical matter. The present entrances, through the north and south porches in Bay 11 and the west door, are not additions or insertions into the built fabric but no doors are referred to in any of these positions in the Will. Indeed, the reference to the small closets 'betwix euery of the same boteraces in the body of the chirche,

28 Eton College: Chapel interior looking east

on bothe sides. . . .' would eliminate the provision of the present side porches in Bay 11. A west door was doubtless intended, both for architectural propriety and for access to the cloister, but again, no door is specified in the Will in this position. While there would be no practical difficulty in providing a west door, it would hardly have been the sole entry, particularly as it lay outside the principal College court. Some direct access from College to Chapel must have been intended, but where? Bays 1 to 6 were to be occupied by the altar area and the stalls, thus blocking the available wall space. Even Bay 3 S with its existing door to the closet was to be blocked in the original scheme. Bays 8 to 11 were to be flanked by closets containing altars, while Bay 12 S was to form the angle connecting the Chapel with the library in the west range. It is possible that the main college entrance to the Chapel was to be through one of the side closets, though they are very small and intended to function as chapels. Perhaps Bay 12 S was to have a lobby contrived under the first-floor library with access to the court next to the Disputation and reading rooms – Willis pointed out that the dimensions of these rooms as given in the Will left an odd 12 ft (3·66 m) with an unspecified use for which he suggested a passage to the south of the library between it and the hall.[18] It might equally have formed a ground-level passage from the court to Bay 12 S of the Chapel, though the depth would be insufficient to clear the buttress without cutting it back. Hence only one bay on the southern side presents itself as a suitable candidate for the principal entrance to the Chapel in the 1448 design – Bay 7 S. This bay was to contain the 'reredos berying the Rodeloft' dividing the choir from the antechapel. The bay was not intended to have a side closet nor were its lateral internal walls to be covered by the stalls. Bay 7 S also lies at the mid point of the north side of the principal college court, the buttress between Bays 6 S and 7 S being dead centre. Thus Bay 7 S could provide a chapel door from the middle of the court with direct access beneath the roodloft to both the choir and antechapel. The reredos supporting the 'Rodeloft' was to be extraordinarily deep, 14 ft (4·27 m), far larger than necessary but quite big enough to contain a walking space. According to the Will, the antechapel was to have at least two 'auters at the queries dore', suggesting a central door through the screen with an altar either side. An exterior door in Bay 7 S would thus lead to a wide walking space, with a single door east and west to the choir and antechapel. The immediate parallel for such an arrangement would be the larger friar's churches where, commonly, just such a walking space separated the aisled preaching nave from the friar's own unaisled choir.[19] Such a model for King's College Chapel would be quite characteristic of Henry VI and might also explain the great and rather useless size of the antechapel.

The placing of the side chapels in small closets between the buttresses at King's represents a trend current in chantry chapel building during the first half of the fifteenth century. Henry himself had ordered the erec-

18 Willis and Clark, vol. I. p. 375.

19 For example, St Andrew's Norwich. For plan see H. Sutermeister, *The Norwich Blackfriars*, Norwich 1977, pp. 14–15.

tion of a similar closet chapel between the buttresses of the Trinity Chapel in Canterbury Cathedral – the chantry of his grandfather, Henry IV, built after 1435, and tucked beneath the main windows in much the same way as the closets at King's. A similar chapel was built outside the north aisle of the Angel choir at Lincoln by Bishop Fleming *c.* 1425. Two others existed between the choir buttresses of Old St Paul's, the Waltham Chantry of *c.* 1325 and the More Chantry of *c.* 1418. However, all these chapels were coincidental to the main church and were all additions to an existing fabric. The closets at King's were to be an integral part of the initial build, though playing only a minor role in the overall appearance of the Chapel. The most obvious parallel, though geographically remote, is the thirteenth-century cathedral of Albi in southern France.

The eight closet chapels specified in the Will and Intent were each to contain an altar. Probably the number chosen reflected the number of priests to be attached to the college – Henry stipulated that there should be ten priests included in the overall numbers of the foundation. If one altar stood either side of the roodloft door as implied in the Will, then the antechapel would contain ten altars in all, one for each priest. The provision of so many antechapel altars, and the decision to place them in 'chantry' closets between the buttresses was another factor in determining the shape and size of the antechapel. The containment of ten altars would also appear to be the only function intended for the antechapel and it is somewhat surprising therefore that in the original proposal they would appear to be quite divorced from the main interior and relegated into small closets shut off from the main space. Possibly, Henry VI simply instructed that his Cambridge chapel was to appoximate the size of his intended Eton Chapel, with its additional parochial nave. King's had no such local function, for though the parish church of St John Zachery was demolished for the new Chapel, it was to be rebuilt 'at our own cost near to our aforesaid college'.[20] The last and most unusual feature of the initial design for King's College Chapel was that the whole building was to be vaulted, presumably in stone and not wood. No university college chapel prior to King's, or for that matter after it, was stone vaulted throughout, and it must be taken as a sign of the special significance and prestige awarded to King's by Henry VI that the choir, antechapel, the closets and even the entry to the vestries were to be vaulted in stone like the great cathedral churches.

G. G. Scott proposed that the model for King's College Chapel was the free-standing Lady Chapel of Ely Cathedral, built *c.* 1320–80.[21] Quite obviously, one aisless rectangular chapel is much like another so what are the architectural features common to both Ely and King's? The *29* Ely chapel has large lateral windows with decorated figure niches within the internal jambs. So has King's. The emphasis placed on the lateral windows in the overall design is also similar to King's. The Lady Chapel at Ely is notably wide for a stone-vaulted structure – the clear span is

20 Willis and Clark, Vol. I. p. 550.

21 G. G. Scott, *Essay on the History of English Gothic Architecture*, 1881, pp. 182–3.

43 ft 6 in. (13·26 m) while the interior width between the glass is 46 ft 6 in (14·17 m). The King's vault is 41 ft (12·66 m), which is also wide by English medieval standards. However, there is no evidence to prove, *30* or even to suggest, that the Ely Lady Chapel was ever intended to be vaulted nor that the present vault was built prior to the commencement of King's College Chapel in 1448. The parallels for the Ely vault would suggest that it was an addition to the basic structure from the second half of the fifteenth century.[22]

Even if the Ely Lady Chapel had been vaulted before the design of King's College Chapel, there are yet more differences that would make it an unlikely model. Ely is a single space while King's was always to be two connected spaces totalling nearly three times the overall length of Ely. The Lady Chapel has no side closets or additional altar areas, its liturgical function and arrangements are entirely different, and unlike King's, it was never intended as part of an integrated architectural complex. Ely belongs to a series of detached, or semi-detached Lady Chapels once also found at Peterborough, Thetford and Bury St Edmunds. Could it be that Scott was attracted by the name of Reginald Ely, the first master mason of King's College Chapel? Despite his name, Ely came from Norwich. More probably, the original design of King's College Chapel

22 F. Woodman, The Vault of the Ely Lady Chapel. *Gesta*, 1984, The Metropolitan Museum, New York, 23, 2.

29 Ely Cathedral: exterior of Lady Chapel from west
30 Ely Cathedral: interior of Lady Chapel looking north-east

followed no precise model, but represents the sum total of its own collegiate requirements – its shape and size determined by the adoption of the
All Souls Oxford variant of the New College plan. The grandness of
the overall design, the polished ashlar exterior elevations, the huge
windows, high vaults and perhaps even the 'two-storey' effect of the
exterior may all be a hazy reflection of Henry's childhood memories of
the Ste Chapelle which probably served as the King's personal chapel
during the English occupation of Paris. Whatever lay behind the 1448
design of King's College Chapel, it need owe no debt to any particular
building in the locality.

The financing of the construction in the reign of Henry VI

The building of King's College Chapel was dogged by lack of money.
Royal grants often went unpaid. In 1461, Edward IV cut off all royal
funds for a number of years as did Henry VII after 1485. The only reason
why the Chapel construction dragged on for over seventy years was the
halting and often dry sources of income. In the Will and Intent of 1448,
Henry VI set out directions for the funding of both King's and Eton,
to be drawn from the revenues of the land held in feoffment by the Duchy
of Lancaster. He ordered that each college should receive £1,000 backdated to Michelmas 1447, and that this grant should be repeated annually
for twenty years, with an extension thereafter if either foundation
remained incomplete.[23] The order replaced a similar grant issued in 1446
that was intended to run for only fourteen years, but by 1448 the larger
scheme for King's had been born, requiring considerably more money.
In the same year, both colleges received a legacy of £1,000 in the will
of Cardinal Beaufort.

Additional royal grants were made in kind, usually free building
materials, oaks from the Duchy estates at Wethersfield in Essex, and
thirty acres of woodland at Quendon, both in 1443, and oaks from Deb-
den in 1446. The King also diverted part of the fee farm due to him
from the City of Cambridge towards the building of King's College,
ordering £10 per annum to be paid over from 23 March 1445.[24] Eventually the entire fee farm of £70 per annum was given over by the King.
Had all these generous grants been paid promptly, the early architectural
history of the Chapel would have run smoothly with considerable progress made possible prior to the overthrow of Henry VI in 1461 – indeed
the Chapel might have been completed by the original target date of 1468.

Two major problems exist regarding the financial history of the Chapel
prior to 1476; the most important is the loss of all the Chapel building
accounts from the reign of Henry VI, while the accounts of the Duchy
of Lancaster appear to be missing for a number of vital years, especially
between 1455 and 1460. The King's College Accounts were divided into

23 Willis and Clark, vol. I. pp. 353–4;
R. Somerville, *The Duchy of
Lancaster*, vol. I *1265–1603*,
London 1953, p. 221.

24 Close Roll 26 Henry VI. p. 9,
under June 18, 1448 makes
reference to a grant of fee farm to
King's College by letters Patent of
23 March, 1445. Close Roll 29
Henry VI, p. 206 of 30 November,
1450 confirms this grant and
orders the City to pay arrears.

two parts: the college expenses, including the cost of the college buildings, and a quite separate Chapel building account. The former were handled through normal college channels but the latter were regarded as records for an independent royal project, accountable directly to the King. All the latter are lost. Hence the picture presented by the documentary evidence is very patchy. Add to this the temporary insanity of Henry VI between August 1453 and January 1455 and again from the June of that year to the following January, the collapse of the English resistance in France and the outbreak of civil hostilities at St Albans in May 1455 and it will not be found surprising that smooth and well-ordered government appears to have broken down.

Some comfort may be found in the surviving building expenses at Eton College, where accounts exist for much of the period to 1460. Both colleges were to be financed by identical grants from the Duchy of Lancaster, so that every pound spent at Eton should represent a pound given to King's.[25] However, the extent to which each college may have supplemented its Royal revenues from its own substantial income is impossible to determine – by 1460, King's College revenues had reached £1,000 per annum.[26] Between 1448 and 1460 it can be estimated that Eton spent over £8,000 on its buildings, that is on the Chapel and the College, while even the most generous assessment of the expenditure at King's Cambridge, admittedly taken from scraps of evidence, totals less than £2,000 over the same period. Either Eton was subsidising its building work heavily from its own income, or the accounts at King's belie the true level of expenditure or the construction of King's College Chapel was way behind schedule.

The organisation of the Cambridge project was placed in the hands of William Waynflete, Bishop of Winchester from 1447, who had impressed the young King Henry with his 'high trought and fervent zele'. The man responsible to the Bishop in Cambridge was the Master of the Works, a post held until 1447 by John Langton, Master of Pembroke and Chancellor of the University. After his elevation to the bishopric of St David's his place was taken by the Provost of King's, William Millington, though a dispute over the statues forced his early resignation.[27] Millington was replaced by Nicholas Close, a fellow of the college, who was in turn created Bishop of Carlisle in March 1449/50. By December 1452, Robert Wodelarke had been elected Provost, and shortly after he took over the additional role as Master of the Works, a post he continued to hold until the overthrow of Henry VI. The King also determined that there should be a Clerk of the Works for the accounting and financial administration. This post was held successively by William Ruskyn, c. 1444–1451/2, Thomas Dekyn, 1451/2–1458 and by John Canterbury from 1458.

The master mason of the Chapel, responsible for designing and constructing the building, was Reginald Ely, named as early as 1443, that

25 D. Knoop and G. Jones, The Building Accounts of Eton College. *Ars Quatour Coronatorum*, XLVI 1933, pp. 70–111.

26 J. Saltmarsh, in *Cambridgeshire, Victoria County History*, vol. III, 1959, p. 379.

27 J. Saltmarsh, *King's College*, Cambridge 1959, p. 5 and n.

28 Calender of Patent Rolls 1441–46. p. 269.

is before the conception of the great new scheme.[28] Ely certainly remained in charge until 1461 and possibly later still. Thomas Sturgeon was the master carpenter from at least 1443 and the King also made provision for a chief smith and two purveyors.[29] The Will of 1448 stipulated the various annual wages of each man: £50 for the Master of the Works, £16 13s 4d to the master mason £13 6s 8d for the clerk, £12 8s 0d for the carpenter, £9 2s 9d to each of the purveyors, and £6 13s 4d to the chief smith. Thus the annual wages bill for just seven men came to £117. 6s 10d.

29 Ibid. p. 247.

It is ironic that in the years preceding the commencement of the new Chapel, financial evidence is at its best. After the grant of £1,000 in each of the years 1444 and 1445, there followed a grant of £1,400 1s 0d in 1446 plus £100 worth of service books.[30] All this money was destined for the original small Chapel and for the abortive Old Court of the earliest scheme. Despite the grant of £1,000 p.a. backdated to Michaelmas 1447, the evidence of Royal financing appears to evaporate during the vital period surrounding the decision to build a new and larger college complex. In 1447, only £400 is known to have been provided while in the crucial year 1448 a mere £299 19s 8d was received from the Duchy, together with a half share of vestments worth a total of £221 19s 3d. In 1449/50, only £377 3s 9d is known to have been made over and after that there is a silence. In each year between 1452 and 1457 a grant of £100 was made by the King, probably from his own personal revenues, but nothing is heard of the major annual grant of £1,000 from the Duchy of Lancaster promised in 1448. Chalices worth £104 were donated by Henry in 1460 and a further grant of £100 to speed the completion of the work. There can be little doubt from a study of the Eton Accounts that Royal payments were on the decline after 1448/9. Between 1443/4 and 1448/9 expenditure at Eton was in excess of £1,000 in each of the five years, being £2,016 in 1443/4, and £1,716 and £1,704 in 1447/8 and 1448/9. Throughout this period, income exceeded expenditure at Eton by as much as £750 p.a. But then expenditure fell to below £1,000 in every recorded year to 1460 save for 1452/3 when £1,560 was spent. The lowest years were 1457/8 when £396 was paid out and 1459/60 with accounts totalling only £360. Nevertheless, between 1448/9 and 1459/60, Eton managed to find £8,082 for building works against an estimated amount at King's Cambridge of only £1,948 13s 9d – this including £328 10s 4d paid from his own funds by Robert Wodelarke in excess of income prior to 1461.[31] Despite the Civil War, the King's illness and the French raids, Henry's interest in the Cambridge project was maintained, if not expressed financially. In February 1459 the King made a fresh attempt to revive the flagging work with an order of impressment authorising Wodelarke and the master mason and carpenter to impress building labour and materials for the continuation of work.[32] In the same month, the King ordered the City of Cambridge to make over the entire

30 Somerville, vol. I. pp. 221–2.

31 Willis and Clark, vol. I pp. 469–70; Colvin, vol. I. p. 221.

32 Calender of Patent Rolls 1452–61, p. 478.

annual fee farm of £70 towards the operations, and in addition to the Royal gift of £100, Henry gave bells to the value of £60, evidently to be used and not sold for bell metal.[33] In this year, the income of King's College from its own revenues topped £1,000.

After the overthrow of Henry VI and the acclamation of Edward IV on 4 March 1461, the new King set about dismantling the income and estates of his rival's foundations. King's College suffered a halving of their income by the sequestration of college estates while what income there had been from the Duchy of Lancaster was stopped. The number of student admissions fell dramatically – there had been 70 scholars in 1451 but by 1465 there were only 23. Against this hostile background, and the uncertain future of the Yorkist dynasty, the work on King's College Chapel could hardly flourish.

Other documents concerning the earliest phase in the construction of King's College Chapel

Evidence for the actual progress of construction upon King's College Chapel prior to 1476 can be gleaned from further documents, mostly from outside the royal administration – letters, property transactions and incidental expenses recorded in the College Accounts, and those known as the Mundum Books. No building work could begin until the ground on which the Chapel stands had been acquired. The site formed part of what was originally intended to be an extension of the Old Court scheme. It was purchased from 1443 though negotiations for certain plots continued into the 1450s. Until recently, it was believed that the foundation stone laid by Henry VI on 25 July 1446 was for the present Chapel, but the evidence for this, contained within a letter, should now be dated to 1444, indicating that the ceremonial concerned the building of the old, small chapel adjacent to the Old Court.[34] Thus there is no known date for the commencement of the present King's College Chapel. Permission to build on the 'whole site' acquired for the second college scheme was granted by Parliament on 30 May 1449, some fourteen months after Henry VI had approved the new layout as detailed in the Will and Intent. This approval may well indicate the earliest date for the commencement of the existing Chapel.[35] The properties of Robert Lyncoln, lying along the High Street (now King's Parade) and extending back to the east end of the Chapel site, were not acquired until 1452, and even then the College agreed to allow Robert and his wife to remain in occupation until their deaths.[36] Such an agreement must signify that the properties were a desirable addition to the site rather than an essential element of it. The continued presence of buildings along the street line may have influenced the position of the new college layout, setting it back behind an existing

33 Close Roll 38 Henry VI, p. 407; Somerville, vol. I. p. 221.

34 Saltmarsh, *King's College*, p. 91.

35 *Rot. Parl.* V. 164a.

36 Willis and Clark, vol. I. pp. 336–7.

37 Ibid. p. 397.

38 Knoop and Jones, pp. 70–111.

39 Ibid.

40 King's College Muniments, College Accounts vol. II; and RCHM, *City of Cambridge*, vol. I, p. 99.

41 A. Oswald, in *English Medieval Architects*, p. 96, quoting College Accounts vol. II. I cannot confirm this from the existing accounts.

42 Willis and Clark, vol. I, p. 489. Burial of John Stok servant to the Provost. There are many precedents for burial within an unfinished or simply projected building once the ground is consecrated.

43 RCHM, *City of Cambridge*, vol. I, p. 99.

44 King's College Muniments. *Custus Ecclesie* 1469/70.

45 Ibid., Mundum Book vol. IV, 1466/67.

46 Ibid., Mundum Book vol. V, 1468/69.

47 Ibid., Mundum Book vol. VI, 1470–74.

ribbon development. Subsequent dating evidence for the building of the Chapel is scant, due to the loss of all the early building accounts, while references in the College Muniments give but the slightest indication of progress. The grant of the Yorkshire quarry at Huddleston to Eton and King's in February 1449 may well have been prompted by a new start on the chapels at both sites.[37] Quarrying, carriage and labour costs at Huddleston are recorded in nearly half the surviving Eton accounts for the eleven building seasons between 1449 and 1460.[38] The payment of 33s 4d rent to Huddleston in the Eton accounts of 1458/9[39] would suggest that a similar sum was paid each year by King's, making a total 'rent' of £3 6s 8d – two pounds less than King's paid alone for a Northamptonshire quarry in 1460.[40] On 15 April of that year, Reginald Ely, master mason of King's, was given 33s 4d when 'riding to the quarry'.[41] No destination is named, but the sum is far greater than normal travelling expenses and it may well represent the King's College share of the Huddleston rent for 1460/61. If the Eton accounts do parallel the lost accounts of King's then Huddleston limestone was in fairly regular supply in Cambridge until at least 1460 at which point the early accounts at Eton draw to a close.

Documentary evidence for the state of the Chapel at King's by 1460 is limited to a few references only. In 1458 a burial occurred in the 'nave of the new chirche', taken to refer to the antechapel, though there is the possibility that it refers to the old small chapel.[42] In 1460, the College Accounts include payment for a key to one of the new chapels, that is one of the side closets of the existing Chapel.[43] Subsequent evidence for the repair of the hangings in the Provost's Chapel in 1470 suggests that the closet referred to ten years earlier was that against Bay 2 N.[44] Thus by 1460, one side closet was sufficiently complete to require locking.

The fall of Henry VI in the following year inflicted severe financial hardship upon King's College and it has been assumed that this calamity brought building work upon the new Chapel to a standstill. Part of this assumption, however, is based on lack of evidence. For example, the College Mundum Books which occasionally record incidental expenditure upon the Chapel are missing from 1459 until 1466, but once these accounts resume the evidence they contain suggests that at least some building work had continued during the early part of the reign of Edward IV. Three references from 1467 will illustrate this point; the 'towers' of the new church were covered over, presumably having been uncovered for some reason, 'large stones' were brought into the college, and reference is made to a mason's lodge.[45] Two years later a second closet was completed, the lock, key and two bolts being entered in the College Accounts.[46] In 1472 the mason's lodge was rebuilt, though by now, the College was also involved with the rebuilding of the Grammar School, known as the Glomery Hall, but in the same year a plumber was paid for 'sawdering over the choir and chapels of the new buildings'.[47] The repeated covering and uncovering of the new Chapel denotes winter protection of building operations, for the expensive lead covering once placed would hardly be removed for any other reason. The additional mention of buttresses in the 1472 accounts is also the first indication that any of the fabric had risen above the level of the side closet roofs that envelop their lower areas.

A second burial took place on 5 January 1473, in 'a chapel on the south side of the new collegiate church', which resulted in damage to the pavement that had to be repaired.[48] Once again a brief secondary reference provides evidence that a third closet, this time one on the southern side, was finished and paved prior to January 1473. A private subscription to further the building of the Chapel raised from the fellows in 1476 realised a mere £10 19s 4d[49] which was followed by a recorded expenditure of at least £77 1s 7d in the next year.[50] These monies have been taken as evidence for a completely new building campaign, picking up work 'abandoned' since 1461. The sums involved however, are comparatively trivial, for example, the annual wages of the seven leading officers as determined by Henry VI came to well over £100 p.a. and, from the previous references from the College Accounts, it would appear that building work had continued, though very slowly, throughout most of the troubled years between 1461 and 1476.

The recorded expenditure of 1476 and the succeeding flood of documentary references in the College Accounts and Mundum Books may indeed signify a new determination on the part of the College to pursue the work on the Chapel, though it might indicate no more than a change in the accounting system away from the entirely separate recording of the Chapel and College expenses.

The documents concerning the first master masons

Architectural control of the Chapel during the first phase to 1476 lay originally with Reginald Ely and subsequently with John Wolryche. Ely was first named as 'Chief mason of our College of the blessed Mary and Saint Nicholas of Cambridge' in letters Patent of 16 June 1444, some four or five years prior to the commencement of the great Chapel. He was referred to by name in a fragment of College Building Accounts covering 6 July to 3 August 1443.[51] Reginald Ely continued to figure in various College records, though the loss of the actual building accounts for the present Chapel precludes any absolute assurance that he was indeed the original designer. Between April 1459 and April 1461, the Provost entertained Ely at table on no less than thirty occasions[52] and he was also one of those empowered to impress masons and materials by Patent of 26 February 1459.[53] On 9 April 1460, Ely's salary was in arrears, Provost Wodelarke finding himself in serious financial diffi-

48 Willis and Clark, vol. I, p. 489.

49 Ibid. p. 472.

50 Ibid.

51 T. Carter, *Notes on King's College Cambridge*, 1867, p. 11.

52 King's College Muniments Kitchen Accounts. See also A. Oswald in *English Medieval Architects*, p. 96.

53 Calender of Patent Rolls 1452–61, p. 478.

54 King's College Muniments College Accounts, vol. II.

55 Ibid. vol. VI.

56 Ibid., vol. II, and see p. 39, n. 41.

57 Ibid., Mundum Book vol. V, 1468/69.

58 Gonville and Caius Muniments Box. xxi. no. 18. See also Oswald, *English Medieval Architects*, p. 96.

59 Willis and Clark, vol. I, p. 12.

60 Ibid., vol. II, p. 450.

61 Carter, p. 11. King's College Muniments Kitchen Accounts.

62 Willis and Clark, vol. I, p. 629.

culties.[54] At one stage, Ely actually lent Wodelarke £10, but within a few months this had been repaid together with £7 8s 8d in part payment of arrears, with a further £8 10s on 5 June 1460, leaving him still £1 10s short. The final payment of £1 owing to Reginald Ely was paid to his executors several years after his death in 1471.[55] Other payments made by the College to Ely whilst acting as master mason included the half share of the quarry rent of 33s 4d paid back to Ely after he had visited the quarry in April 1460,[56] and even after the fall of Henry VI the College continued to utilise Ely's services as purveyor or supplier of building materials: in 1468 they purchased from him coping stones for a College wall.[57] By this time, Reginald Ely was an old man. He had made his will in 1463 though it was not proved until 16 July 1471.[58] Occasional payments by the University Proctors in 1463 show that Ely was still active, but the making of his will in the same year must indicate that he considered himself to be at the end of his working life. The original provisions of the will make no reference to King's College Chapel, instead Ely left money to Queens' College whose President, Andrew Doket, was at one time his neighbour in Silver Street. By the year of his death, in 1471, Ely must have been sixty at the very least, being first mentioned as a practising mason in Cambridge in 1439.[59] There is no clear evidence as to when Reginald Ely relinquished his position as master mason of King's College Chapel. If indeed, work did come to a brief standstill during the first few years of the reign of Edward IV, then Ely may have taken that opportunity to withdraw. The making of his will in 1463 must be some indication of his state of health and his ability to recommence so great an undertaking in such difficult circumstances.

The second master mason, John Wolryche, is the most sketchily known of the four successive architects. A possible background for Wolryche may be provided by King's Hall, now Trinity College Cambridge, where 'John Wolryche, mason, and supervisor of the masons' was paid in connection with their new chapel in 1468/9.[60] It had been under construction since at least 1464. Master mason of King's Hall, as implied by the entry, was a post of considerable prestige in Cambridge, indeed, John Wastell, the last master mason of King's, held that post whilst concurrently master mason of Canterbury Cathedral. It is quite possible, therefore, that Wolryche was master mason for both King's College and King's Hall at once. Reference to him at King's College is scant: between January and June 1476, Wolryche was a constant guest for dinner in hall,[61] and in the same year he was named in a legal case as 'Master mason of the King's College Royal of our Lady and Saint Nicholas'.[62] The College Mundum Book for 1476/7 specifies that £6 17s 2d was paid 'at divers times' to Wolryche and his son, masons, working on the said new church. Later in the same Book, Simon Clerk is called master mason of the Chapel. John Wolryche had either died, retired or moved on elsewhere.

The constructional progress of the first phase using the evidence of building materials

The constructional progress of King's College Chapel prior to 1476 is very difficult to determine what with the loss of all the principal building accounts and only the most fleeting secondary references as compensation. After 1476, the surviving documents do give some indication of the state of the fabric as it then stood but, as it has been shown, it is not possible from purely documentary sources to establish how the building was erected, in what order, and which of the two masters was responsible for the various parts of the design. However, the secondary evidence that does exist would tend to discredit the rigid division of the work into two entirely separate campaigns – one ending in 1461, another beginning in 1476. The arrival of Simon Clerk as master mason in 1477 and the patronage of Edward IV from 1479 would seem a more obvious starting point for any 'second campaign', allowing that the first work may only have ticked over during the lean years of the 1460s. Given the lack of documentary information about the precise date at which Wolryche replaced Ely, coupled with the vague indication of the amount and level of the structure built prior to 1476, it is difficult to assess the relative contributions of the two architects of the first phase without a very detailed analysis of materials, style and structure.

The employment of a hard white magnesian limestone from Yorkshire as a date marker is one of the best-known features of the architectural history of King's College Chapel. King's College acquired the right to quarry the fine white magnesian limestone of Thefsdale in 1447.[63] Two years later, they were granted, together with Eton, the right to quarry at Huddleston, close by.[64] The stone was evidently free, subject to the payment of an annual rent, the rent 'shared' with Eton. Both colleges financed its quarry and carriage jointly. In 1460, King's College was acquiring a beige brown oolitic limestone from the Northamptonshire quarry of King's Cliffe for use on the Chapel.[65] Willis, in the nineteenth century, pointed out that, as the acquisition of the white Yorkshire stone was known to date from 1447 and 1449, and as the brown Northamptonshire oolitic limestone was bought in 1460, then the employment of the white stone should define all the building work carried out between 1448/9 and 1460.[66] This demarcation has won general acceptance and has formed the basis of all subsequent discussion.[67] The use of the white magnesian to identify the greater part of the 'first campaign' has one important consequence for the history of the Chapel. All the side closets have exterior base courses in white Huddleston as do the north and south porches and some of the interior antechapel vault support bases. Thus for Willis, and for all subsequent writers, the whole Chapel with its side closets and porches, was laid out to a height of at least 4 ft (1·22 m) prior to 1460. The provision of the present eighteen closets and north and south

63 Willis and Clark, vol. I, p. 466.

64 Ibid., vol. I, p. 397.

65 King's College Muniments College Account vol. VI and vol. II. See also Colvin, vol. I, p. 275.

66 Willis and Clark, vol. I, pp. 486–95.

67 RCHM, *City of Cambridge*, vol. I, pp. 99–100.

31 King's College Chapel: numbered plan as used throughout the text

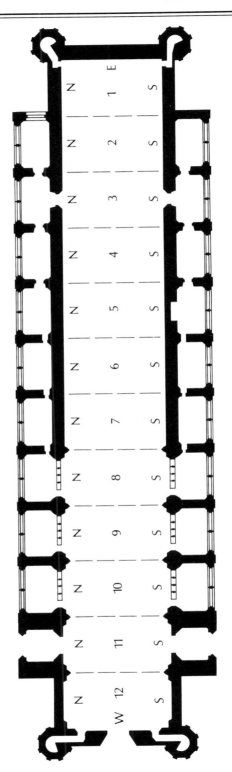

32 King's College Chapel: interior of closet Bay 3 N showing junction of white magnesian limestone from Huddleston and the brown oolitic limestone from Northamptonshire

33 King's College Chapel: interior of closet Bay 4 N showing extent of the employment of brown oolitic limestone from Northamptonshire

34 King's College Chapel: interior of south porch showing the white Huddleston base mouldings

68 Not all of the closet walls have been cleaned of their plaster.

porches has long posed a problem, since they are contrary to the Will and Intent of 1448, but the 'evidence' of the base course material seemed so strong that it is assumed that the plan must have changed dramatically between March 1448 and the commencement of the work. The idea that the whole Chapel was laid out from the very beginning and that this initial work dictated every succeeding building campaign has determined the direction of all the scholarship devoted to King's College Chapel since 1886.

The truth is somewhat different. The recent cleaning of the Chapel interior, the removal of the sanctuary panelling and the lowering of the floor area in Bays 1 and 2 has revealed that the white magnesian limestone was neither the first nor the only material in use at King's before 1460. The interior base courses visible in bays 1 to 3 N are, with the exception of the door jambs in Bay 3 N, of a brown oolitic limestone, probably from Northamptonshire. The white magnesian begins some way above, at the original floor level. The reverse walling of the choir bays visible within the north and south closets can be seen to be of brown oolite in Bays 2, north and south, 3 N, 4 north and south and in 5 N, though *32* in some bays the lowest course of all is in white magnesian limestone. The brown oolite is also used extensively in the cross walls within the *33* closets in Bays 2 N, 3 north and south, 4 north and south, 5 north and south (?) and in 6 north and south.[68] Within the choir, all the walling visible above the base courses appears to be in white magnesian limestone up to the level of the Angel frieze that runs directly beneath the cills of the main lateral windows. Hence, all the obvious areas intended originally to be visible within the choir are faced in the finer, more expensive white magnesian from Yorkshire, whilst the backing material, all out of sight within the closets, is the cheaper oolite from Northamptonshire. More than half the material employed in the lower sections of the eastern bays of the Chapel and side closets is a brown oolite, probably from King's Cliffe. It is this section that was regarded by Willis and many others as being pre-1460 due to the 'sole use' of white magnesian limestone. Unless the base courses of the eastern bays post-date 1460, which is hard to imagine, then the isolated ordering of a delivery from King's

Cliffe in 1460 was not the first acquisition of stone from Northamptonshire.

The loss of any early reference to the purchase of brown oolitic limestone between 1449 and 1460 must raise corresponding doubts as to the 'abandonment' of the use of white magnesian in 1460, since it has always been assumed that the brown King's Cliffe replaced the white Huddleston. The fall of Henry VI, and even a brief cessation of the building operations thereafter, may not have prevented the College from continuing some acquisition of materials, indeed, the College Accounts for 1467 show payments for 'bringing large stones into the College'. The source of this stone is not specified, but it could just as easily be white magnesian limestone from Huddleston as brown oolite from King's Cliffe.

The pier bases that form the vault supports in the antechapel further discredit the notion of a 'sole use' of Huddleston in any phase of the construction. Only four of the clustered moulded bases are made entirely of Huddleston; VS 7/8 S, VS 8/9 S, VS 10/11 N and VS 12/13 S.[69] The majority of the bases are made of the brown oolite though standing on at least one course of the Huddleston. Two vault support pier bases, VS 8/9 N and VS 12/13 N, have moulded sections in Huddleston but stand on top of base courses of Northamptonshire oolitic. Similarly, the north-west tower has exterior base courses of Huddleston but interior base courses in King's Cliffe. The moulded bases within the north and south porches are also of Huddleston but they too stand on pedestal courses of brown oolite. *34*

The cleaning of the Chapel interior has further revealed that the choir interior has a 'two-tone' design, with white Huddleston below the Angel frieze and a fine beige brown stone above, a Northamptonshire oolite. This particular stone is finer, smoother and paler than the brown oolites elsewhere and may be King's Cliffe or perhaps an excellent Clipsham. Only a few odd blocks of Huddleston have found their way into the lateral elevations above the Angel frieze and they are now very obvious to the eye.

The extensive use of Northamptonshire oolitic limestone in some of the lowest sections of the Chapel interior changes signficantly previous notions about the early history of the work and in particular about the 'necessary' order of its building. The employment of the rougher, brown stone as a backing material for the smoother Huddleston and the overwhelming use of a fine Northamptonshire stone for the interior elevations above the Angel frieze suggests strongly that the white Huddleston was reserved from very early in the work to be used only in those areas of prominence such as the plain walls around the high altar, for some of the detailed carved work and for the moulded sections of the antechapel vault supports. It was also kept for the major external features: the base course plinth moulding and for the great buttresses. This selection of materials may have been both aesthetic and practical, the finer

69 The vault supports divide the lateral window bays and are consequently numbered VS 0/1 N and S to VS 12/13 N and S.

Huddleston being less susceptible to damp, an important consideration when building next to a river. A similar 'colour scheme' was used for the riverside Chapel at Eton, with the hard white Yorkshire stone for the base plinth and less durable Teynton above. The reservation of Huddleston at King's may well have continued after 1460 either from source or using material stored away in the lodges. After all, no one at the quarry could have foreseen the fall of Henry VI. Stored Huddleston might still have been available during the 'second campaign' under Simon Clerk from 1477, especially if the College had supplemented the supply in the late 1460s.[70]

In the light of this discovery, several well-established 'facts' concerning the phased construction of King's College Chapel must now be re-examined. The entire ground plan, as expressed by the continuous exterior plinth, has been attributed to the earliest phase of construction in the late 1440s due to the employment of Huddleston. Hence it was assumed that the antechapel had at least been laid out when the elevations of the choir were under way. With the reservation of Huddleston precisely for this feature, the antechapel could have been laid out on the ground at any time up to 1477 and possibly later still. The whole layout no longer *has* to be an early feature of 1448.[71] However, as early as Hammond's aerial view of 1592, confirmed by Loggan's view of 1690, the present plinth in Bay 12 S was already intact. Unless this section of the plinth was rebuilt between 1508 and 1515, then the westernmost bay may not have been laid out until after the abandonment of the great court to the south. This is unlikely to have happened before the overthrow of Henry VI in 1461 and perhaps not until after his death in 1472. With this in mind, the dating of the progress within the antechapel becomes an enormous problem. It is not even possible to pinpoint the speed of construction by matching the occurrence of particular materials in the building with those specified in the various references, for the Huddleston was reserved, and one brown oolite looks much like another. The antechapel contains at least three oolites, of which two, King's Cliffe and Clipsham, come from closely neighbouring quarries. The same situation exists in the choir bays, with three similar oolitic limestones from Northamptonshire in use before 1480.

The use of materials to provide a dating procedure is thus no longer reliable and the central plank of the established theory has collapsed. Having disposed of the previous methodology for tracking the constructional progress of the Chapel prior to the arrival of Simon Clerk as master mason in 1477, from which point things get a lot easier, we are still left with the same basic questions: In what order was the Chapel erected and, what can be attributed to Ely and what to Wolryche? This can only be accomplished now by an analysis of the structure, from the documents after 1476 and from stylistic considerations.

70 Huddleston was still available in London in the early sixteenth century. The vault support springers within the Henry VII Chapel are Huddleston. At least one block of Huddleston occurs in the last campaign at King's from 1508 in side closet Bay 8 N.

71 This might explain the curious state of Bay 12 S, which was to have formed the junction with the intended west range. The entire plinth is modern but as early as 1592 there was no sign of the projected toothings as could be seen in Bay 1 S until the nineteenth century. Loggan's print of 1690 confirms this point. Unless Wastell rebuilt the bay from plinth level, it may only have been laid out after the abandonment of the great Court after *c*. 1472. For Hammond's map of 1592 see J. Clark and A. Grey, *Old Plans of Cambridge*, pt II, 1921; D. Loggan, *Cantabrigia Illustrata*, 1690, pl. X and XI.

35 King's College Chapel:
interior of closet Bay 2 N
looking east

36 King's College Chapel:
interior of closet Bay 3 N
showing vault

72 The eastern window was remade in
1841 after the removal of the
through passage to the old
Provost's Lodge.

The work of 1448–1461

Throughout the first phase of the work upon King's College Chapel between 1448 and 1477 we are confronted by a lack of helpful documents, a multiplicity of materials and the changeover of architects at a point unknown. What was seen until now as a 'first campaign' running more or less smoothly until 1461 and creating a 'wedge of cheese' from east to west has become a muddled confusion with various possible computations. One area of the work, however, can be dated and attributed by secondary references and by heraldry – the side closets behind Bays 2 and 3 N. At least one closet was in use in 1460, from later evidence, the **35** Provost's Chapel against 2 N. The vault of Bay 3 N contains two Lancas- **36** ter bosses, indicating a date of pre-March 1461. These two closets have stellar vaults that are quite different from those in any of the succeeding closets, indeed they are certainly the two closets omitted from the number specified to be vaulted in 1513. The existence of two vaulted closets prior to 1461, when Reginald Ely was still master mason, and the possibility of a third, unvaulted closet against Bay 2 S as implied by the burial of 1473, would all indicate at least the existence of the lower walls of the choir bays common to these closets.

The documentary and heraldic evidence would seem to confirm that the side closets behind Bays 2 and 3 N represent the earliest substantial section of the fabric and that both closets are the work of Reginald Ely. Therefore, they should be investigated closely for indications of his style and technique so that points of comparison may be sought in other parts of the Chapel fabric. The interior of the closet behind Bay 2 N is constructed almost entirely in brown oolitic limestone, the only major use of the white Huddleston being the tracery of the eastern and northern windows.[72] The main interest in the closet lies in the design of the tracery pattern. The northern windows are paired under a single, depressed four-centred overarch, with the resulting top spandrel pierced and glazed. Closets Bay 2 N and 3 N have an alternating tracery scheme, with a matching A B A B pattern, where A, or the easternmost, has regular Perpendicular tracery with simple subdivided lozenge panels above four main lights, flanked by side elements with pointed dagger lights. The **37** alternating design, B, differs radically, with flowing tracery supporting a central wheel. The basic elements are a quatrefoil of dagger lights *à saltire*, enclosed within the vertical extensions of the ogee gables that couple the major lights below. As the four daggers do not fill this shape completely, other smaller lights are introduced. The remaining outer angles above the ogee gables have pairs of Flamboyant mouchettes. The combination of two such opposing tracery traditions within a single

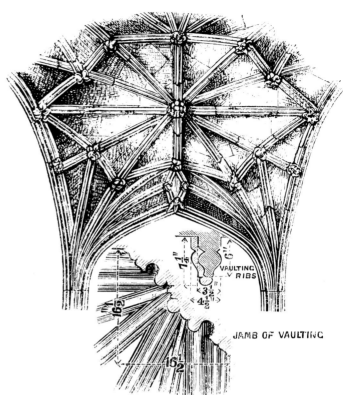

VAULTING
RIBS

JAMB OF VAULTING

37 King's College Chapel:
exterior of Bays 2 and 3 N
showing closet tracery
38 King's College Chapel:
vault and mouldings of
vault respond in closet Bay
3 N

ensemble is without parallel in English fifteenth-century architecture –
one design, rigidly vertical, orderly and 'Perp.', the other, flowing and
sinuous, revolving around a central point.

The closet interiors also contain many mouldings. The moulding profile, literally the drawn pattern from which the stonework was cut, is
one of the most useful tools in the dissection of a medieval building. Every
master mason had his own personal and favourite forms and the occurrence of unusual profiles can be of great assistance in the attribution of
a particular design. The principal moulding profiles in the closets by
Reginald Ely are on the vault responds, the window jambs and the
entrance door. The vault supports rise directly from a sloping glacis base
and occupy nearly all the available wall space within the angles. The
respond mouldings that flow straight into the vault without capitals are
unusually complex in design, their elaboration being greater than any
other vault responds after those in the closet against Bay 3 N. The vaults
spring without either moulded bases or capitals, hence the very French
feeling. The responds have half brackets, hollow casements and rolls, *38*
and an unusual display of wedges, rare in their tightness and density.
The jamb mouldings of the windows and of the connecting door between
the two closets have quite different types of moulding, with a flattish,

incised feeling and a predominant combination of slight raised fillet, half bracket and raised fillet, sometimes with a tiny roll squeezed in between. Such shallow profiles, hardly breaking into the surface of the ashlar, were popular in Cambridge in the mid fifteenth century, especially on small-scale works such as chantry chapels.[73] Perhaps the most useful moulding profile within the early closets is that of the ribs and wall ribs of the vault, the ribs having an odd polygonal lower order that is very distinct, while the wall ribs have a hollow chamfer, half bracket and roll combination. This profile was not used by Wastell in his completion of the closets in the sixteenth century, nor did he use the demi-angel half boss at the apex of the wall ribs. It is relatively easy therefore to plot the progress of the side closet construction in the first campaign by referring to the design of the wall-rib profile and the integral provision of the demi-angel half bosses. This combination forms a sequence from the east and reaching to the closet behind Bay 6 N, though occurring there only on the east and west walls, and stretching to the west wall of Bay 7 S, the wall that commences behind the antechapel vault support VS 7/8 S, while the east wall of the closet behind Bay 8 S has Ely's wall-rib profile but without the angel. Of course the southern wall of the northern closets and the northern wall of those on the south are the reverse sides of the plain socle walls of the choir. Equally, the north–south cross walls of the side closets are the lowest section of the great buttresses that divide the lateral window bays, and despite the fact that the buttresses above the roof level are built of Huddleston, the sections within the closets are made almost entirely from a Northamptonshire oolite.

39

The stylistic evidence would suggest that Reginald Ely embarked upon a horizontal campaign stretching to the east wall of the closet behind Bay 7 on the north side and to the east wall of Bay 8 on the south. It would seem that Ely's initial purpose was to build the choir socle walls and flanking buttresses to at least the height of the lateral window cills, which almost coincidentally involved the basic construction of the side closets.

The main choir door from Bay 3 N into the closet is also an early piece (compare the angel stops with those at the extreme east end of the Angel frieze) though, plainly, the door has been inserted into a gap left for it in the ashlar of the surrounding wall. As with the closet vault responds, the jamb mouldings of the choir door rise directly from a sloping glacis without individual moulded bases – all that is except for one shaft which is provided with a high stepped pedestal base. This shaft is also the only element within the door jamb to be provided with a moulded capital, all the other mouldings rushing off uninterrupted to perform their various functions. The door jamb-mouldings repeat some of the motifs found within the two early closets – especially the fillet-half bracket-fillet combination, used once again to terminate the profile and to turn the

40
41
42

73 For example, the mouldings of the Lane Chantry in St Mary the Less of 1443.

39 King's College Chapel: detail of vault from Bay 2 N showing demi-angel wall rib boss

40 King's College Chapel: interior, choir door in Bay 3 N

angle to the main wall face. Perhaps the most interesting feature of the door jamb moulding is the triple shaft effect of the central projection, where a concave sided shaft is pinched into an additional roll at its extremity. The use of such rippling mouldings enjoyed a peculiar popularity in parts of East Anglia from the 1420s – it appears on the arcades of St Mary's Bury St Edmunds, and it continued in use through a group of churches mostly on the Suffolk/Essex border well into the 1490s.[74] Both the north and south doors in Bay 3 have hood mouldings supported by figure sculpture. The north door has demi-angels carrying shields with the Royal Arms to the right and St Edmund to the left. The south door has images of St Catherine of the left and St Margaret opposite. The hood moulds are crocketed and are carried up as ogee arches topped with a foliate finial. The spandrel has a simple tracery infill containing the arms of St Edward the Confessor on the north, the patron saint of the Lancastrians, and a scene of the Assumption to the south. The north and south doors in Bay 3 mark something of a change in the bare wall surfaces of the choir bays. The walling east of the doors is rather haphazard in appearance, with misalignments and irregular coursing. West of the doors the visible ashlar is finer, larger and more even. This smooth, white walling continues behind the present choir stalls to reach Bay 7 N, where the reverse walling in the flanking closet appears to be Huddleston under a thick coat of whitewash, while on the southern side of the choir the white Huddleston ashlar wall reaches from the door in Bay 3 right up to the commencement of Bay 8 S and accounts for nearly half the height of the vault support VS 7/8 S. Despite the irregularity of the walling in the easternmost bays beyond the doors in Bay 3, it must be assumed that the bare walls of the choir bays were constructed in a single horizontal campaign as they also provided the 'back walls' of

43

44

74 See also p. 150. This group includes the nave of Cavendish *c.* 1471, the chancel arcades of Lavenham from the 1480's, the Lady Chapel of Long Melford of 1496, and the chancel arcades of Glemsford and the chancel aisle of Boxford. They are all probably the work of John Melford of Sudbury.

41 King's College Chapel: choir door in Bay 3 N showing demi-angel end stop with Royal Arms

42 King's College Chapel: interior, Angel frieze in south-east corner with Arms of Edward the Confessor

3 King's College Chapel: mouldings used by Reginald Ely. A: External plinth, B: Jamb of choir door Bay 3 N, C: Door jamb north porch, D: Entrance arch of north porch, E: Arch moulding between closets Bays 3 and 4 S

4 King's College Chapel: choir door in Bay 3 S end stop with St Margaret

the closet chapels, without which they could not be roofed and brought into use. The date of the choir walls to the level of the Angel frieze can be fixed by the completion of two closets behind the north wall before 1461 and at least one behind the southern wall before 1473. The building of the socle walls in the choir to the level of the Angel frieze would enable work to proceed on other flanking closets and allow for their roofing, as well as providing a uniform base level from which the next phase of the elevation could be taken up.

Unfortunately for any analysis of style, the plain walls of the choir are the least helpful feature with the Chapel, one plain wall being much like another. The walls are defined on the interior by an Angel frieze of high quality, though this doubtless reflects the skill of the sculptors not the abilities or stylistic background of Reginald Ely. The frieze is carved from blocks of a Northamptonshire oolite and its marks the general upper limit of the use of Huddleston within the choir bays. The Angels are placed in pairs immediately beneath the wall ribs of the upper elevation. They carry emblems, and some hold scrolls containing traces of former inscriptions indicating that they represent the Heavenly Orders.

This is all that can be said of Ely's work on King's College Chapel at this stage. The dating evidence so neatly provided by the completed side closets is abruptly cut off at the level of the Angel frieze. What remains unknown is exactly how much of the upper elevation was designed and built by Ely before 1461 or possibly during the 1460s. The next date marker within the elevational history comes in 1476 with the building of the two window arch heads in Bays 1 and 2 N, by which time the work is in the hands of John Wolryche. If we next examine those upper areas definitely attributable to the 1470s it may be possible to work downwards in the hope of establishing the exact point at which the work of the two masters coincides.

John Wolryche and the progress of the 1470s

Reginald Ely died in 1471. At some point, John Wolryche took over as master mason, though whether this occurred prior to Ely's death is unknown. Work upon the Chapel appears to have been in progress once again in 1473, when a reference to the covering of the towers and buttresses indicates that some of the buttresses, and hence the main walls and lateral window jambs, had now risen above the interior Angel frieze and clear of the closet roof level – the first time that the buttresses become exposed. The expense of covering the work, particularly in lead, suggests that it had been uncovered recently for some reason and this costly exercise is unlikely to have been permitted for anything but construction, presumably now under the direction of John Wolryche. No reference is made to the east wall save for the covering of the angle towers which could have stood at any height. It is interesting, therefore, to compare the occurrence and condition of the stonework both on the interior and exterior of the north-east angle of the Chapel, the corner adjoining the earliest of the side closets to be completed. Outside, the material employed in Bay 1 N, which has no side closet, is predominantly the white magnesian limestone from Huddleston, though some brown oolite does occur below the springing level of the lateral window. On the adjacent north-east turret, the white magnesian limestone continues up to the level of the adjoining lateral window apex, though from the equivalent height of the lateral window transom, the stonework of the tower is made up from odd blocks jigsawed together. This is in marked contrast to the fine ashlar of the lower section. The made-up nature of the second level of the tower displays a need to salvage every bit of the white stone, suggesting that the supply was then under threat, or even suspended temporarily.

The interior of the north-east angle of the Chapel exhibits a similar

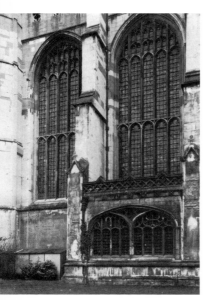

45 King's College Chapel: exterior of Bays 1 and 2 N and the north-east corner stair turrett

6 King's College Chapel:
interior with vault support
VS 0/1 N

47 King's College Chapel:
exterior with Bays 1, 2 and
3 S and the side closet Bay
2 S. The Wolryche tracery
design in central bay,
Clerk's altered design to
the left

admix of stone but above the Angel frieze it is predominantly built of the fine beige Northamptonshire oolite. The vault support in the north-east corner, VS o/1 N, appears to be made up from the beige oolite for the first few courses, and not in the white Huddleston as thought previously. The texture and colour of the oolite is hardly as 'pure' and glassy white as the Huddleston on the immediate areas of the east wall. The use of Huddleston on the east wall is random and rather odd, but as the material will be shown to be still in use in the 1470s, and odd blocks of it can be found in work from post-1508, no special dating signifiance should be attached to its use on the east wall above the Angel frieze.[75]

When we return to the documents, the most significant entry in the College Accounts for 1476/7 is the part payment for the ironwork for the lateral window in Bay 1 N. This one reference indicates that at least one bay had reached the height of the window springing level.[76] What we are missing from the documents and the fabric evidence is the constructional history of that bay between the Angel frieze of *c.* 1460 and

75 See also the interior of the closet behind Bay 8 N from the last campaign.

76 Willis and Clark, vol. I, p. 472, quoting the Mundum Book vol. VII, 1476/77. There is no reference on either fol. 63 or 64v. to the purchase of any material for the east window of the Chapel as is implied by Oswald, *English Medieval Architects*, p. 303, and repeated in RCHM, *City of Cambridge*, vol. I, p. 101, and in Colvin, vol. I, p. 277.

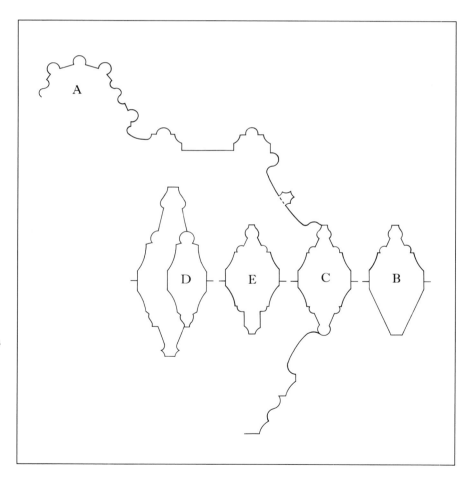

48 King's College Chapel: jamb and mullion moulding profiles 1448–1515. A: Antechapel vault support and window jambs by Ely *c.* 1448, B: mullion profiles by Ely and Wolryche *c.* 1448–77, C: mullion profile by Clerk 1477–85, D: east window major and minor mullions by Clerk *c.* 1480–85, E: mullion profile by Wastell 1508–15

the arrival at the window springing level in 1476. The only way to determine the sequence of this missing section, with its vital evidence concerning the design of the vault, is to examine the information derived from the accounts after 1476, when the documentary evidence is considerably more plentiful, and to use it to work in reverse upon the fabric itself.

Structural evidence suggests that the main lateral window tracery was inserted from top to bottom, that is, the tracery head was built first as a suspended structure integral to the construction of the main window arch moulding. The tracery lights must be held in place by ironwork, with all the stone bars bolted together and on into the arch moulding. At a subsequent date, the lower mullions and transom could be inserted beneath the hanging tracery, the springers for the transom having been provided previously as part of the jamb construction. In this way, the risk of buckling the tall mullions was reduced. The clearest evidence in support of this constructional sequence is the blatant change of mullion profile that occurs in Bay 2 north and south, where the moulding within the tracery head follows that in Bay 1 N,[77] whereas the lower mullions display mouldings associated with all the succeeding windows from Bay 3 westwards to Bay 6 N and 7 S. The change of mullion profile in Bay 2 can be attributed quite safely to Simon Clerk, who was master mason by the summer of 1477. Ironwork for the completion of the windows of Bay 2 and for that in Bay 3 N was purchased in 1480/81,[78] indicating the likely date of the mullions of Bay 2. The combination of the known date for the window in Bay 1 N, the matching tracery heads of Bay 2, presumably also of 1476/77, and the Clerk mullions introduced from Bay 2 westwards in 1480/81, all indicate that Wolryche erected the four tracery heads of Bays 1 and 2 prior to his departure in 1477.

One other important piece of information regarding the extent of the work accomplished before the arrival of Simon Clerk in that year can be found outside at the cill level of the lateral windows. Clerk abandoned the earlier wedge shaped profile of the exterior mullion in favour of a more decorative form. Hence, the early tracery heads in Bay 2 have wedge-shaped mouldings on the outside, while their 'supporting' mullions have the more complex profile. However, the base block for each mullion forms an integral part of the window cill construction. The cills throughout the choir bays have a two-stepped sloping glacis design, inside and out. The base blocks for the mullions and window jambs are cut from the same blocks that make up the upper step of the glacis. The occurrence of the earlier wedge-shaped base blocks for the equivalent shaped mullions will, therefore, pinpoint the number of lateral window cills built prior to the change of the external moulding profile of the mullions after 1477. Clerk and Wastell both continued their mullion profile

77 The mullion mouldings in Bay 1 S were replaced in 1841 with a profile taken from the sixteenth-century antechapel windows.

78 Willis and Clark, vol. I, p. 473.

47

48

right down to the window cill. The earlier wedge-shaped blocks occur in Bays 1–5 N and 1–6 S, confirming the one-bay-westward advance of the south side indicated by the greater extent of the white Huddleston lower walling within the choir. The exterior of Bay 7 S is unhelpful in this respect as the sloping glacis of the cill and the base blocks have been restored and are therefore no longer reliable. The cill of the great east window of the Chapel has wedge-shaped base blocks for the mullions throughout, on to which Clerk has placed moulded mullions of his own design. This must indicate that either Wolryche or Ely determined the width of the east window, and the number of lights – despite the fact that the number deviates from that specified in the Will and Intent of 1448.[79]

79 The base blocks of the window in Bay 12 N are all wedge shaped, though Victorian restorations. The two western mullion blocks in Bay 11 N and the central pair in Bay 12 S are also wedge shaped. The restoration and refacing of this end of the building has been so aggressive that it is almost impossible even to guess what the significance of these base blocks might be. The restored string course beneath both the windows of Bay 12, now badly weathered, contain no heraldry and are in every other way unlike the Wastell string courses of post-1508. If the restoration of Bay 12 is at all accurate, then the walls of the westernmost bays of the antechapel alone, a bay possibly not even begun until after 1472, may have risen to lateral window cill height before the summer of 1477.

The evidence of the vault supports

A number of important and characteristic features occur between the lateral window cill level, reached *c.* 1460 in the easternmost bays, and the tracery heads commenced in 1476/77. It is self-evident that they must belong to the first phase of the work and represent the intentions of either Ely and Wolryche, or both. These features include the form and level of the corbelled vault supports in the choir, the transom level of the main lateral windows, the springing level and arcature of the lateral windows and the sequence of figure niches introduced into the deep window splays at the level of the vault support corbels. The level and form of the lateral windows, and of the vault supports, was dependent upon one factor, the decision to vault. Henry VI stated quite clearly that the Chapel was to be vaulted and the design and level of the vault supports may reveal something of the intended vault of 1448, or any possible later revision of Ely's first scheme by Wolryche.

The vault supports vary in design between those in the choir proper and those in the antechapel. The choir vault supports are lifted well clear of the lower socle walls and are carried on corbels let into the upper elevations at the height of the lateral window transoms. This was simply in 49 order to allow wooden stalls to run uninterrupted from the pulpitum to the sanctuary as at present. The antechapel was free from such fittings, so that the vault supports rise directly from the floor. Thus it is possible that at least some of the antechapel vault supports pre-date any of those further east in the choir bays due to the fact that they stand immediately above foundational level. The support at the southern end of the existing pulpitum, VS 7/8 S, is one of the most critical pieces of all the structural evidence concerning the architectural history of the Chapel. It is bonded 50 into, and is part of the first campaign on, the southern socle wall of the choir, now hidden behind the stalls – a wall finished by *c.* 1473 if not earlier. The vault support is constructed from fine Huddleston in one build up to the height of the inserted Tudor portcullis on the eastern bay of Bay 8 S, to which height the work appears uniform. It is the only vault support in the whole Chapel to contain a large quantity of Huddleston and it shows no evidence of piece-meal or jigsawed construction. The signficance of VS 7/8 S is that it separates the antechapel from the termination of the southern socle wall of the choir. Hence it belongs as much to the choir design as to that of the antechapel. The base of VS 7/8 S is in the antechapel beneath the southern end of the pulpitum loft, and, as it stands on the Chapel floor it almost certainly pre-dates any of the choir vault supports which are corbelled out at a higher, that is constructionally a later level.

VS 7/8 S consists of a tall socle with individual polygonal basement pedestals responding to the various moulded elements above. The

49 King's College Chapel: interior of choir Bays 1 to 5 N

moulded bases are in groups of seven, with profiles similar to those on the choir doors in Bay 3. The vault support, here more of a wall pier, is roughly semi-circular in plan with a group of three bases for the vertical shafts around the mid point. The shafts flanking the central group are inset into the plane of the pier, causing their moulded bases to step back from the remaining members of the group, while the outermost bases return to the major plane of the pier. The vault support VS 7/8 S now vanishes into the dark recesses of the Henry VIII screen which is most annoying, for when it emerges from the top of the pulpitum it has quite changed its character. Now, the four easternmost shafts start all over again, with high stepped bases perched on top of the Angel frieze that runs under the lateral windows of the choir bays. At some point, invisible 51 within the woodwork of the screen, the lower shafts have been terminated – all that can now be seen is the rough-toothed edge of a projected block,

50 King's College Chapel: interior, with vault support VS 7/8S and tracery screen of closet Bay 8 S

51 King's College Chapel: interior, with raised base of vault support VS 7/8 S at cill level of Bay 7 S

52 King's College Chapel: interior, damaged Angel frieze beneath vault support VS 7/8 S in Bay 7 S west jamb

0·56 m east to west and (0·38 m) out from the Angel frieze. This single block supports not only the new group of upper vault shafts but also an angled extension of the Angel frieze complete with damaged angel.　　*52*

The most curious feature of the new beginning of VS 7/8 S is the treatment of the mid-point shaft, for half of it belongs to the antechapel Bay 8 S while the eastern half belongs to the choir Bay 7 S. In order to accomodate this dual function, the shaft is split vertically in two, the eastern half sitting on a new base on top of the Angel frieze while the western half bypasses the new base altogether and shoots on down to the antechapel floor. Presumably, the projecting block and the subdivision of the central vault shaft were to form some part of an intended pulpitum between the choir proper and the antechapel – a screen evidently to be executed in Huddleston. VS 7/8 S may therefore have been regarded as the southern 'terminal pier' of the pulpitum, hence it was to be constructed entirely from the same material. The consistency of the stonework, the height of the uniform Huddleston and the apparent bonding of VS 7/8 S into the southern socle wall of the choir would all suggest that its design and execution formed part of the earliest work upon the Chapel.

Possibly, the intention during the first few years of construction was to erect the Chapel only as far as a stone screen between Bays 7 and 8, and to seal the choir bays behind a temporary wall at that point. It may then have been planned to bring the seven bays of the choir into use whilst construction of the antechapel progressed. Lack of funds and the fall of Henry VI dictated that things would be otherwise. The western side of VS 7/8 S that forms the eastern jamb of Bay 8 S pre-empts three vital features of the design of the Tudor antechapel campaign – the openings into the closets from the antechapel interior, the socle panelling beneath the lateral windows and the introduction of lower jamb niches with tall crocketed pinnacles. These elements are all integral to the original design and build of VS 7/8 S, though the final form of the closet openings was subject to Tudor alterations. Why VS 7/8 S should have been constructed so far in advance of the rest of the Chapel is not clear, though it does form the termination of the southern choir wall. On the other hand, VS 7/8 N, which forms the termination of the opposite northern socle wall of the choir, is of a later, sixteenth-century build, with only one base course in Huddleston, the rest of the pier being of a brown oolitic limestone. While it has been demonstrated that both materials were in use concurrently, the sole use of the finest Huddleston in the lower half of VS 7/8 S indicates that it formed part of the specific reservation of that material seen in the eastern bays of the choir. The early date of VS 7/8 S is also another indication that in the first phase of construction, the southern side of the Chapel stood at least one bay ahead of the north, a progression already indicated by the evidence of the mullion base blocks and later to be confirmed by the lateral window campaign of 1480/81. The last important fact concerning VS 7/8 S is that for the first time on the interior elevations, the Huddleston level reaches above the defining line of the Angel frieze, which hitherto has formed the upper limit of all the uniform magnesian limestone walling within the choir bays. This is due simply to the fact that the frieze terminates at the eastern face of the intended choir screen and it was not to reappear as part of the antechapel design. The Angel frieze is cut from a fine beige oolite, and it formed a colour demarcation within the choir, with white below and beige above. The vault support VS 7/8 S had no such restrictions, as the two-tone colour scheme was not evidently to be employed in the antechapel. Its all-white colour was dictated by the proposed Huddleston screen, of which it was to form a major part. Thus the Huddleston structure of V 7/8 S was continued as high as conditions in the early phase of the work would allow.

The contribution of VS 7/8 S to the architectural history of King's College Chapel is clearly of great importance. Its early date suggests that it was designed by Reginald Ely, and the pre-empting of much of the design of the later Tudor campaign on the antechapel will cause us to review that design in a later section. But the major problem raised by the design and date of VS 7/8 S is the evidence it contains for the history of the vault.

All the evidence suggests that VS 7/8 S was the first vault support actually to be built. Therefore, its design represents that proposed by Reginald Ely at the commencement of the project. However, by the time that the corbelled vault supports were begun further east in the choir bays, a significant change in the design had taken place, one that affected not only the design of the vault supports, but by implication the intended design of the vault, or possibly even the intention to vault at all. Since these implications are considerable, it is vital to make a detailed comparison of the unique nature of the early vault support VS 7/8 S with that of the later corbelled vault supports to the east.

53 King's College Chapel: interior, with vault support VS 1/2 N and niche Bay 2 N east jamb

The vault supports of King's College Chapel pose a very famous and knotty problem. The early vault support VS 7/8 S stands on the floor, hence it can and almost certainly does pre-date any of the choir vault supports further east which are corbelled out from the walls at window transom height. As was demonstrated previously, the earliest of the corbelled vault supports must be those in Bay 1 N, which includes for obvious structural reasons the eastern support of Bay 2 N. These are designated VS 0/1 N and VS 1/2 N. These supports must have been under construction if not in place when the window tracery of Bay 1 N was projected in 1476/77.

The corbels are supported visually by nodding ogee arches slung between the wall shafts that flank the window bays. The choir vault supports rise from a sloping glácis base that itself highlights the important   53 difference between them and the vault support base of VS 7/8 S on the antechapel floor. Instead of seven shafts grouped around the pier as on VS 7/8 S, the corbelled vault supports of the choir bays have only five, retaining the central group of three but omitting the next pair completely. Their omission is made all the more obvious by leaving the ashlar face of the support quite plain. This change from seven to five shafts has become one of the most celebrated (and misunderstood) features in the history of King's College Chapel. Willis and many others have pointed out the main arguments.[80]

80 Willis and Clark, vol. I, p. 495.

It is argued that since the easternmost choir vault supports VS 0/1 N and S occur within the 'Huddleston' area, a material hitherto believed to have been used exclusively before 1460 and no later, then these vault supports must have been in place before the fall of Henry VI in 1461. It was also thought that the lowest sections of VS 0/1 N and S were actually made of Huddleston, though the cleaning has shown them to be a fine beige Northamptonshire. Some sections of the antechapel bases, including of course VS 7/8 S, were also known to be partly composed of Huddleston and were, for Willis, also pre-1460 for similar reasons. Before the cleaning of the Chapel, nobody could see that about half the total height of VS 7/8 S was also made of Huddleston. The problem for Willis was that the easternmost vault supports were of a different design from those in the antechapel. The conclusion must be that either two different vault designs were intended from the outset, with a simple vault over the choir bays adjoining a more complex vault over the antechapel, or, one of the vault support designs has been subject to later alteration.

The five-shaft system now seen in the choir was more easily adapted for the present fan vault, commenced in 1512, than the seven-shaft system of the antechapel which provided an excess of shafts, two of which are simply ignored in the existing Tudor vault design. With the advantage of being able to see the final vault design, Willis proposed the famous 'cut-back' theory. According to this, Reginald Ely, the first master mason, built seven shaft supports throughout, both in the choir and antechapel, intending to erect the kind of stellar lierne vault seen in the closets against Bays 2 and 3 N. Subsequently it was decided to cover the main Chapel with a fan vault, a design requiring but one shaft plus a transverse arch occupying the central group of three – that is, the present design over the choir. This decision, it is argued, happened between 1476 and 1485, a time when the choir bays were known to be approaching completion, but the antechapel was in abeyance. What happened, according to the protangonists of the 'cut-back' theory, was that either Wolryche or Clerk chiselled off the offending extra shafts in the choir vault supports, so reducing the number from seven to five. The antechapel bases with their seven shafts were left intact for the time being, as no work, it was believed, was then in progress beyond the line of the intended stone pulpitum screen between VS 7/8 N and S.

The 'cut-back' theory makes two major assumptions, both of which have profound consequences for the architectural history of King's College Chapel. First, there was the 'certainty' that the easternmost vault supports of the choir were partly of Huddleston and that they must, therefore, pre-date 1460 and second, there was a specific decision to 'alter' the design of the choir vault supports already built, prompted by the proposal to erect a fan vault over the whole Chapel *c.* 1480. Clearly, the first assumption is made questionable by the unreliability and wrong identification of material evidence discussed earlier. The second assumption is also questionable, for the upper sections of all the eastern bays of the Chapel, built from 1480, have been mutilated in the attempt to erect the present fan vault, and the relationship between the existing vault and the choir vault supports as they are now represents a most unhappy compromise. It seems difficult to believe, therefore, that the decision to build a fan vault as opposed to a rib vault was taken before the completion of the present choir vault supports, indeed evidence that this decision was taken only in the sixteenth century will be presented later.[81]

The greatest flaw in the 'cut-back' theory, however, is that the extra shafts assumed to have been removed from the choir vault supports, but still remaining in VS 7/8 S, cannot be chiselled off. They do not project beyond the plane of the vault supports, as do the other five shafts, but are recessed into it. The shaft is in fact a wave or roll moulding formed   *54* by cutting two hollow chamfers into the face of the pier. This is why the moulded bases provided for them step back into the pier and break the line established by all the other bases. The only way to remove these shafts would be to plaster in the hollow chamfers. This has clearly not happened on any of the choir vault supports which now have only five shafts. The extra shafts have never existed. Either Reginald Ely intended   *55* two vault designs at once, which would seem unlikely, or a major change in the intended vault design occurred between the building of the early VS 7/8 S and those in the choir further east. What Willis got wrong was not that a change had occurred, nor particularly the date at which it happened, but by adopting a too rigid dating scheme for the use of materials he overestimated the amount of structure built pre-1460, he overlooked much of the early structure that does exist because it was not at the eastern end of the Chapel, and he attributed far more of the existing design to Reginald Ely than can now be substantiated, whilst missing other areas that he clearly did design. Lastly, the 'cut-back' theory assumed that radical alterations were made about 1480 to allow for the building of the present vault design. What actually appears to have happened was that Ely proposed and began a seven-shaft vault support system in 1448/9. By the late 1460s or early 1470s, and presumably under Wolryche, a simpler five-shaft design was adopted and begun in the choir bays, perhaps indicative of the reduced circumstances of the College coupled with the possible abandonment of the high vault altogether, and even possibly

54 King's College Chapel:
   interior with a choir vault
   support. Had additional
   recessed mouldings been
   'cut out' the flat plane of
   the pier would be set back
   in a deep casement and this
   would also affect the
   moulded capital string
   course
55 King's College Chapel:
   section through vault
   supports, A (left):
   antechapel vault support
   c. 1448, B (right): choir
   vault support *c.* 1475

82 See pp. 93–8.

of the antechapel. The probability of such drastic measures will be discussed in a later section.[82]

The division of the vault supports between the complex Ely design seen in the antechapel and the simpler corbelled design in the choir by Wolrchye also raises the pertinent question of who designed the choir vault support corbels with their elaborate sculptured angels?

The moulded corbelled vault supports within the choir bays spring from nodding ogee arches slung between the vertical walls ribs. They are accompanied by flanking ogee gables with internal cusping. Every alternate corbel beginning with VS 2/3 N and S is further enriched by the addition of magnificent demi-angel figures with outstretched wings, some holding emblems. All the corbel blocks of the south elevation of the choir share the same moulding profile, and the alternating demi-angels form a consistent sculptural sequence. These two factors suggest that they are products of a single campaign, including the westernmost VS 6/7 S. The same sequence is seen on the north side but only until VS 5/6 N, that is the support between Bays 5 N and 6 N. This has different mouldings and the flanking ogee gables within the adjoining wall ribs have simple, three-part cusping rather than the usual five. Throughout the choir bays up to the east jamb of Bay 5 N, and the east jamb of Bay 6 S, the wall rib gables have five cusps internally. Between Bays 5 N, west jamb, and 7 N, east jamb, and between Bays 6 S, west jamb, and 7 S, east jamb, the design changes to one with only three cusped sections. These sections will be shown later to be by Simon Clerk. In the antechapel, Wastell returned to the original five-part cusped design for his wall rib ogee gables, indicating that it was he and not Clerk who built the upper section of the Ely Antechapel vault support VS 7/8 S.

The corbel blocks are the wrong shape for the vault responds that they carry. They have odd angles jutting out that are redundant in the five-shaft choir supports but which would have been suitable for Ely's seven-shaft system as seen in the antechapel. It would appear from this one feature that the original vault design with seven shafts was maintained at least to the corbel height within the choir, whilst the decision to simplify the supports was taken at a later stage when the vault supports were actually built. The conflicting design of corbel and vault support would suggest that the former were at least designed by Ely before 1461 and existed in the workshop if not actually placed, while the latter reflects the more modest design of John Wolryche from the 1470s.

The choir vault support corbels occur at a crucial level within the design of King's College Chapel. They are one stone course below the next elevational feature – the window jamb figure niches, which represent one of the most difficult problems of date and attribution within the history of the Chapel.

The window niches of the choir bays

The lateral windows and the great east window are flanked by figure niches at transom height. The attribution of the niches in the eastern bays of the choir is one of the most complex problems in the early history of the Chapel, as they may have been cut at any time after 1448, and being of a standard size, their positions were interchangeable. This raises the possibility that the easternmost canopies were not necessarily the first to be made, merely the first to be put in place. Furthermore, a stylistic examination of the various canopy designs and their tiny interior vaults does not reveal which, if any, were by Ely and which were by Wolryche. It might be hoped that the analysis of such a regularly occurring feature almost exactly half way up the elevational wall could assist in defining the point at which Wolryche took over design control from Ely. However, in Bays 1 to 5 there are almost as many different niche canopy designs as there are niches, and no clear development can be traced before Bay 4 N west jamb and Bay 5 S west jamb, where a regular series of canopy and interior vault designs is initiated. Prior to that, the canopy and vault designs vary considerably.

The use of material may here be significant as there is a clear preference for the white Huddleston when available, though any number of niches could be made at one time and stored until required. The east window

56 King's College Chapel:
interior, niche in Bay 1 S,
west jamb

niche canopies and the four canopies of Bay 1 all appear to be made of
Huddleston, the most obvious being that in Bay 1 S west jamb where
the white stone can easily be distinguished from its oolitic background. *56*
But all these niches present very different canopy designs, those of the
east window suggesting that they are of a considerably later date than
those in the lateral windows – this despite being carved from Huddleston.
This may be yet another indication of the reservation of the finer stone
over a long period for the more important features.

The ironwork purchase of 1476/77 must signify that both the niches
of Bay 1 N were already in place by that date and while on first sight
they appear a pair, they contain considerable differences that highlight
the problems of attribution for all the early niches. The design closest
to that on Bay 1 N, east jamb, is its southern fellow, Bay 1 S east jamb
and its partner, Bay 1 S west jamb. What is so confusing about the
canopies of the eastern bays is that, whereas the south side begins with
a consistent series of three niches, the north side has two designs in the
first bay alone. The north side then settles down to a fairly consistent
sequence of four canopies in a row, while the southern bays run riot with
an assortment of shapes, facades and vaults. Order only returns to the
south side at a time when a radical change is also introduced on the north
– the introduction of two-sided canopies rather than three, and with stellar vaults. This design begins at Bay 3 N, west jamb, and Bay 4 S, west
jamb. From the documentary evidence alone, the next, fan-vaulted
design from Bay 4 N west jamb and Bay 5 S west jamb can be attributed
to the last phase of the choir construction and can be attributed to Simon
Clerk who arrived in 1477.

The canopy designs of both the east window niches are unlike any
others in the eastern bays of the choir, indeed, they can be related stylistically to only one other pair in the whole Chapel – those in Bay 2 S west
jamb and Bay 3 S east jamb. The vault within the east window south
niche leaves no doubt that it comes from a later hand, being by far the
most sophisticated and well executed in the whole Chapel, and unrelated *57*
to any other east of Bay 4 N and 5 S. The implication drawn from this
is that the building of the east wall lagged behind that of the lateral bays
and that the east window north jamb, had reached only niche height when
work was already in progress at the same level as far west as Bay 3 S,
while the east window south jamb, was even farther behind.

After this fruitless examination of the lateral window niches of the choir
bays, there is an understandable reluctance to introduce yet one more
niche into the discussion, but it is perhaps most important of all. The
lower niche of the east jamb of Bay 8 S, which forms part of VS 7/8 S,
is probably the only niche that can be definitely attributed to Reginald
Ely. The cleaning of the Chapel has made clear the differences between
this niche and the sixteenth-century canopy that faces it to the west. The
east jamb canopy is three-sided, with slightly ogeed gables, uncusped

57 King's College Chapel:
interior, east window south
niche

subarches and a teardrop lobe within the spandrel. The polygonal pro- *58* jecting corner buttresses carry tiny ogee gables and the main spirelet has broad, spreading crockets. The canopy is supported by demi-angels, a unique feature of this niche. The side angels are in prayer, while the suspended pendants have angels carrying shields. The internal vault is a complex lierne pattern centred on a four-lobe radiating design, recalling the flowing tracery of the early side closets. The base of the niche is *59* heavily moulded and was castillated originally. The whole niche, minus the very top of the spirelet, is an integral part of the first Huddleston build of the vault support. This niche is, therefore, probably earlier than any other niche in the Chapel. It does not bear any particular resemblance to any of the others in the choir bays, which strongly suggests that none of them are by Ely. However, the form of the antechapel niche is quite unlike that of the choir canopies and a direct comparison may therefore be considered unfair. Nevertheless, there is a notable difference in conception and where a direct comparison can be drawn, as with the interior vaults, the antechapel niche stands in isolation.

One other factor that may end up more of a hindrance than a help is the gatehouse niche of Queens' College, attributed to Reginald Ely, and dating from after *c.* 1446.[83] The evidence for this is rather circumstantial and is discussed at greater length below. The niche is a combination of the tall spirelet canopy of Bay 8 S east jamb lower niche, and the vaults of Bay 1 S east and west jambs, which themselves resemble those in Bay 1 N west jamb, and Bay 3 N east jamb and the northern niche of the east window. Given the uncertainty concerning the identity of the designer *60* of Queens' and the varied distribution of the vault type within King's College Chapel, what should we make of the obvious parallels?

The combination of vault and canopy type must be significant, for the two niches in Bay 1 S with vaults that most closely resemble the Queens' gatehouse niche vault have canopies quite unlike any others in the Chapel except that in Bay 1 N east jamb which has some points in common. Both the southern niches in Bay 1 appear to be made of Huddleston set into an oolite, either King's Cliffe or Clipsham. These two canopies may well have been designed and prepared during the master masonship of Reginald Ely, perhaps as early as 1460. However, there is no reason to suggest that they were placed that early, nor should we expect John Wolryche to throw out anything stored in the lodges left over from his predecessor.

Equally, it is important to remember that Ely was not personally responsible for cutting these canopies, that would be done by one of the leading masons expert in such matters. Neither they, nor the current designs, were dropped from the project immediately upon the departure of Reginald Ely. There was bound to be a considerable overlap, and many of Wolryche's own niche designs that follow may have been developed

83   See A. Oswald, *Andrew Doket and his Architect*, pp. 8–26.

58   King's College Chapel: interior, lower niche canopy of Bay 8 S east jamb

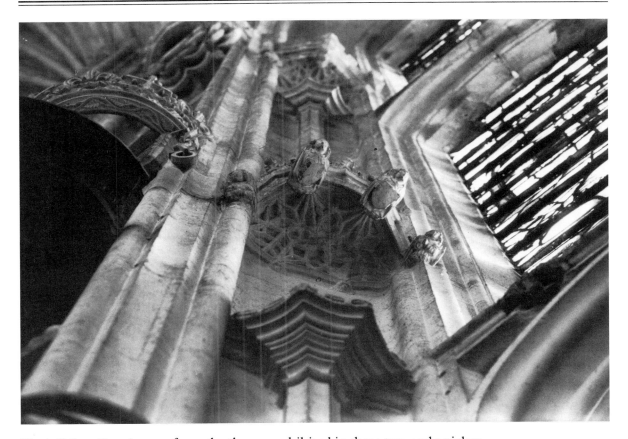

59 King's College Chapel: interior, lower niche of Bay 8 S east jamb interior vault

60 Queen's College Cambridge: Gatehouse niche

from the themes exhibited in these two early niches.

The inevitable conclusion is that most of the lateral window niches of the choir bays must be divided between Wolryche and Clerk, with the only possible exceptions being the niches in Bay 1 S, and that the profusion of designs apparent in Bays 1 N to 3 N and S, was an intended element of Wolryche's revised scheme, perhaps of the late 1460s or early 1470s. Alternatively, it may be symptomatic of the rather desultory building progress through the troubled years after the fall of Henry VI. The arrival of Simon Clerk is indicated by the move to a more ordered and uniform design, beginning with Bay 3 N west jamb and Bay 4 S west jamb. The niches of the east window would appear to be by Wolryche on the north and Clerk on the south. It must be pointed out that some of the 'early', that is more easterly, niches within the choir are executed in brown oolite, while some of the 'later' niches are in Huddleston. This may be an indication of the infrequent supply, but it also raises the general spectre of storage. All the niches, except those of the east window, are of the same size and are interchangeable, and some may have been intended for a location other than that which we now see – after all, the dynastic squabbles of York and Lancaster dragging on until 1472 could hardly have been forseen by the sculptors of Cambridge and any number of finished niches may have been held in the lodges for months or even years before being incorporated into the fabric. What can be demonstrated from the niches, however, is that the east wall did not keep up with the construction of the adjoining lateral bays, and once again we see that the southern side of the choir had achieved a one-bay advantage over the north at quite an early stage.

One other feature of the niche design illustrates the complex nature of the building operations prior to 1477. The niches have polygonal bases, supported by shafts rising from the sloping glacis of the window cills. The bases have simple mouldings which exhibit a constant design throughout Bays 1 to 5 east jambs, both on the north and south sides. The bases are narrower than the casement moulding of the jamb in which they are placed, the extra width being filled with a horizontal string course extension of the base moulding across the face of the jamb. This early design is also found on the eastern jamb of VS 7/8 S and on the base of the lower Ely niche in Bay 8 S east jamb, in the antechapel. The remaining choir niche bases, those from Bay 5 west jambs, N and S, are slightly different, being larger and filling completely the expanse of the casement moulding. Wastell returned to the original, smaller-scale bases in his antechapel niches, though he decorated their main faces with tiny square panels and they are thus easy to distinguish.

The niche bases in the choir occur at the transom height of the lateral windows, while being one stone course above the top of the vault support corbel on the main elevation. The consistency of the bases up to Bay 5 east jamb suggests that there was a concerted effort to build all the bays evenly at least to transom height for the first four bays, and consequently building the eastern jamb of Bay 5. In addition, this could suggest that the niche bases in Bay 5 east jambs are actually earlier than the niche canopies in Bay 1, that is, the window jambs of Bays 1 to 4 were erected in one horizontal campaign to the height of the transom and niche bases, before a second horizontal campaign began, which added the upper sections of the window jambs from transom level to window springing point, and included the niche canopies and the corbelled vault supports. What we may see here is an indication that, at least in the four eastern bays of the choir, a horizontal building programme was in operation, whereby the elevations were built up in a series of layers, returning each time to the east end for the commencement of the next one up. The link between the niche bases of Bay 1 to 5 east jambs and the earliest niche in the antechapel, Bay 8 S east jamb, would suggest that Reginald Ely was responsible for the first horizontal campaign above the Angel frieze and up to the transom height, whilst the profusion of niche canopies suggests that Wolryche took over for the second phase.

The slight alteration in the niche base design after Bay 5 east jambs provides one more important piece of evidence in deciding exactly what features of the elevational wall were built by Ely. The niche bases are just above the great corbel blocks that form the base of the choir vault supports. The niche bases would indicate that at least the corbels must belong to Ely's work as far as VS 4/5 N and S, the actual vault supports being from a later phase. It is not possible to estimate exactly how much of the wall beneath vault support VS 5/6 N was built before 1477, as it did not, evidently, reach as high as the level of the vault support corbel. Directly opposite, the vault support VS 5/6 S has the earlier moulding profile and five-part cusping in the wall-rib ogee gables, and thus it dates to before 1477. Yet the flanking jamb niche bases only one stone course above have Clerk's wider niche base mouldings. This adds one more vault support on the south side to the list partly built by 1477, though not quite to niche base height. The general division between the early corbels and the later vault supports now proposed, giving the former to Ely and the latter to Wolryche, might also help to explain the provision of the lavish sculptured demi-angels of the former which extend as far west on the southern elevation as VS 6/7 S. Such expensive sculpture could *61* hardly have been countenanced after 1461. One puzzle however, is the plain design of the easternmost vault corbels beneath VS 0/1 N and S. The system calls for alternating moulded and angel corbels, the eastern corbels are moulded, they should be angels. Were they in fact built later on by Wolryche as part of his work on the east wall? One last indication that the lower sections of the choir elevation to transom height formed a separate campaign from the area above is indicated by the change in the method of scaffolding. In Bay 1 to 5, the scaffolding, or putlug holes, are very obvious in the walls below transom height and have been filled

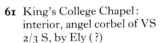

61 King's College Chapel: interior, angel corbel of VS 2/3 S, by Ely (?)

in with small stones. In the section above, and throughout, the Tudor antechapel, such putlug holes are not easily visible and appear to be few in number. Thus, an integrated scaffold was built into the lower walls of the choir elevation to transom height, while the upper sections were erected using a scaffold built through the window openings.

The introduction of Clerk's first niche canopy design from Bay 3 N west jamb and Bay 4 S west jamb, and his niche base designs from Bay 5 N and S west jambs defines the exact moment when he took over responsibility for the design of the Chapel. It is the Summer 1477 date line. It also indicates that Wolryche's last horizontal campaign, adding the window jambs from transom to springing height, had restored the constructional lead of the south side, evident in Ely's very first work upon the lower socle walls.

The evidence from the niche designs indicates that both Wolryche and Clerk were intent on completing the choir bays at the expense of the antechapel. The reduced circumstances of the College after 1461 may have led them to abandon any hope of building the antechapel at all, and the work appears to have been concentrated on just the five eastern bays of the choir. The niches may not help us in determining when Wolryche took over from Ely, but they can tell us where – above transom height from Bay 1 westwards to Bay 3 N east jamb and Bay 4 S east jamb.

The contribution of Reginald Ely

The dissection of the choir elevation reveals that Ely's contribution to the existing fabric of King's College Chapel is less than had been supposed previously. The elements of the choir that can now be attributed definitely to him are the side closets against Bay 2 and 3 N, the socle walls, the vaults support VS 7/8 S and the window jambs from Bay 1 to 5 east jamb to transom height with the corbels ready for the vault supports. The major part of the elevations above transom height, including the vault supports and the lateral window tracery, must be attributed to Wolryche, or at least, they were erected during his term of office as master mason.

But if Ely's contribution to the building of the choir was small, his influence on the present state of the antechapel was considerable, despite the fact that little of it appears to have been built prior to 1508. Once again, the crucial evidence is associated with the vault support VS 7/8 S. The springing of the blind panelling beneath the lateral window in Bay 8 S from the vault support VS 7/8 S is an integral part of the early section of the pier, and has been damaged by the later Tudor insertion cut into the Huddleston. The lower section of the 'through jamb' into the closet

62 King's College Chapel: interior, cut-away view of Bays 1 to 5 N as existing *c.* 1475

is again part of the same first build of the vault support. The existing Tudor tracery screen between the antechapel and closet has destroyed the original evidence of the form of the closet opening intended by Ely but the existence of the through jamb confirms that there were indeed to be openings into the side closets beneath the lateral windows of the antechapel. The need to insert a tracery head for the Tudor screen implies that the original intention was different. From the Huddleston evidence within the closet, the side chapels were to be enclosed by a low wall, the beginning of which is again pre-empted in part of VS 7/8 S, which includes a plinth moulding ignored in the later Tudor completion. 63 Similarly, the closet interior against Bay 8 S reveals that a moulded over-arch was intended and partly begun, which would frame the opening from the closet into the antechapel. A doorway was proposed in the 64 present position at the north-west angle of the closet, the western jamb being built as part of the base course of VS 8/9 S. Despite the loss of the exact design of the closet opening, it can be seen that Ely intended the socle panelling of the main walls extending below the lateral windows,

63 King's College Chapel: interior of closet Bay 8 S with Ely work, right, and Wastell, left, showing discontinued plinth moulding

64 King's College Chapel: interior of closet Bay 8 S north-east angle by Ely, and Wastell screen

84 G. G. Scott, *Essay on the History of English Gothic Architecture*, 1881, pp. 182–3.

the closet openings from the antechapel with low retaining walls and benches along the base within the antechapel, doorways to the west of each closet, and additional jamb niches flanking the cills of the main lateral windows. Thus the richness of the present antechapel is, in great part, due to the original design of Reginald Ely with the full approval of Henry VI. The later completion, especially the work under Henry VII, should therefore be seen as a revival of the approved 1448 design and not as an entirely inappropriate Tudor embellishment.

It has been shown that Ely's original conception of the antechapel was much as Wastell actually built it in the sixteenth century – indeed, the College was instructed by Henry VII to finish the Chapel 'as it was ordered and devised' by the King's uncle, Henry VI. Thus, the elevation that we see today is not far removed from Ely's design *c*. 1448.

But what of the choir bays? The evidence for Ely's choir elevation ends at the mid-height transoms of the lateral windows. Below this there are blind panels with ogee gables flanking the windows, suggesting that what little wall space existed between window and vault support was to be panelled like the antechapel. The lower walls are blank to allow for the stalls and canopies. The relationship of the window arch heads and the vault supports as built by Wolryche is clearly a compromise solution of the 1470s, as will be shown later, so what then did Ely intend?

Ely's original design for the choir elevation is difficult to envisage given the limited amount of his actual construction. Our only evidence is the Will and Intent (with which Ely's work does not always agree), the fabric executed by Ely to lateral window transom height, and the guidelines of the main Chapel contained within the side closets, which need not necessarily pre-empt any of the design features of the Chapel proper. For example, it would be unwise to propose that the main lateral windows were to have alternative 'flowing' and Perp. tracery or that the vaults would burst out from the support shafts without capitals.

The Will and Intent is no real help: the Chapel is to be ninety feet high, it is to have lateral windows and a vault. The reconstruction as proposed by G. G. Scott and based upon the Ely Cathedral Lady Chapel[84] had a sharp, steep lierne vault framing harsh, angular windows. The result is strangely Victorian. Obviously, some sympathetic design relating the vault to the windows existed from the start, but not necessarily one that brought them closer together. Reginald Ely may well have intended a higher springing point for the vault than we now see, one level with the window apices. This would enable the vault capitals to line up with the top of the square framing above the windows, actually built by Wolryche. It would also create regular lunette spaces beneath a vault, quite independent of the framed windows and unmolested by the vault wall ribs. The existing compromise scheme, with a lower spring-

IN MEMORY OF ARTHUR HENRY MANN
16 MAY 1850 – 19 NOVEMBER 1929
FELLOW AND FOR FIFTY-THREE YEARS
THE BELOVED ORGANIST OF THE COLLEGE

IN MEMORY OF
HERBERT WILLIAM
RICHMOND F.R.S.
SENIOR FELLOW
BORN 17th JULY 1863
DIED 22nd APRIL 1948

ing point, has led to a clash between the vault and the square frame, while the sixteenth century blind tracery within the lunettes looks rather squashed.

A vault springing from the window apex height would immediately recall the interior of St Stephen's Chapel, Westminster, which until Wren's alterations had a glazed clerestory above square-framed lateral windows and enclosed within the wall ribs of the vault. Was this Ely's proposal for King's Cambridge, including the glazed clerestory? There is no mention of a clerestory in the Will and Intent but thereagain a great deal of the Chapel as begun by Ely is not in the Will, for example all the closets, while much of what does appear in the Will did not materialise, such as the two-storey vestry. The design of the Chapel as commenced by Ely was clearly one stage further from the Will of March 1448. The suggestion that Ely might have intended a glazed clerestory would also help to explain why Wastell filled the eventual lunette space with vertical blind tracery – was he completing the design as near as he could, remembering that the upper section of the Chapel as erected by Simon Clerk from *c*. 1480 has a double-wall, stone-clad brick construction?

Ely must have intended to do something with the upper section of the elevation, as the Chapel was to be ninety feet high, and, while his window campaign rose no higher than the mid-height transom, the presence of this feature some 39 ft (12 m) above the floor, dictates that his lateral windows were not to be much taller overall than at present. What else then was he proposing above? This is all, of course, pure specu-lation, but it is possible that, after a period of compromise in the 1470s, followed by a different scheme in the 1480's, the original design for the upper elevation of the Chapel as proposed by Ely was attempted by John Wastell in the early sixteenth century, accommodating as best he could to the actual condition of the building as he found it. Thus, due to a second change in the elevation after Ely's departure, it was no longer possible to glaze the vault lunettes, so Wastell added them 'blind'.

The present vault is another matter. The Wastell vault was to his own design and by no one else. Ely probably intended a lierne vault, based on one transverse, diagonal, two tiercerons, a ridge rib and a cross axial. Such a relatively straightfoward design would fit on to the seven-shaft support system as built by Ely in the antechapel, whereas Scott's proposal does not. It would mean, however, that the transverse would be a single rib, not a great arch as now, and that the main diagonals would spring from the smallest, inset support – the one eliminated later from the design by Wolryche. Thus, the smallest element would take on the greatest role, the sort of game Ely doubtless enjoyed.

The style of Reginald Ely

Having redefined and reduced the amount of Ely's work at King's College Chapel, it is now possible to examine something of his style and to see where his architecture fits in to the development of Perpendicular in the mid fifteenth century. Ely probably came from Coltishall, a village near Norwich in Norfolk.[85] His will of 1463 contains references to 'tithes forgotton' to be paid to the parish church of Bungay, Suffolk, suggesting that he also resided there at some stage in his life. Ely's first appearance in Cambridge in 1438[86] came at a time when the influence of the London workshops over those in eastern England was on the decline, and the counties of East Anglia were beginning to establish regional architectural centres of their own, especially Norwich and Bury St Edmunds. No particular emphasis on Ely as a place name should be forced upon Reginald Ely as the name is a standard corruption of 'a Lee', 'a Leigh' and 'Lee'. Ely may have come from Norfolk, but does his style, as seen at King's, conform to that current in East Anglia in the first half of the fifteenth century or can other influences be detected in his work that might suggest additional areas of training and practice?

From the limited area of the fabric actually built by Ely several stylistic points come to the fore. The two eastern towers are Ely's work at least to the transom height of the lateral windows. The towers are severely plain, their angles softened by the addition of pilaster strips that effectively remove the basic polygonal plan. Yet, the plinth moulding of the tower is allowed to peep through the smaller bases of the added pilasters and re-establish the original form at least in the mind. Other features of the exterior attributable to Reginald Ely include the four-centred overarches of the closet windows, and the use of sharp angular mouldings to express the downward extension of the niche bases of the porches, the actual niches being by Wastell. The closet interiors betray a number of stylistic traits: the absence of moulded bases, the complexity of the vault responds, particularly those in the closets behind Bay 2 and 3 N, the use of sharp wedge-shaped responds in tight clusters, and the total absence of capitals so that the vault simply bursts out from the corners. The window tracery is also most puzzling – the strict Perp. versus the blatant 'flowing'. The doors in Bay 3 share many features of the closets; the general lack of capitals and bases, the moulding repertoire and the forceful use of the ogee arch.

The remaining evidence for any assessment of Ely's style at King's is contained in the vault support VS 7/8 S with its elaborate bases, complex pier moulding and its implications for the elevation intended for the antechapel. The vault support has a tight cluster of small moulded bases, slightly staggered in height and position by the insetting of the minor shafts. The use of a wave moulding as a vault shaft, complete with base and presumably to have its own capital, is most unusual and quite

85 Oswald, *English Medieval Architects*, p. 98.

86 Willis and Clark, vol. I, p. 12.

at odds with the general avoidance of bases and capitals found in the closets.

King's College Chapel is the only building that can be linked by documentary evidence to Reginald Ely, though it would seem reasonable to assume that, as master mason of 'our College Royal' he had also designed the layout for both the new and the Old Court. One section

65 Cambridge, King's College Old Court Gate

87 Ibid., vol. I, p. 228–9.

of the Old Court survives, though heavily restored, and it now forms part of the western entrance to the Old Schools.[87] The gatehouse fragment has a standard plan, with polygonal turrets flanking a sharp, four-centred entrance arch. It is faced entirely in cut stone, and it provides *65* several points of comparison with Ely's work within the Chapel. The base mouldings peep out from additional plinths in a fashion similar to Ely's angle towers on the Chapel. The gate jambs have mouldings that rise from a glacis, with wave elements utilised as shafts just as on the doors in Bay 3 and on the antechapel base VS 7/8 S. Only one element of the gatehouse jambs is provided with a capital and base and some shafts are hollowed into 'triple shafts' – all features found in the doors of Bay 3. Once again, the favourite Ely moulding, raised fillet–half bracket in combination, is used to terminate the jamb. The western entrance arch is severely four-centred, reminiscent of the overarches of the closet windows, while the inner arch has an ogeed overarch with infill tracery as on the choir doors. The cornice of the main outer facade is decorated with demi-angels like the Angel frieze around the choir bays, while the inner face of the gatehouse has a central niche with a tall crocketed spirelet similar in form to Ely's lower niche in Bay 8 S east jamb.

Unfortunately, the excessive restoration of the gate renders the niche interior vault unreliable for the purpose of comparison, it is entirely new and its design cannot be vouched for. On the main facade the unfinished central niche is flanked by panels containing radiating tracery, a pointer perhaps to the flowing tracery of the later closet windows. Despite the zealousness of the restoration and the uncertain accuracy of some of the existing design, it would appear safe to attribute the Old Court gate to Ely on stylistic grounds, which would establish his 'Chapel' style to at least 1440.

Like many master masons of the period 1420–50, Reginald Ely displays an extraordinary awareness of both English and continental forms. Something happened to English architecture during the 1420s that has not yet been adequately explained. The speed of the transformation of the grand and rather austere Perpendicular of *c.* 1400 into the exotic and fantastic monumental style of many mid fifteenth century workshops happened surprisingly fast and was remarkably uniform around the major architectural centres of the south, the east and the east Midlands. The difference of approach between, for example, New College Oxford of the late fourteenth and early fifteenth centuries and the first design of the Oxford Divinity School *c.* 1430 is most revealing. By the late 1420s even leading masons brought up in the sober traditions of late fourteenth century London seem to have been overtaken by the desire to elaborate and to reduce all architectural elements down to an unrealistic scale. How this movement might be defined in stylistic terms is complicated by the extent of local variations, itself a significant reversal from the previous half-century. There are, however, detectable common themes that high-

PLEASE
KEEP OFF
THE GRASS

66 Canterbury Cathedral
south-west porch

light the extent and nature of this architectural revolution, and as some appear in the work of Reginald Ely at King's their origin and development should be examined. Elements and motifs that had hitherto been purely decorative began to take on an architectural significance, sometimes quite at odds with their actual purpose. Tracery forms began to break down the structural and logical regime of Perpendicular and, from *c.* 1425, patterns that are distinctly 'anti-Perp.' became increasingly popular. Architectural motifs were employed inappropriately and with a casual attitude to structural and visual integrity. Most of all, there arose an interest in plasticity, complexity and illusion that ran counter to the strict tenets of 'Classic Perp.' Some have tried to explain these developments as a 'Decorated Revival', especially in those areas where Perpendicular was still a relative newcomer, or it has been seen as a reaction against the rigidity of, and boredom with, Perpendicular. To a certain extent this may be true, but the suddenness and extent of the reaction suggests that it was more than just a general sense of artistic dissatisfaction. Something else happened beyond the usual throw-away excuse that all the 'great names' of the fourteenth century – Yevele, Winford, etc. – had died off and that a new generation of master masons simply saw things differently. Men like Robert Winchecombe had worked on one of the most austere and severe buildings, New College Oxford, as late as 1418, yet by *c.* 1430 his style had become so fantastical and extravagant that it caused the celebrated condemnation by the University Proctors over the Divinity School project. Thomas Mapilton was trained in the classic London style of Stephen Lote yet by 1424 he could design the casket-like porch of Canterbury Cathedral where the excess of decoration has usurped the structural architecture to an unprecedented degree.   *66*

What brought about this sudden change in the attitudes of so many of the leading master masons in the south and south-east? The catalyst in the transformation may well have been the war.

The English occupation of Normandy

The English war with France, the so-called Hundred Years War, is blamed for many of the interruptions in the development of architecture on both sides of the Channel. The reality is somewhat different. The war was intermittent and, while large areas of northern and western France changed hands from the French to the English and back again, the impact of the fighting rarely affected the people, or the Church. Ironically, the English occupation of Calais from 1337 accelerated the development of brick architecture, for Calais had no indigenous building materials and the French could hardly be persuaded to send their enemies stone for its defence. For centuries, English masons fortified and refortified the town with brick, and the production of 'Calais brick' was sufficient to permit a considerable export trade to the mother country. Most of the earliest all-brick buildings in England are defensive, for example the Cow Tower in Norwich *c.* 1398, a town, like Calais, where the local production of brick was a useful alternative to expensive imported stone. By the early fifteenth century, Calais brick had become so established in England that it was considered suitable for the building of the Royal Palace at Sheen by Henry V.[88]

Whilst Sheen was under construction, Henry was invading Normandy. The thirty-year English occupation of the Duchy of Normandy led to a remarkable period of artistic and architectural patronage. Henry V invaded not for warring destruction but to claim the throne of France. He came as king not conqueror, hence he had every reason to protect and develop his promised land. The most significant aspect of the invasion for the future of English architecture was the constant flow of masons to France to work alongside, and sometimes under the direction of, some of the greatest French architects of the day. Hundreds of English masons went to Normandy from 1416, including Thomas Mapilton, the future Master of the King's Works and of Canterbury Cathedral.[89] In Normandy, they would have met and seen the work of such men as Alexandre de Berneval, who had himself been to England, Pierre Robin, the master mason of Charles VII, and Jean Salvart. Berneval was master mason of St Ouen in Rouen until his death in 1441 and was responsible, with his son Colin, for some of the most remarkable work in Flamboyant architecture: the upper parts of the transept, the extraordinary south porch and the second stage of the central tower. Berneval was appointed Master *67* of the King's Masonry in the baillage of Rouen by Henry V, a post he held for life. Jean Salvart had been master mason for Rouen Cathedral since 1406. He was responsible for the completion of the great west front with its fretted screenwork of Flamboyant tracery, finished in 1421. Salvart was appointed Master Mason for Henry's new Palace at Rouen, *68* begun in 1420. Robert Westerley, later to be master mason of Eton and Westminster Abbey, worked under Salvart in the early 1420s.

Throughout the three decades of the English occupation, Rouen was a thriving architectural centre with the new Palace, St Ouen, the cathedral and the important church of St Maclou, all under construction. *69* The latter church highlights the artistic freedom enjoyed by the leading masons, for it was designed by Pierre Robin, master mason for the rival King Charles VII, yet it was built in the heart of the English occupied territory. A similar situation existed in Paris between 1423 and 1436. In 1431, an English mason, John James, was appointed master mason of Notre Dame, as well as Master of the Works of the City of Paris.[90] This may seem natural enough during the brief English occupation but James continued in his post even after the French recapture of the city, resigning from the Cathedral only in 1447 but retaining his civic position until 1455.

88 Colvin, vol. II, pp. 994–1002.

89 Ibid., vol. I, pp. 457–64. From 1423, master mason of Canterbury Cathedral.

90 C. H. Bauchal, *Nouveau Dictionnaire des Architectes Français*, Paris, 1887, p. 307.

67 Rouen, St Ouen central
tower
68 Rouen Cathedral, detail of
west facade screen

It is unthinkable that two countries that had such strong military, economic and administrative ties should not have influenced each other's cultural, artistic and architectural development. It has long been established that French Flamboyant was a direct offshoot of the English Decorated Style, and, more recently, the development of English Perpendicular has been seen as a new awareness of Rayonnant and its regional variants from late thirteenth-century France. The English masons who travelled back and forth between England and France during the years 1416 and 1449 cannot have failed to cast a critical and appreciative eye on the latest Flamboyant architectural developments en route. The effortless soufflé creations of northern France must have seemed heady stuff to men brought up on a strict diet of regimented geometry and disciplined correctness. It was not that the style that confronted them was altogether new, they too could create some exotic filagreed conconctions for a screen or tomb, but it was its application to 'real' buildings that must have impressed them. It cannot be doubted that many of them came home with their heads, and notebooks, filled with Gallic recipes. Similarly, most of the great English architectural patrons of the first half of the fifteenth century, both nobility and ecclesiastics, were exposed to the new French style and its fabulous vitality. Thus the combination of patrons and leading master masons, with first-hand experience of the latest in French taste, was to have a considerable impact on the direction of Perpendicular architecture for the rest of the century.

69   Rouen, St Maclou: interior of crossing and north transept

91   Colvin, vol. I, p. 458.

92   Ibid., Later master mason of Eton and Westminster Abbey.

93   For St Ouen see J. Daoust, *L'Abbaye Royale Saint Ouen*, Rouen, 1966. For St Nicholas des Champs see Y. Christ, Saint Nicholas des Champs, *Dictionnaire des Eglises de France, vol. IV c. Paris et ses Environs*, Paris 1968, pp. 97–9.

94   M. Alline, *Bulletin des Amis des monuments rouennais*, 1912; M. Aubert, Rouen, la Cathedrale, *Congres Archaeologique*, LXXXIX 1926, pp. 50–51; J. Bony, *The English Decorated Style*, p. 67. n. 45.

95   The nearest English parallel, though remote in date, would be the chancel windows of St Helen's Norwich of c. 1385. Similar 'Flamboyant' tracery occurs over the Shrine bays in the choir of Ely, inserted into the thirteenth-century work c. 1450.

The English style that they evolved was not, of course, Flamboyant, but neither was it a 'Decorated Revival' – it was the fantastic strand of Perp. overlaid and undermined by memories of France. What came out of it was a style that was suitable, or at least usable, for any situation, from the thinnest screen to the greatest church. For perhaps the first time since the thirteenth century it becomes possible to speak of a single style that could embrace all the elements of ecclesiastical building. It is not without significance that this new era of Fantastic architecture coincided with a distinct shift towards brick in domestic building and for the first time in the history of medieval architecture, the domestic and ecclesiastical traditions began to part and go their own separate ways.

Whether Reginald Ely was amongst the hundreds of English masons who went to Normandy, Calais or Bordeaux is impossible to tell, but the numbers involved in this cross-channel venture would suggest that at times the English workshops were depleted seriously. For example, in 1415, over one hundred masons were sent to Normandy from London and the Home Counties alone, another batch went in 1416, and yet more including Mapilton in 1417/18,[91] and another group of thirty went with Robert Westerley in 1421.[92] After the English took possession of Paris and most of northern France in 1421, English masons would have had direct access to nearly all the major buildings of French Gothic, past and present.

The activities and whereabouts of Reginald Ely prior to 1438 are unknown but his style as exhibited at King's Cambridge from 1441 contains significant traits suggesting that he possessed more than a passing knowledge of contemporary French architecture. The flowing tracery patterns in the closet windows of the Chapel are far more French than English in conception – the excessive accent on the depressed ogees over very flat, segmental lights, the bringing of the ogees further forward than the rest of the tracery, and the filling of the upper lights with revolving tracery and coupled mouchettes all speak of an East Anglian interpretation of something very French. The twin ogee window is so common in France that it hardly needs illustration but interesting examples amongst the hundreds that would have been seen by English masons include the west end of St Nicholas des Champs in Paris from the early 1420s, and the lower blind tracery in the north transept of St Ouen at Rouen of pre-1441, both works in progress during the English occupation.[93] The French were also fond of coupling different and entirely inappropriate tracery patterns within one design, as on the west front of Rouen Cathedral, completed in 1421,[94] and on the central tower of St Ouen, before 1441, both major undertakings in the English capital of Normandy. It would certainly be difficult to find an English mid fifteenth century parallel for the closet tracery combination at King's Cambridge.[95]

70 King's College Chapel: exterior detail, base of the north-west stair turret

The base mouldings of Ely's corner towers of King's College Chapel have extraordinary 'peeking' bases, vestiges of the buried and actually non-existent polygonal angles. This is the grossest misuse of this favour- 70 ite tiny trick of tomb architecture but one that the French had taken up with a vengeance, for example the multiple cluster of homeless bases on the west porch of St Germain d'Auxerrois in Paris, begun during the English occupancy and completed *c.* 1439. Ely also demonstrates the 71 complete degeneration of vault responds, using complex rolls and fillets, wave mouldings with entirely illogical bases and capitals, and even groups of angular wedges. The employment of such elements should have been heresy to English masons but they were all standard elements of French Flamboyant before the middle of the fifteenth century. Wave mouldings were used as vault responds complete with capitals and bases as early as *c.* 1420, again in St Nicholas des Champs in Paris, while wedges and every conceivable complexity of rolls and fillets were used as vault responds in Rouen, both at St Ouen and St Maclou. Reginald Ely also 72 displays a cavalier disregard as to the employment of capitals and bases, the closet vault responds lack either element, the responds jumping straight from a corner glacis while the vault responds become vault ribs without interruption. The total abandonment of bases and capitals had become a common feature of Flamboyant as early as *c.* 1400, e.g. Riom, Notre Dame du Sablon in Brussels, and the choir of Souvigny, but it is a feature rarely found in England prior to the 'revolution' of the 1420s.[96]

The antechapel bases are also characteristically Flamboyant, not only the use of a wave moulding with a base, but also in the tight cluster of

96 For Riom see J. Bony, fig. 394; for Notre Dame du Sablon see R. Sanfacon, *L'Architecture Flamboyant en France*, Quebec 1971, figs. 14.15; for Souvigny see Bauchal, p. 392.

71 Paris, St Germain d'Auxerrois: exterior detail, west porch pier base

97 Lierne ribs of a kind occur as early as *c.* 1220, i.e. Anjou.

72 Rouen, St Maclou: interior detail, choir base

individual pedestals and the syncopation of the size and height of the bases themselves. The closest parallels to the King's antechapel bases of post-1448 are in Notre Dame du Sablon *c.* 1400, in the Cathedral of Seville begun in 1406 but soon after taken over by a Norman workshop, and the choir bases of Mont St Michel, rebuilt late in the English occupancy from *c.* 1446.

Yet Ely's style is not French, nor is it English Perpendicular in the conventional late fourteenth century interpretation. The English elements are strong, the rigidity of the Perp. tracery in every alternate closet window, the capital mouldings, where they exist, the standard lierne vaulting, though this too had been assimilated into French Flamboyant at an early-stage,[97] while the larger-scale mouldings are more typically English with only occasional excursions into Flamboyant extravagances. It is notable, for example, that the major mouldings such as the lateral window jambs of King's revert to standard Perpendicular conventions whereas the less obvious and smaller-scale mouldings tend to be more experimental. Ely had not lost all sense of Perpendicular propriety and there is a suggestion in the disposition of the 'English' and 'Flamboyant' elements that he kept to the surer ground of his 'Perp.' training for the essential structure such as vaulting techniques and major mouldings, while allowing his alien tendencies to affect only the less essential and peripheral sections. Such a stylistic division could well be indicative of a mason who knew how to build in one style, but who was taken with the purely decorative attractions of another.

This mixture finds a notable parallel in the design of St Peter Mancroft in Norwich, begun *c.* 1440. Reginald Ely, of course, came from the Norwich area and may even have worked on some of the projects of the Mancroft workshop, the Erpingham Gate or the Norwich Blackfriars, perhaps on the first stages of St Peter's. The main arcade walls display all the standard, large-scale mouldings of the period, whereas all the periphery work shows a far more adventurous attitude. The aisles, porches and west door ensemble of St Peter Mancroft contain mouldings and other details so alien to the body of the church that one might be forgiven for thinking them the work of another hand altogether. The moulding profiles, particularly those of the inner west and north doors, are amongst the most complicated of their day, certainly as elaborate as anything in Oxford or Canterbury. The use of 'boss-less' vaults and the Yorkshire ogee elements of the eastern facing windows of the church, and throughout the clerestory, suggest a workshop, or at least a master, whose knowledge of northern developments was matched by his infatuation with a growing Fantastic style of the south and east. The contrast between the intricate and complex work on the perimeter of the nave of St Peter's with the austerity of the main arcade walls within is as marked as the simplification enforced upon the upper level of the Oxford Divinity School during construction. St Peter Mancroft also contains

3 Mont St Michel: interior
detail, choir piers

98 An observation to be published in F. Woodman, *Early Brick Architecture in Norwich*, 1986.

99 Oswald, Andrew Doket and his Architect, pp. 8–26.

a lot of brick, all discreetly out of sight, but denoting the sudden popularity of that material around 1400. St Peter's is in fact substantially brick built and merely clad with Ancaster.[98] Brick architecture finally 'came out' in spectacular fashion during the 1430s and 1440s – Caistor and Tattershall Castles and Queens College Cambridge, the latter most notably attributed to Reginald Ely.[99] The Mancroft style of the 1440s is evident in much of Ely's work at King's College Chapel. Many of his moulding profiles find parallels in the products of the Norwich team, the tightness and variety of the profiles within the choir doors at King's are similar to those on the west and north doors of St Peter's and to the mouldings of the earliest product of the workshop, the Erpingham Gate to the Cathedral of *c.* 1430–50. Other Mancroft elements in Ely's repertoire include the use of wave mouldings, and 'triple shafts' are used repeatedly at St Peter's and on the Erpingham Gate. Both the west door of St Peter's and the Erpingham Gate display a total disregard for the niceties of providing shafts with capitals and bases, while the north porch of St Peter's and another of their works in the city, the south porch of St Mary Coslany of *c.* 1450, provide a parallel for the side closet vaults in Bays 2 and 3 N at King's, with the ribs bursting out from the angle responds without capitals or any break at the springing point. While such similarities might provide a workshop background for Reginald Ely, the works cited are generally of the same date as his work in Cambridge and the parallels lack the absolute exactness to strengthen the connection any further. The one notable exception is the link between the inner west door of St Peter Mancroft and the two choir doors in Bay 3 at King's. These three doors are remarkably similar and, notably, the Norwich door is probably the earliest. The rich stylistic mixture evident in the Mancroft workshop – indigenous Perpendicular, elements drawn from the north plus strong traits of the French-inspired Fantastic Style – raises the problem as to whether Reginald Ely was exposed to the latter movement in the 1420s and 1430s through Norwich, or directly through experience gained in northern France. Whatever the answer, and one would suspect a mixture of the two, the Mancroft workshop stands out in eastern England as being one of the most precocious and sophisticated of the early exponents of the Fantastic Style, though its influence upon the architecture of Norwich appears to have been shortlived.

Reginald Ely is also linked with the church of Burwell, some twenty miles north-east of Cambridge. Burwell is one of the finest products of East Anglian Perp. and its design has long been attributed to the architect of King's College Chapel. What documentary basis there might be for this local mythology is not clear. However, a stylistic analysis of the building can lend considerable weight to the legend.

Burwell was a prosperous small town in the late Middle Ages, the town was 'wool rich'. The advowson of the church belonged to the University

74 Norwich, St Peter Mancroft: interior

100 Bury Wills, ii, f. 23.

101 Ibid., 256v.

102 P.C.C. 20 Godwyn.

103 This feature was to reappear in Norwich and Cambridge *c.* 1500. i.e. Great St Mary's Cambridge, St George Colegate, St Andrew's and St Stephen's Norwich.

104 See also Walpole St Andrew's Norfolk, another product of Bury?

of Cambridge, while two of the manors belonged to Sir John Tiptoft. The large church, with an aisled nave and aisleless chancel, was rebuilt from *c.* 1450 and its progress can be followed from wills. The nave aisles, and presumably therefore the arcade walls, were under way in 1454, when construction of the north aisle is mentioned.[100] The south aisle was glazed in 1460.[101] In 1464, as appears in an inscription on the chancel arch, the nave roof and parapets were under construction. The chancel was begun prior to 1467, when the vicar, John Heigham, requested that the 'chauncell newly begun' should be 'entirely built and completed', to which end he made a bequest.[102] The whole church, minus the west tower, can therefore be dated with some confidence to *c.* 1450–70. The church is very handsome and is one of that elite group in eastern England of high-quality late medieval parish churches that can hold their own against any works of architecture. The nave arcade walls are treated architectonically from floor to roof, a rare feature in the east, with the arcade linked to the 'triforium' area and on up to the clerestory. Needless to say, such work was expensive, and the quality of Burwell, both in design and execution, confirms instantly that it is the product of a major workshop.[103] Cambridge would be the natural source, both geographically and architecturally, and quite obviously by the patronage of the living. The workshop of King's College Chapel would seem the obvious candidate. But can an attribution be made directly to Reginald Ely on the evidence of his work at King's?

The most celebrated parallel between the two buildings is the tracery of the east windows of the aisles at Burwell and the 'flowing' tracery of the early side closets at King's, built prior to 1461. It must be said immediately that they are identical and provide the firmest evidence for a common design authorship. The known dates would confirm that the Burwell windows are no mere copy: the aisles of Burwell were in progress in 1454 and finished by 1460. The earliest closet at King's was first 'locked' in 1460 so that the tracery cannot realistically pre-date *c.* 1455. The Burwell windows may well pre-date the building of the first closet at King's. The occurrence of such rare tracery, executed in high quality, some twenty miles apart and perhaps within months of each other, is strong evidence for a direct design connection.

Other features in the church are perhaps less helpful. The general repertoire of moulding profiles are of a standard East Anglian form. The arcade bases resemble those in the south chancel aisle of St Mary's Bury, and are not particularly like Ely's bases in the antechapel of King's. The capitals, however, are very like those on the choir doors in Bay 3 of King's College Chapel, but not absolutely identical. The Burwell piers include a 'triple shaft' element, with corresponding capitals and bases, a feature that occurs on the choir doors in Bay 3 and on the Old Court gate at King's, though in the latter case they are rather muted and lack the answering capitals and bases.[104] One interesting feature of the Burwell

75 Burwell: interior of nave
76 Burwell: exterior, east window of south aisle

105 Built by Alexandre and Colin de Berneval. See Bauchal, pp. 46–7.

elevation is the downward extension of the clerestory mullions directly on to the extrados of the main arcade arches. Such an arrangement was not new, it dates back at least to Gloucester in the 1330s, but its application to parish church architecture was rare. It may reflect the original antechapel design at King's, where VS 7/8 S predicts that Ely intended an overlay of blind tracery extending beneath the lateral windows. The interior of the side closet against Bay 8 S further predicts a low four-centred arch opening directly into the antechapel interior and tempts one to see the combination of the blind tracery descending to the arch very much in the manner of Burwell.

One motif within the blind tracery of the Burwell chancel arch of 1464 is very curious and has a French parallel – the slight twisting of the wheel pattern so that the regular lobes become gentle mouchettes. A similarly *77* subtle arrangement of wheel tracery occurs on a massive scale on the interior of the end wall of the north transept arm of St Ouen at Rouen, built before 1441, during the English occupation.[105] *78*

The chancel of Burwell is more rigidly Perp. with regular tracery forms and bare wall surfaces. Perhaps the contrast with the nave was intentional, like the austerity of the choir bays at King's compared to the intended

77 Burwell: interior detail, blind tracery above chancel arch

78 Rouen, St Ouen: interior detail, blind tracery in north transept

elaboration of the antechapel. The Burwell choir is decorated with a series of large figure niches, two on each wall. The southern pair immediately recall the Ely niche on the lower section of VS 7/8 S. They have identical canopies with ogee gables and segmental subarches, lobed infilling, suspended demi-angels, crocketed spirelets and interior vaults supported on tiny heads. The vaults, however, are different, the King's niche vault *79* being more angular, while the Burwell vaults are flowing and 'fan-like'. The execution of the Burwell design does not stand comparison with that at King's.

Stylistically, the attribution of Burwell to Reginald Ely has a strong case – the dates make it stronger, but the execution, particularly that of the chancel, would cast something of a shadow. Of course, by the time that the chancel was under way in 1467, Ely was an old man and may no longer have been active. The work was probably farmed out to a member of his workshop.[106] John Melford of Sudbury, the prolific parish church master mason, is the most likely candidate. He is known to have served his apprenticeship under Ely and he made a bequest to the church of Burwell in his will.[107] It is entirely possible that Ely controlled the nave campaign directly, leaving Melford to build the chancel. The church of Burwell may well provide hints as to the original design of King's College Chapel in 1448. The socle tracery motif has been explored already. The terminal windows of the aisles may also provide a clue as to Ely's intended design for the lateral windows at King's – four-centred lights, flowing tracery, and transoms at mid height.

It has been suggested that Reginald Ely was the designer of Queens' College, founded as St Bernard's in 1446 by Andrew Doket, rector of St Botolph's Church.[108] The link between Ely and Queens' is somewhat circumstantial: Ely and Doket were neighbours, each remembered the other in their wills, Ely left a house and money to Queens' while Doket bequeathed an obit at St Botolph's on the anniversary of Ely's death. However, if we were to infer that the reference to Queens' in Ely's will was sufficient for an attribution to be made concerning the design authorship, then should the lack of any reference to King's in the same will be taken as evidence that Ely did not design that College?

Quite clearly, in view of the lack of any documentary evidence concerning the identity of the master mason of Queens' the building itself will have to be examined for any points of comparison it might have with known Ely works.

The main problem with any analysis of the architecture of Queens' College is that it is almost entirely built of brick, the only stone features being the various gate, door and window jambs, tracery and the odd vault. Furthermore, it would be wrong to assume that any mason who normally worked on all-stone buildings would necessarily adopt the same approach when confronted with brick. We can, however, divide quickly those stone elements that are similar to known Ely designs from others that are not. On the negative side, the base mouldings in the gatehouse and in the hall are not like any known to be by Ely, though equally these two examples are also unlike each other. The tracery in both the hall and chapel has no known Ely counterpart while the general repertoire of mouldings is heavier and bolder than those associated with Ely at either King's or Burwell.

On the positive side, the gatehouse entrance arch is similar to the Old Court Gate of King's just a few years earlier, the arch mouldings are

106 Reginald Ely made his will in 1463, see Oswald, *English Medieval Architects*, p. 98.

107 Ibid. and P.C.C. 22 Bennett.

108 Oswald, Andrew Doket and his Architect, pp. 8–26.

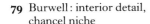

79 Burwell: interior detail, chancel niche

very close, the spandrel decoration identical. The Queens' gate also has demi-angels for end stops. The interior vault is similar but not identical to the Ely closet vaults against Bays 2 and 3 N of King's College Chapel, but the unusual vault rib profile with its polygonal termination is common to both sets of vaults. The execution of the Queens' vault is poor when compared with King's. Above the gate entrance is the most frustrating of all the features at Queens', the central niche canopy. This has a tall crocketed spirelet rising from a triple-sided canopy made up from ogee gables with segmental subarches enclosing tear-drop lobes – identical to the Ely niche in Bay 8 S east jamb but without the demi-angels. The niche vault at Queens' is very much like the niche vaults in Bay 1 S east and west jambs of King's College Chapel, while it also bears a family resemblance to the niche vaults in Bays 1 N west jamb, 3 N east jamb and the northern niche of the east window.[109] One other feature at Queens' that is reminiscent of Burwell is the set of mouchette circles in the spandrels of the doors to the kitchen offices. Such Flamboyant motifs are not common in fifteenth-century England, but they do recall the decoration of the chancel arch of Burwell.

It will be seen that there is as much evidence against the attribution of Queens' College to Reginald Ely as there is in favour. The most compelling evidence, the niche canopy, merely complicates the existing problem of the attribution of the King's niches, for the parallels within King's College Chapel are rather oddly spread about the early, pre-1477 work. With such uncertainty concerning the identity of the designers of the King's niches, it would be rash on the evidence of only a single niche to attribute Queens' College to Reginald Ely. On present evidence, the verdict must be 'not proven'.

The analysis of Reginald Ely's work at King's College, both on the Chapel and the fragment of the Old Court, can provide an outline 'life story' for him, based on style and a very little documentation. The gatehouse fragment and the distinctive design of the side closets at King's place Ely into the select group of leading master masons who display an awareness of French Flamboyant, suggesting that he probably spent some time early in his career in Normandy, perhaps in the 1420s. His East Anglian roots are strong, and the Mancroft workshop parallels in Norwich are highly suggestive, especially given Ely's Norfolk origin. Burwell demonstrates that the Ely workshop, if indeed that's what it was, continued working in Cambridge after the fall of Henry VI.

The contribution of John Wolryche

If it is now proposed that the contribution of Reginald Ely to the interior design of King's College Chapel is less that suspected hitherto then, conversely, the second master mason, John Wolryche, must gain in signifi-

109 See p. 65.

cance. The limit of his work is easier to define – the change in mullion moulding profile in Bay 2, the slight alteration to the tracery pattern of the lateral windows from Bay 3 and the introduction of a more orderly sequence of window jamb niches – all assist in pinpointing the changeover from Wolryche to Clerk in the summer of 1477. Thus the area of the Chapel attributable to John Wolryche can now be defined as follows: the window jambs from Bay 1 to 5 east jambs from the level of the transom to that of the window springing (the lower section being by Ely), the jamb niches from Bay 1 to 3 N east jamb and Bays 1 to 4 S east jambs, the mullions of the lateral windows in Bay 1, the window heads and tracery in Bays 1 and 2 and sections of the east wall up to the transom height on the north jamb of the great east window, but slightly below that on the south.

In addition, a number of vital decisions affecting the present internal appearance of the Chapel were made and implemented by Wolryche prior to the summer of 1477. They include the design of the vault supports in the choir and the number of shafts to be employed, the level of the vault springing and the design of the capitals, and the arcature and the height of the lateral windows. The change of mullion moulding profile as early as the windows of Bay 2 would suggest that Wolryche had only just completed the tracery heads in that bay by the middle of 1477. This in turn would signify that a number of major design decisions were not made by Wolryche but by his successor, Simon Clerk – the final decision to vault, the stone-clad brick structure of the upper walls above the lateral windows, the inclusion of brick-lined passages to give access to the intended vault, the present overall height of the building, the east window tracery and the design of the blind panelling that wraps around it.

It might be expected that such basic decisions as to whether or not to vault, or the overall height of the Chapel, had been determined from the outset and indeed they had in principle. The Will and Intent of 1448 specifies that there was to be a vault and that the Chapel should be ninety feet high. But much had happened since those confident days of Henry VI, and much had failed to happen. The money supply had all but dried up after 1461, the new King had tried to impoverish the College, and the fellows and scholars had been forced to live in half-finished and 'temporary' accommodation. By the early 1470s the great scheme for the new College buildings apears to have been shelved reluctantly and there can have been little hope for completing the vast Chapel according to the initial design. At Eton, similar reduced circumstances had led to the total abandonment of their large antechapel, while the choir bays were summarily finished off without a vault but with an open timber roof.[110] Moreover, the choir of Eton College Chapel was nearer to completion in 1460 than that of King's and it was brought into use as early as 1476. Thus the response of King's to the same unwelcome conditions

110 The existing vault over Eton College Chapel dates from 1956–9.

might have been even more severe. Could they ever have hoped to see the whole project completed, with the enormous antechapel and expensive high vaults? The logical answer must be no. By the late 1460s it would have been optimistic of the College even to expect the completion and roofing of the choir bays of their Chapel and undoubtedly, the first thing to go was the vault. High vaults were very costly, those of King's College Chapel would be extremely expensive as the Chapel has an unusually wide span of 41 ft 6 in. (12·66 m). Bishop Waynflete, who was still responsible for the financing of the building operations at both King's and Eton, had already ordered the completion of Eton College Chapel without vaults and this probably set the precedent for the Cambridge Chapel. After all, the comprehensive stone vaults of King's are a most unusual feature for any university college chapel, and with such prestigious examples as New College and All Souls, Oxford, having open timber roofs, there would have been little compunction to follow this established and less-expensive form.

There are a number of structural indications that suggest that the vault was abandoned for a time, and these occur around the level of the lateral window arch heads. Previously, Reginald Ely had provided corbels at the lateral window transom level as part of his last horizontal campaign when building the lower jambs of the windows from Bays 1 to 5 east jamb. Thus, at that stage, the intention to vault persisted. The difficulty in determining exactly when transom level was reached in these bays makes the dating of this lingering intention difficult to establish, but some indication may come from the original state of Bay 1 S, where the lateral window was blinded below the transom to allow for the intended eastern range of the College buildings. Hence when this level was reached in Bay 1 S, the College had not yet given up hope of erecting the great court of the Will and Intent. While the fall of Henry VI in 1461 may have caused the College to postpone any decision concerning the great court, his eventual death in 1472 must have made the total abandonment inevitable. Thus at least some of the corbels for the choir vault supports are likely to have been in place before Ely's death in 1471. Having once started the series, it was probably felt best to continue them, and to erect the modified vault supports upon them, whatever decision had been taken over the actual vault. The design of the choir vault supports, that rise from the polygonal corbels, illustrates the reduced circumstances of the College in the period after 1461. The design had been revised and simplified, eliminating one pair of the vault shafts altogether and replacing the rather sinuous profile of the support with something altogether smoother and cheaper than that proposed and begun by Reginald Ely in the antechapel. The simplification of the vault supports suggests that the vault design had also undergone a radical reduction, or indeed that it had been dropped from the plan altogether.

A proposal that the high vault of King's College Chapel was abandoned at this stage would fit well with the financial situation of the College and it would also make considerably more sense of the arrangement of the lateral window design and its relationship with the vault supports as adopted by Wolryche in the 1470s. To explain this, it is necessary to examine exactly what now happens at this vital juncture of the main elevational wall. The existing interrelation between the lateral windows, the vault springing and the present vault is the least happy feature in the appearance of King's College Chapel. The vault supports as built are carried some way above the springing level of the lateral window arch heads to a point where no vault of reasonable design could both spring from the supports and embrace the lateral windows in a sensible manner. Added to this, the vault supports are distanced from the windows by tall blind panels with intermittent ogee gables. The arch heads of the windows are squared off internally with ribs that extend up from the inner jamb mouldings, and the resulting spandrels are treated with cusped lobes and odd-shaped quatrefoils. The squaring is not complete, for the present sixteenth century fan vault slices the extremities with its own wall ribs. The geometry of the fan vault, springing from so great a height, causes the empty space above the windows, now filled out with blank panelling.

Of course there is no positive proof that the high vaults were abandoned during the 1470s, but the present design does suffer difficulties which are unlikely to have been included deliberately. Had Wolryche still intended to vault in 1476/77, when he began the window arch heads in Bay 1 and 2, he would surely have raised the window springing level with the vault, or lowered the vault supports accordingly. Alternatively, he might have raised the vault springers to the apex level of the windows, so that a vault could have sprung clear of the window bay as an independent upper feature of the design i.e. in the manner of St Stephen's Westminster. The only way in which a vault could be added to the Wolryche design as built by *c.* 1476, without radical rebuilding, was to elevate the interior considerably, and to build a vault lifted well clear of the lateral windows, as was done in the sixteenth century. However, the Wolryche *80* vault supports were not rebuilt higher, freeing the vault from the window bay, and the result is the present 'blind spot'. But, if Wolrchye had intended no more than an open wooden roof, then the level of the supports vis à vis the windows, plus the squaring of the window bays, all *81* make perfect sense.

By the summer of 1477, Wolryche had not built any higher than the apex level of the lateral windows of Bays 1 and 2 – this we know from the ironwork purchases of 1476/77. He may not have intended to raise the interior elevation any higher at all. The decorated squared spandrels of the lateral windows may represent a new compromise upper limit to

80 King's College Chapel: interior of choir looking east

81 King's College Chapel: interior detail, the clash between the square-framed window bay and the sixteenth-century vault

111 C. Wilson, The Original Design of the City of London Guildhall. *Journal of the British Archaeological Association,* CXXIX, 1976 pp. 1–14.

112 See also F. Mackenzie, *Observations on the construction of the roofs of King's College Chapel Cambridge,* London 1840, pl. II.

82 London, the City Guildhall: interior reconstruction (Wilson)

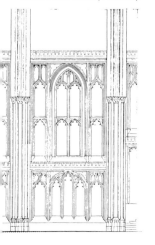

the stone elevation, with the vault supports adapted to carry no more than the wall posts of an open timber roof construction. Alternatively, the vault springers might have been intended to carry stone overarches supporting the wooden roof in the original manner of the London Guild-hall.[111] With the existing vaults and their support walls removed, the remaining squared elevation of the lateral window bays at King's College Chapel, would resemble strongly the reconstructed elevations of the earlier London work. Such a design would eliminate the need for the existing upper walls, the passages and square lights on the exterior. The subsequent provision of this section, with a passage floor only 8 in. (0·20 m) above the window spandrels, signifies that once more the Chapel was to be vaulted.[112] This section is also 8 in. above the level reached by Wolryche in 1477.

82

The level of the passage floor above the windows marks a dramatic change in the structural technique of the fabric, seeing the abandonment of an all-stone structure in favour of a lighter, cheaper and easier brick construction, with stone cladding on the exterior and exposed interior surfaces. This changeover from stone to clad brick occurs immediately on top of the level reached by Wolryche in the summer of 1477 and is another indication of the arrival of Simon Clerk as master mason.

Any temporary abandonment of the high vault in the early 1470s would have allowed a major reduction in the height and hence the cost of the Chapel project and would certainly have encouraged the College in their attempts to complete at least the choir bays. The battlements could have stood more or less directly above the apices of the lateral windows, thus

113 The string courses on the south-east turret are confused by an additional string related to the intended height of the proposed southern range of the great court.

114 This level is picked up within the design of the buttresses.

cutting over nine feet from the overall elevation. The compromise height intended by Wolryche *c*. 1476 may be indicated by the fourth string course of the exterior of the north-east turret,[113] which occurs above the string course that marks the apex level of the lateral windows.[114]

Whether or not Wolryche did adopt a compromise open timber roof design for King's College Chapel, as suggested above, will be discussed further as part of the examination of the problems faced by Simon Clerk upon his arrival. What we do now know is that Wolryche contributed more to the existing design and fabric of the Chapel than has been thought previously. But what can we tell of his architectural background and stylistic training? John Wolryche is a shadowy figure and only the sketchiest impression can be caught of his history. As master mason of King's College, and perhaps also of King's Hall, he was clearly a man of some standing and reputation. Unlike Ely, he has left us no will from which a life history can be assembled, merely the blankest of references to his position. However, Wolryche must have achieved something before coming to King's, either a building of merit, or a job of sufficient seniority to inspire the confidence of Bishop Waynflete and the College.

The architectural analysis of his work at King's is hampered by the relative uncertainty as to precisely where his sections of the Chapel commence, and by how much of his first work might still continue the proposals of his predecessor. There are, however, some 'safe areas' and it is best to concentrate upon these.

115 See p. 171.

As with the work of Ely, the areas known to be built by Wolryche contain such architectural evidence as niches, mouldings, tracery and decoration. Vaults are present only in the niche canopies – the closet vault contract of 1513 providing the vaults for all the side chapels save those vaulted by Ely prior to 1461.[115] Many of the mouldings were inherited from the Ely campaign, including the closet vault responds and the jambs of the lateral windows. The design of the choir vault supports represents a dilution of Ely's original and more complex proposal. It is perhaps the most significant decision made by him, not only for its implications concerning the future of a high vault, but also for the problems it raised when it was finally decided to revert to a vaulted scheme.

116 For example, Kenilworth great hall and the London Guildhall.

Two further and important elements of the choir elevational design can be attributed to John Wolryche: the window spandrels and the lateral window tracery patterns. The infilling of spandrels within a square frame was a common design feature of Perpendicular, but one usually employed on the exterior, i.e. the porches of Westminster Hall and Abbey, the crypt windows of Canterbury Cathedral and the cloisters of Old St Pauls. Few buildings can be cited that incorporate decorated squared window spandrels on the interior, mostly due to the provision of vaults or timber roof constructions that embrace the window overarches.[116] One notable exception was St Stephen's Chapel Westminster, where the wooden vault sprang from the window apex level, leaving a considerable spandrel area exposed, which was square framed and filled with vertical panelling. *83* The original design of the spandrels at King's has been mutilated by the subsequent imposition of the sixteenth century fan vault but the basic pattern of two cusped lobes supporting some cusped foil shapes in the corners appears to be sound. The present blind panelling within the vault lunettes is an addition to the choir bays inserted after 1508 and was part of the construction programme of the existing vaults – a horizontal break can be detected above every lateral window from Bays 1 N to 6 N, and from Bay 1 S to 7 S, whereas in the sixteenth century bays further west the blind panelling forms an integral part of the lateral window bay.[117] The base level of the added panelling in the choir bays has destroyed any evidence concerning the uppermost level of the Wolryche design pre-1477. When the intention to vault was re-introduced, sometime after the arrival of Simon Clerk, it was necessary to supply additional height against which a vault could then be constructed. Hence, the Wolryche elevational scheme in Bays 1 and 2 now merges into Simon Clerk's additions, which are in turn overlaid by the sixteenth-century solution to the problems of the vault and the lunettes.

Whereas the spandrel decoration is unusual, the tracery introduced by Wolryche in Bays 1 and 2 is exceptional. The tracery patterns of the lateral windows of King's College Chapel are amongst the rarest forms in England. Their uniqueness lies in the unresolved ogee arches of the

117 For the construction of the high vault, see pp. 182–90.

83 Westminster, St Stephen's Chapel : interior detail of spandrel (Carter)

84 King's College Chapel:
exterior showing tracery of
Bays 1 and 2 S

85 Bury St Edmund's, St Mary's: exterior detail, nave window

86 Map showing distribution of the King's College Chapel lateral window tracery type

118 Walpole St Peter Norfolk. For a distribution map see fig. 86.
119 St Stephen's Norwich.

middle ranks and in order to explain their peculiarity it is necessary to examine the tracery in some detail and to search back to the end of the fourteenth century for its origin.

The tracery of Bays 1 and 2 is divided into five lights, with four-centred arch heads. The mullions continue unbroken to the main arch moulding and each main light is subdivided within the tracery by lesser mullions that stand directly upon the apices of the main lights. Thus far, the tracery 84 is standard 'Perp.'. The side lights above one and five have cusped lobes joined at the heads and a single regular sub-light-plus-lobe arrangement. This element would seem to be a reflection of the 'flowing' tracery of the closet windows by Ely. The three central lights are subdivided into regular sub-lights but are coupled by ogee arches that spring from the major mullion extensions, and are carried up to form the minor mullions of the top tier. The resulting apex spandrel is in the form of a concave lozenge. The top tier of lights is again regular, though the outermost have triangular heads. A cusped quatrefoil and odd-shaped lobes fill the very top.

The curious and extremely unusual element of the design is the coupled ogee lights which create one-sided descending lights immediately above and which are at first sight more 'Dec.' than 'Perp.' It would have been perfectly simple, and far more standard, to resolve the asymmetry of the top lights by making them cusped lozenges, that is regular elongated ovals. The asymmetry of the lowest tier is an inevitable outcome of a subdivision above a regular four-centred main light, whereas the top tier displays a deliberate disregard for Perpendicular propriety that would have been unthinkable in most workshops of the fifteenth century. The wilful nature of the King's tracery becomes apparent when it is compared with more orthodox London forms, for example, the aisles of St Mary's Bury St Edmunds or the Holland Chapel in Canterbury 85 Cathedral.

The geographic distribution of the King's tracery type is very revealing. Only about ninety buildings have been noted so far that employ variations of this asymmetrical tracery. The largest number occurs in Norfolk, with thirty-six buildings, dating from *c.* 1420[118] to the mid sixteenth century.[119] This figure must be set against well over 700 churches and med- 86 ieval stone buildings in the county, most of which have Perpendicular tracery of some kind. Lincolnshire has ten examples out of more than 420 buildings, but the list is notable in a county that contains little first-rate architecture post-1400, as this tracery form is found in nearly all the major fifteenth-century projects that do exist: the Russell Chantry in Lincoln Cathedral, Tattershall, Boston, Spalding, Burgh le Marsh, etc. The City of York has four examples, with five more out in the East Riding out of a total of around 150 medieval stone buildings with tracery. A further six buildings containing this tracery type can be found in the

West Riding of Yorkshire out of nearly 190. Suffolk has eight out of 430, while Cambridgeshire, including the Soke of Peterborough, has six examples out of approximately 160 – one of which is King's College Chapel. Three examples only can be cited in Northamptonshire out of over 250, while Bedfordshire, Essex and Hertfordshire each have one out of a combined total of over 550 churches. Two exist in Oxfordshire, one in the West Country and one post-Reformation example in the West Midlands.[120] No others have yet been noted in any other southern or eastern county.

The dating of the surviving examples would point to a Yorkshire origin. The initial idea of using coupled tracery lights under an ogee over-arch, thus providing an asymmetrical base for the next tier, seems to have evolved in the east window workshop of York Minster, of *c.* 1400. The immediate inspiration for that tracery may have been the new east window of Holy Trinity, Hull, of *c.* 1380. The ogee overarches at York are further complicated by the extension of the dividing mullion straight through the top spandrel and on to the ogee head. This additional element also occurs in the west window of Hull *c.* 1418, and in the south transept window of Merton College Oxford, a work of 1414–24.[121] Another feature of the York east window is that, unlike King's College Chapel, the

120 See Appendix II. The total for each County represents medieval stone structures with at least some tracery.

121 Perhaps by Robert of Hulle, master mason of Winchester Cathedral *c.* 1411–42.

87 York Minster: exterior detail of east window

122 Demolished 1900.

major mullions become the minor subdividing elements within the tracery head – the additional mullions taking on the major role of framing the ogees and carrying on to the window head. This unexpected syncopation of major and minor mullions can also be seen in some of the other early windows of the group – St Crux *c.* 1402–8[122] St Martin le Grand *c.* 1411–37, both in York, as well as in the western clerestory windows of Bridlington Priory, the west window of Burgh le Marsh, the east end, south porch and aisle west windows of Boston *c.* 1425, the east window of Heydon in Norfolk and in the east windows of the aisles of St Peter Mancroft in Norwich *c.* 1440.

A second variation of this tracery type also appears at an early date, with a regular major-minor mullion arrangement similar to King's, but with extensive subarcuation within the tracery head. This group includes the Merton College south transept window and the west window of Hull, as well as the east windows of Patrington *c.* 1420(?), St Peter's Bradford *c.* 1430, and St Mary's Beverly *c.* 1440, plus the north-west window of St Margaret's King's Lynn *c.* 1458, the west window of Peterborough *88* Cathedral, said to be *c.* 1478,[123] and several of the windows of St Peter Mancroft in Norwich dating from *c.* 1440–55. But by far the largest number within the total group have single vertical divisions taken from the direct continuation of the major mullions, forming a rigid grid between which a variety of single or groups of coupled lights with ogee overarches are arranged. The absence of subarcuation in the majority of windows is not a matter of scale. Some, like the east windows of Great Cressingham, Norfolk, and of Lowestoft in Suffolk, are very large – the lateral *89* windows of King's College Chapel being the largest of all without subarcuation. The earliest datable example of this grid group would appear to the chancel windows of Walpole St Peter's, Norfolk, lying close to the Wash. They are a Boston work, whose workshop was itself York based, and they can be dated to *c.* 1423 from dates formerly inscribed in the glass. On present dating evidence, however, it will be seen that the York examples predate any others by almost a generation, ignoring the variations of major–minor syncopation and subarcuation, and it would be appropriate to name this type as Yorkshire Ogee Tracery. It must be said immediately that the lateral windows of King's College Chapel cannot be linked directly with any of the other ninety or so known examples. The only guidelines present are that the tracery type itself is rare, it developed in those areas where a strong indigenous Decorated tradition successfully resisted London Perpendicular for much of the fourteenth century, that the King's windows reject the earliest York arrangement of syncopated major-minor mullions and resist the temptation to subarcuate, despite their great size. Hence, they fall into the grid group stemming from but surely not originating at Walpole St Peter's, a group centred around the Wash, with an offshoot in Norwich which in turn inspired a group of churches in its vicinity. The only exam- *90*

123 R. Marks, The Patronage of Sir Reginald Bray *Friends of St George's Windsor*, vol. V, 1973–5, p. 199. This date is that proposed for the glass fragments.

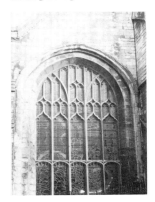

88 King's Lynn, St Margaret: north-west window

89 Gt Cressingham, Norfolk, east window

90 Walpole St Peter, Norfolk: chancel windows

91 Tattershall: south transept

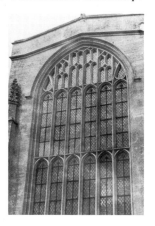

124 See p. 55.

125 For Auntell see Oswald, *English Medieval Architects*, p. 21.

126 Curiously, Clerk's alteration to the tracery makes the resemblance to Tattershall closer still.

ples of the grid group outside these areas are Aldborough in the east Riding of Yorkshire, and Dedham in Essex, where the late fifteenth-century choir is probably a Norwich work.

The tracery at King's was inserted from 1476, though its design date is unknown.[124] Its employment on such a prestigious building sparked off a new series of imitators such as the south transept of Holy Trinity Cambridge, and the churches of St Andrew and St Stephen in Norwich, all around 1500. The use of the Yorkshire Ogee Tracery in Norwich is extremely interesting for, as in Lincolnshire, the tracery type can be found on the most important works of the period, from St Peter Mancroft begun after 1440, the chancel of the Blackfriars by the same workshop *c.* 1440, in the towers of St Clement Fyebridge Street and St George Colegate *c.* 1475, in the marvellous church of St Michael Coslany and in the two splendid sixteenth-century churches already mentioned. The re-introduction of Yorkshire Ogee Tracery into Norwich *c.* 1480 was probably due to John Auntell, who moved to Norwich about that time having worked previously on King's College Chapel.[125] Of course, Reginald Ely came from the Norwich area, and the relative popularity of Yorkshire Ogee Tracery in that city might suggest that the design of the lateral windows of King's was in fact his, merely built by Wolryche. Yet while Ely's closet tracery at King's includes elements that are distinctly 'anti-Perp.', there is no suggestion of the Yorkshire-based motifs in any of his surviving works. While many of the Norwich windows in this style fall into the same rigid grid group as the lateral windows of King's College Chapel, they cannot be said to have any more than a family resemblance to the Cambridge example. The nearest in both feeling and scale to the King's lateral windows is the south transept window of Tattershall, built by Lord Cromwell *c.* 1450, though even there the similarity is one of organisation rather than style.

The rarity of the Yorkshire Ogee Tracery form nationally, and its relative popularity around the Wash, would appear to be the only pointers to the origins and architectural background of John Wolryche. The tracery form was clearly anathema to Simon Clerk, who altered the side elements in his lateral windows, and abandoned the form altogether in his east window tracery design.[126] But with four of the lateral window heads already in place upon his arrival, Clerk evidently felt unable to replace them with a new and more regular Perpendicular design, and in any event, the financial state of the project in 1477 would hardly have tolerated their removal.

91

Summary

In Part One, the idea of a 'first campaign' based on the 'sole' use of Huddleston prior to 1460 and ending with the fall of Henry VI in the following year has been rejected in favour of a longer phase of construction using various materials and continuing, though at a reduced level, until the departure of John Wolryche in the summer of 1477. The notion that the Chapel was built like a 'wedge of cheese', with the easternmost bays always ahead of anything further west, also requires a degree of modification,[127] and a new summary of the building progress over the period would now be as follows.

The entire base of the Chapel was laid out sometime between 1448/9 and 1477, and not necessarily all at once. Work then commenced on the building of the lateral socle walls of the choir bays from Bays 1–7 N and 1–8 S. Why the southern side was carried one bay in advance of the north is not clear. The lateral walls of the choir were built up to the level immediately beneath the interior Angel frieze under the cills of the lateral windows in one campaign, the inner face being almost uniformly of Huddleston.[128] The vault support VS 7/8 S was built somewhat above this level, taking advantage of the one bay lead on the south side. Reginald Ely also completed at least three of the side closet chapels – two on the north including their vaults, and one on the south, with the considerable evidence that he completed the walls of nearly all the other choir bay closets. The main elevations were taken up again with the building of the Angel frieze, a feature that also denotes an important change in the material and colour of the main interior. The blank walling below is made of white Huddleston from Yorkshire, the frieze and the majority of the upper elevation is of beige Northamptonshire oolite. Very little Huddleston occurs above the Angel frieze, with the exception of the east wall where its use continues somewhat erratically. The dramatic change in materials is in contrast with the exterior walls, where, at least in the more easterly bays, the white stone was employed as far as possible to the springing height of the lateral windows.

The new phase of the work upon the lateral walls also saw the construction of the main window cills, including the base blocks for the lateral window jambs and their intermediate mullions. These were built in a horizontal campaign that included the cill of the east window, and which included Bays 1–5 N and 1–6 S.[129] The cill of Bay 7 S may also have formed part of this work, but its restored state has removed any positive proof. The lateral window jambs followed in a further horizontal campaign, adding the jambs of the windows from Bays 1–5 N and S to the height of the window niche base and including the corbels for the vault supports, and the ogee gables that flank them. This campaign reached the east jamb of Bay 5 N and S, while the corbels of VS 5/6 S and VS 6/7 S appear to have been built but stopping one course lower. It was prob-

127 As suggested in RCHM, *City of Cambridge*, p. 100.

128 Clerk introduced a different moulding profile for the glacis cill exterior commencing at Bay 6 N. Unfortunately the exterior cill of Bay 7 S is in modern cement. For some unknown reason, Bay 12 S may also have been built to cill level at this stage.

129 The lower sections of the next jambs westwards may also have been begun at this stage, but did not rise to niche base level.

ably during the building of the jambs and vault support corbels that Wolryche took over from Ely as master mason, perhaps *c*. 1465–70. With the completion of the east jambs of Bay 5 to niche base level, Wolryche returned to the east end and commenced the upper sections of the jambs, together with their niche canopies and intervening vault supports. At this stage the various changes in the design of the upper parts of the elevation and of the vault proposal appear to have been executed. The first complete campaign by Wolryche consisted of the upper sections of the window jambs and extended to Bays 1–3 N east jamb, and Bays 1–4 S east jamb, re-establishing the one-bay lead of the southern side. The next horizontal addition saw the construction of the arch heads, tracery and   *92* internal spandrel decoration of Bays 1 and 2, the ironwork purchases indicating a date for this work of between 1476 and the summer of 1477. Thus when Clerk took command during that summer, a 'wedge of cheese'   *93* profile did exist, but it was one built up from a number of horizontal layers, each slightly shorter westwards than its predecessor. For some

92 King's College Chapel: exterior cut-away of Bays 1 and 2 S as existing *c*. 1477

93 King's College Chapel: exterior Bays 1 to 7 N with 'wedge of cheese' in white Huddleston

reason, the east wall had hardly reached transom height.

Clerk's mastership saw a new determination, both financially and architecturally, which is more truly a 'Second Campaign' upon the Chapel, rather than desultory progress made during the 1460s and 1470s. When Wolryche succeeded Ely, he modified and watered down the original design, tailoring his building work to the reduced circumstances of the time. The major loss was undoubtedly the high vault. Within a few years, Clerk was able to replace this piece-meal approach and to begin a vigorous campaign aimed at completing at least the choir bays and reinstating the provision for a high vault, even though the sections of the eastern bays already completed by Wolryche rendered the final execution of that intention extremely difficult.

CHAPTER 2

THE YORKIST CAMPAIGN

Architectural patronage in the reign of Edward IV

The conflict between the deposed Henry VI and the usurper Edward IV brought about a sudden and understandable halt to Royal patronage and, to a lesser extent, to ecclesiastical and building projects. Edward IV showed little interest in architecture during the early years of his reign, and he took active steps to frustrate the completion of the Lancastrian foundations at both Eton and Cambridge.[1] The restoration of Henry VI in 1471 was too brief for any real progress to be made and it was only after the return of Edward and the death of Henry in 1472 that the Crown turned its attention to building works. Once again, a Bishop of Winchester was instrumental in prompting the continuation of one of Henry's pious works. William Waynflete was the Wykham of his age, building Magdalen College Oxford from 1474, completing Eton College Chapel and promoting the continuation of King's College Chapel. Waynflete had been in overall charge of the Cambridge project since his elevation to the see of Winchester in 1447 but under the political circumstances following the events of 1461 and the financial constrictions inflicted upon the College by Edward IV, the Bishop had been unwilling to provide any major financing for intensive work upon the Chapel.

As the King grew older, so his thoughts turned to ecclesiastical patronage, and in 1473 Edward undertook the complete rebuilding of St George's Chapel Windsor, and within a few years Royal money was devoted once more to King's College Chapel.

The new church at Windsor is the major ecclesiastical building of the period 1460–90. It was built on to the west of Henry III's smaller church, thus the thirteenth-century building became the eastern axial chapel of a large ensemble, with an aisled choir, transept and aisled nave. In planning terms, the project at Windsor was even more ambitious than the 1448 designs for the Chapels of either Eton or King's. The most unusual feature of the plan of St George's is the use of polygonal elements, particularly on the south flank where the hexagonal transept arm is balanced by smaller polygonal chapels terminating both choir and nave. While, like King's Cambridge, the south side represents the major facade of St

1 Edward's actions appear to have been harsher on Eton than on King's. See, for example, Cal. Patent Rolls Edward IV 9 June 1461, p. 33, Close Roll 6 Sept. 1461–2, p. 34. and 6 May 1462, p. 110.

94 Windsor, St George's
Chapel: exterior from
south-west

2 P. Kidson, The Architecture of St
George's Chapel. *The St George's
Chapel Quincentenary Handbook*,
Windsor, 1975, pp. 29–39.

3 For a summary of the progress see
Colvin, vol. II, 1963, pp. 884–8.

George's, this romantic symmetry was unintentional. The westernmost *94*
bay of the nave, with its flanking polygonal chapels, is an addition to
the original plan, probably of the Tudor period. The geometry employed
in the chapel is very complex and has been examined in some detail,[2]
but there would appear to be no answer to some of the oddest features
of the building: Why are the bays so narrow? Why was the crossing tower
to be oblong? Why were the transepts polygonal? Whatever reason lay
behind the strange layout of the Chapel, St George's is the epitome of
the 'Fantastic' style of Perpendicular as revived under Edward IV.

The choir, with its cube-like aisles and eastern ambulatory, was nearly
completed during the two Yorkist reigns and this early work was to
determine much of the flavour of the successive Tudor campaigns on
the transept and nave.[3] St George's is by no means a small building – *95*
at 233 ft (71·02 m) it is the length of all but two bays of King's College
Chapel, 15 ft (4·57 m) longer than Bath Abbey and more than twice the
length of the Henry VII Chapel at Westminster. Yet despite its size,
the scale of St George's is minuscule, with tiny bays, crowded details
and intricate vaults. The choir proper is hardly larger than the Henry
III Chapel to the east, while the narrowness of the aisles is emphasised
by the relatively low vaults. One reason for the intimate arrangement

95 Windsor, St George's Chapel: interior north choir aisle looking east

96 Winchester Cathedral: interior, north nave arcade

of the choir may have been its function as that of a private chapel for the Knights of the Garter, and the wish of Edward IV to be buried in close association with the spiritual and ceremonial heart of the Order. The choir aisles were to provide tomb space for the expected Yorkist dynasty and the Chapel is imbued with something of the spirit of the Royal tomb chapels of contemporary Spain, i.e. St Juan de los Reyes in Toledo of 1478.

The Spanish parallel is quite apt, for much of western Europe was littered with a display of lavish funerary chapels built in the eclectic and diminutive Flamboyant style or its derivatives. St George's shares a number of stylistic features common to late Gothic architecture in Europe, most notably the clusters of tiny bases staggered at various heights around the piers and the baffling complexity of the moulding profiles. Despite these and many other elements, St George's Windsor remains a very English, Perpendicular building albeit in the miniaturist tradition.

The elevational design exhibits a particular debt to the nave of Winchester, not only in the general ratio of arcade to clerestory heights, but in the detailed handling of the spandrel design and the horizontal stress at the base of the clerestory. Of course, the scale is quite different, the *96* Windsor bays being a mere twelve feet wide, and the width of the choir

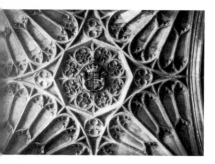

97 Windsor, St George's Chapel: interior detail of choir aisle vault

4 D. Knoop and G. Jones, *The Medieval Mason*, Manchester, 1949, p. 98.

in proportion to the narrow aisles is far more marked than at Winchester. The overall panelling of the aisle interior elevation is also taken from Winchester, though at St George's it is far more insistent. Fortunately, the vault springing at Windsor, if it was indeed intended for a vault, rejected the cowering top-heavy design of Winchester in favour of a higher level, leaving room for only the slightest and flattest of lierne vaults. The choir aisles are covered with fan vaults of a singularly angular design, with the unusual feature of polygons filling the central vault spandrel. The architect of the Chapel, Henry Janyns, was the inheritor of the rich stylistic traditions formulated under the Oxford–Winchester axis that had crystallised its own distinctive style of Perpendicular during the middle decades of the fifteenth century.[4] Architectural initiative had flowed freely between the two cities ever since the foundation of New College Oxford by Bishop Wykham of Winchester in the 1370s, and both centres continued to display a particular awareness of both London and West Country developments. St George's Windsor was also the happy beneficiary of the abandoned project at Eton. The Eton workshop in the 1440s and 1450s had been a melting pot for a variety of Perpendicular traditions – Westminster, Canterbury, Oxford, Bury St Edmunds and Norwich. The Oxford and Canterbury input was especially strong, and of particular significance as the current work in both centres was at its most elaborate and fizzy. The promise of the Eton project was not to be realised, but its influence on Oxford survived the Wars of the Roses and appeared in full blossom at Windsor.

With the exception of St George's Windsor, the reign of Edward IV was not marked by any particular architectural endeavour and is only saved from artistic obscurity by the patronage of a number of builder bishops, Waynflete of Winchester, Morton of Ely and then Canterbury, Alcock of Ely, Suger of Wells, etc. Their ecclesiastical works were either small-scale or personal, such as chantry chapels or subsidiary domestic projects such as palaces. Large screens were built in both Winchester and York, a tiny fan-vaulted Lady Chapel built off the cloister at Wells together with the crossing vaults of that cathedral. York saw the completion of its tower scheme with the building of the north-west tower, and Bishops Lyhart and Goldwell initiated the complete high vaulting of Norwich Cathedral after the fire of 1463, the latter Bishop also contributing the new spire.

Monastic patronage was at something of a low ebb, the principal works being the extensive vaulting project at Bury St Edmunds after the fire of 1466 and probably to the designs of Simon Clerk, the vaults of St Fridewide's Oxford from *c.* 1478 and the completion of the nave vaults at Westminster Abbey from *c.* 1482. The nave of Sherborne was revamped from *c.* 1475 as part of the total late Gothic transformation of that church, and the north arcade wall of the nave of St Werburga's

Chester, now the Cathedral, was rebuilt about 1485. That, plus the central tower of St Augustine's Bristol *c.* 1466, the great reredos of St Alban's *c.* 1476 and the completion of the central tower of Durham *c.* 1483, would appear to be the sum total of major monastic projects in England over the years *c.* 1460–90, remembering that some of the episcopal works were built within their own monastic cathedrals.

Non-ecclesiastical architecture, in contrast, formed a major part of episcopal building – Waynflete with Magdalen Oxford and his palace buildings at Esher and Farnham, whilst Morton built a new palace at Hatfield, and Thomas Rotherham constructed a new palace for the Bishops of Lincoln at Buckden. All these domestic buildings were in brick, as indeed was the Norwich spire. Brick dominated the great private houses of the period like Kirby Muxloe and Oxborough, indeed, one of the few contemporary domestic buildings in the south and east that was not completely brick built was the great hall added to Eltham Palace by Edward IV *c.* 1475. The brick buildings of the Yorkist era mark not only the shift in episcopal and private patronage towards non-religious building, but also the rise of that most unprepossessing material that was to sound the death knell of medieval architecture.

London seems almost to have disintegrated as a major architectural centre after the 1450s. The Court patronage under Henry VI had concentrated on projects outside the capital and as the regional centres of Perpendicular grew in strength, London suffered a decline that saw an end to its longstanding workshop traditions which had flourished since the late thirteenth century. When building on a large scale was resumed in London and Westminster, the style employed, and the architects, came from Oxford, which had surfaced from the general architectural malaise due to the personal interest and patronage of William Waynflete. The bishopric of Winchester was very powerful and, more to the point, wealthy. Waynflete poured money into several projects whilst encouraging others to do likewise. His own chantry in Winchester Cathedral is the perfect example of the Oxford style of the 1480s, with all the elements of small-scale Fantasy architecture combined into a sharp and aggressive reworking of the adjacent Beaufort chapel of some forty years earlier. The Waynflete Chapel represents a conscious attempt to match its fellow and to form a balanced and harmonious grouping within the retrochoir, but the inevitable stylistic changes over the four decades serve to highlight the differences between the London-based Beaufort Chantry and the Oxford version of the 1480s. The most notable change is in the sharpening and squaring of the architectural elements – soft clusters of Purbeck shafts have given way to hard right-angled stone pilasters, gentle curves are replaced by clear-cut depressed four-centred arches. The decoration too has become more deeply incised while the bepinnacled top has evolved into a defensive forest hung with barbed wire. Here, the favourite *98* Oxford motif of criss-cross tracery is seen to best advantage, replacing

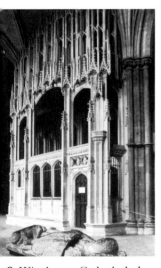

98 Winchester Cathedral, the Waynflete Chantry *c.* 1480

99 Winchester Cathedral, the Beaufort Chantry: detail

100 Winchester Cathedral, the
     Beaufort Chantry: interior
     vault

5 For details of his life see J. Harvey,
   English Medieval Architects,
   London, 1954, pp. 199–201.

101 Winchester Cathedral, the
     Waynflete Chantry:
     interior vault
102 Oxford, Magdalen College
     main quad

the transoms and supertransoms of the earlier design. The interior vaults
form another strong contrast – the Beaufort fan vault, light, delicate and
blossoming, the Waynflete lierne, harsh, angular, a starburst of interlock-
ing lozenges prefiguring the same workshop's high vaults at St George's
Windsor.

Magdalen College Oxford was Waynflete's personal foundation and
was conceived on a grand scale. The instructions to the master mason,
William Orchard, that the cloister windows should be 'as good as All
Souls, or better' might well have been the motto for the whole scheme.[5]
The general feeling of Magdalen, with its oriel windows and squat,
passage-like cloister, is indisputably domestic, resembling a large ram-
bling house rather than a quasi-religious institution. Only the slender
bell tower, begun *c.* 1490, sounds a restorative monastic note. Orchard,
master mason of Magdalen, was probably responsible for the two remarkable pendant vaults in Oxford from the 1480s – the Divinity School and
that over the choir of St Frideswide's, now Oxford Cathedral. Both are
clever engineering solutions to the building of low-pitch vaults over relatively wide spaces, and their origin is doubtless related to similar feats
of carpentry such as Crosby Hall in London.

The Oxford workshop had its roots in Winchester. It grew parallel to
the existing London–Canterbury axis that had been established in the
1380s, and for the first sixty years of the fifteenth century these two
schools of architecture were unrivalled in the south and east. But whereas
the London–Canterbury axis died out with the Wars of the Roses, the
Oxford workshop survived through Eton and became the basis of the
Royal workshop at St George's Windsor and later for that of the

3 Oxford, the Divinity
School: interior vault
4 Oxford, Christchurch
College, St Frideswide's
now the Cathedral:
interior, choir vault

Henry VII Chapel at Westminster. Thus by *c.* 1500, the Royal Windsor–
Westminster workshop was the most important in London and the south-
east, the only major rival being the Bury–Cambridge workshops centred
on that of John Wastell, the last master mason of King's College Chapel.
Simon Clerk, Wastell's predecessor at King's, provides a link between
these two important traditions, for he was the only East Anglian to work
at Eton as master mason. His reputation as master mason of Bury St Edmunds was such that on the resignation of John Smythe from Eton, Clerk
was appointed his successor even though he had had no previous connection with the project. Clerk's work at Eton, drawn as it is from a different
architectural background, is something of a stylistic aberrration rather
than representing a positive East Anglian contribution to the future stock
of the Windsor–Westminster style. Equally, what Clerk later brought
to King's College Chapel was not an injection of the current Royal workshop style but rather his own East Anglian tradition, if a little crispened
by his recent experience.

Edward IV and King's College Chapel

The second campaign of King's College Chapel was made possible
through a change of heart by Edward IV. When he had first siezed the
Crown in 1461, Edward took active steps against both Eton and King's,
stripping them of estates, rents and profits. Edward's spleen seems to
have been vented more on Eton than King's, perhaps because Eton was
all too visible from Windsor Castle. Some of the Eton estates were actually made over to King's College and as the 1460s wore on, Edward

appears to have softened towards the latter foundation. His Queen, Elizabeth Wydeville, took an active interest in Cambridge life and became the second 'founder' of Queens' College. The change in Edward's attitude can be seen as early as February 1462 when he excused the College of any monies they might owe the Crown, but he still repudiated financial responsibility for the projects begun by his predecessor.[6]

After the final fall and death of Henry VI in 1472, Edward took a more generous attitude towards King's, allowing them to accept the Prebendary of Chalk in Wiltshire from the Royal Abbey of Wilton.[7] By 1478, the financial position of the College had become secure enough for it to purchase new estates from its own funds, and by the end of the decade the annual income had recovered to about three-quarters of that received under Henry VI.[8] Most of the income was, of course, spent on the running of the College, for example, the Grammar School was rebuilt, but some at least was spared to keep the Chapel building work ticking over.

Then, around 15 October 1479, the King finally agreed to supply regular funds – at least 1,000 marks over three years.[9] This important concession was won by the Lord Chancellor, Thomas Rotherham, Bishop of Lincoln, who had been one of the earliest fellows of King's College and who was anxious to expedite the completion of its Chapel. Simon Clerk, now master mason of the Chapel, also appears to have played some role in these negotiations between College, Chancellor and King, for on Michaelmas Day 1479 Clerk was rewarded by the College for 'coming from the Bishop of Lincoln at Wobern'.[10] The Royal grant promised much for King's, for the College had won not only the patronage of the Yorkist Crown, but guaranteed funds spread over several years, thus enabling them to plan a constructional campaign aimed at completing and roofing the choir bays and so bringing the east end of the Chapel into use. The grant would not pay for everything, but it augured well for the future. In fact, between 10 January 1480 and 14 June 1483 the College expended £1,296 1s 8d upon the Chapel building, more than twice the total Royal grant.[11] The figure was evidently £56 more than receipts from all sources and it indicates that the College was able to find about half the expenditure from revenues other than the Royal Treasury.[12] This is some measure of their determination to finish the Chapel.

Edward IV fulfilled his financial commitment to the project right up to his death in 1483. In addition, he provided letters Patent allowing the College to take wood from Stanstead Park and from the estates of the Abbot of Walden (June 1480) and later from the King's own forest at Weybridge, north of Huntingdon between March and May 1482.[13] The timber was partly for scaffolding but most of it was felled for the construction of the high roof over the eastern bays. When finally Edward was succeeded by his brother Gloucester, the new King committed himself fervently to the completion of the whole Chapel, and he sent orders

6 Cal. Patent Rolls. Edward IV 20 Feb. 1462, p. 106.

7 Ibid. 15 Edward IV 5 May. 1475, no. 518.

8 J. Saltmarsh, *Cambridgeshire, Victoria County History*, vol. III, 1959, p. 379.

9 Colvin, vol. I, p. 277.

10 King's College Muniments Mundum Book 1477/79, vol. VII.

11 Willis and Clark, vol. I, pp. 472–3.

12 Ibid.

13 Ibid., p. 473.

14 Colvin, p. 278.

of impressment and offered financial assistance to bring this about.[14] On 28 August 1484, Richard III issued a new order of impressment, appointing

Robert Brewes, Simon Clerk, Thomas Stonham, John Sturgeon, Martin Prentice and William Wright, to take stone-cutters, smiths, carpenters, masons, glaziers, and other workmen, and timber, iron, lead, glass shingles, tiles, stone, lime and sand and other necessaries for the works within the royal college of St Mary and St Nicholas, Cambridge, and carriage of the same.[15]

15 Cal. Patent Rolls 1476–85, p. 472.

The 'necessaries' reveal a heavy concentration of glazing materials with little emphasis on stone, which comes well down on the list of requirements. A year later, almost to the day, Richard III lay murdered upon the field of Bosworth and once again, King's College Chapel found its financial security shattered.

There are many reasons for calling the master masonship of Simon Clerk a 'Second Campaign'. Clerk was a new man on the scene, having no previous connection with the work. He was an established architect with his own ideas and strong regional training. From the moment of his arrival during the summer of 1477, he appears to have engendered a new urgency for the work, and within two years the previous desultory programme had been replaced by a consistent and uniform campaign. The patronage was also new, as was the Provost, Walter Field, appointed by Edward IV in October 1479, indeed Field's appointment may have been central to the King's decision to advance financial support for the Chapel.[16] The late 1470s are also marked by a distinct improvement in the amount of surviving documentary evidence, so that a new master mason, documents, and at least five years of determined construction coincide to provide the first sharp picture of the state and condition of the Chapel project since its inception.

16 Field had been chaplain to Edward IV. See Willis and Clark, vol. I, p. 472n.

Clerk was, however, an old man. He resided in Bury St Edmund's where he had been master mason for the Abbey since at least 1445.[17] This would put his date of birth no later than *c.* 1415–20. The post at Bury was no sinecure, for the Abbey had been involved in considerable building work since the collapse of the west tower in 1430 which happened during the almost complete rebuilding of the adjoining church of St Mary. Clerk took over responsibility for both projects, and the choir aisles of St Mary's are to his own design. In 1465, fire devastated the Abbey church and prompted a complete programme of high vault construction similar in appearance, no doubt, to the contemporary high vaults of Norwich Cathedral.[18]

17 B.M. Add MS. 7096 and Oswald, *English Medieval Architects*, pp. 60–66.

But Clerk's appointment at King's came not through his local connections but through Eton. The second master mason, John Smythe, became master mason of Westminster Abbey in 1453, though Eton College retained his services on a consultative basis. Clerk took over the project,

18 M. R. James, The Abbey of St Edmund at Bury. *Cambridge Antiquarian Society Octavo Publications* XXVIII 1895, pp. 205–12.

already altered and rebuilt from the late 1440s. Eton soon found itself facing the same financial insecurities as affected King's Cambridge during the last years of the reign of Henry VI. The choir of Eton Chapel was considerably more advanced by this time than that of King's, but nevertheless, Clerk was forced to complete and roof the Eton choir in a rudimentary fashion, abandoning any intention to erect high vaults, and placing the battlements immediately above the lateral windows. The great aisled nave was also scrapped and it was left to another, later, workshop from Oxford, to build the small transverse antechapel seen today.

Clerk must have left Eton soon after the fall of Henry VI in 1461, at which time work upon the choir bays of the chapel was suspended. In 1469, William Waynflete, Bishop of Winchester and a former Provost of Eton, managed to complete and glaze and choir bays at his own expense, the work being finished by 1476.[19] If Clerk returned to Eton as master mason to complete the choir, then it is possible that Waynflete, who had been responsible for overseeing the work at King's Cambridge since the time of Henry VI, simply transferred Clerk from one compromise solution at Eton to execute another at Cambridge. Clerk certainly did not return to Eton to design the antechapel from 1479, by which time the Royal grant from Edward IV had transformed the prospects for completing the entire project at Cambridge along the lines of the Will and Intent of 1448. On his appointment to King's in 1477, Simon Clerk must have been in his sixties. By 1489 he was dead.

For the first two years of the second campaign, money was still short. During the year of Clerk's appointment a total of only £77 1s 7d is known to have been expended upon the Chapel, or in material terms, equivalent to 300 tons of Weldon stone, though roughly half the annual expediture would be absorbed by wages alone.[20] From the October of 1479, however, the College could look forward to an annual Royal grant and in the ensuing thirty months £1,296 1s 8d was spent on the work, with receipts of at least £1,240. In the period from 2 May to the following Christmas another £746 10s 9d was spent. In February 1485, Richard III allowed the College £300 from the fruits of the vacant see of Exeter,[21] by which time, the glazing of some of the choir windows at King's was under way.[22] The documents of the campaign can provide a fair indication of the nature and speed of the work, though the College Mundum Books are missing for the years 1480–88. During 1476/77 ironwork had been purchased for the two windows in Bay 1 and 2 N, or at least for their traceried heads, both of which had been inserted prior to Clerk's arrival. The southern windows of Bays 1 and 2, being identical to those on the north, are also likely to have been built by then.[23] Stone purchases were made from 'Peterborough', probably indicating a load from King's Cliffe, and from Clipsham in Rutland.[24] The amounts were not large. By 1480, another side closet was complete and in use – a key

19 Willis and Clark, vol. I, pp. 380–413.

20 Ibid., p. 472.

21 Colvin, p. 278.

22 Willis and Clark, vol. I, p. 490.

23 They are not referred to but they share the same tracery pattern as Bay 1 N and originally both had the same moulding profiles.

24 Willis and Clark, vol. I, p. 472.

25 Ibid., p. 473.

26 King's College Muniments Day Book of Thomas Cliff.

27 Willis and Clark, vol. I, p. 473.

28 Day Book of Thomas Cliff.

29 Cal. Patent Rolls 1476–85, p. 203.

30 Willis and Clark, vol. I, p. 473.

31 King's College Muniments College Accounts vol. IV and Day Book of Thomas Cliff.

32 Ibid., College Accounts vol. IV.

33 Willis and Clark, vol. I, p. 473.

34 College Accounts, vol. IV.

35 Ibid., Kitchen Accounts.

being bought to lock the closet against Bay 4 S.[25] On the 27 April of that year, nails were bought for the scaffold cleats, and poplar boards for 'centours', the latter probably for the erection of the lateral window arch heads. On 3 May a parchment was purchased for the 'chief mason'.[26]

The accounts for 1480/81 include further important ironwork purchases for Bay 2 N and S, which must refer to the placing of the mullions and transoms as the heads were already built, and for the windows of Bays 3 to 6 S.[27] There is no surviving reference to the building of the northern lateral windows after Bay 2 N but some progress can be assumed from the purchase in 1480 of a parchment for Martin Prentice, master carpenter, on which to draw the roof.[28] This surely implies that the north side was keeping up with, or was not far short of the progress known on the south side. Between May and June 1480, considerable tree felling took place both at Stanstead and Walden.[29] In the three years up to 1483, stone from Weldon and Hasilborough was purchased,[30] the sum total recorded being only £36 3s 10d representing a tiny fraction of the overall expenditure of nearly £1,300 during the same period. Unless the accounts for stone are deficient or the College held large stocks in store, then the current work involved only very limited amounts of stone. With perhaps half the recorded expenditure going on wages, there would still be nearly £600 laid out for materials other than stone if the surviving documentation is complete. The Day Book of Thomas Cliff, clerk of the works (one of the most important surviving documents of the period) records that in 1480, Simon Clerk was in receipt of £10 per annum, and in the following year the College granted him an additional pension of 40s p.a. for thirty years or until his death.[31] The persistent purchase of parchment for Clerk is something of a mystery, two sheets were bought on 9 August 1481, and another on 16 December the following year, yet most if not all of the design details for the choir bays must have been determined well before the former date as the roof was designed as early as 1480.[32] There can have been few outstanding masonry details for Clerk to design from scratch after this date, unless of course, the parchments were bought for the preparation of drawings for a new high vault scheme, or, for a revived antechapel project.

By this time, the dry roof construction must have been well under way, with further tree inspections at Huntingdon during August 1481, and felling at Weybridge and Sapley between March and July 1482.[33] The date of the final erection of the roof over the choir bays is not known, although two items of equipment are mentioned which may be relevant: the 'fferne', which had to be removed in 1481, and 'le crane' which was repaired on 1 August 1482.[34] From January to May 1483, Simon Clerk was constantly in Cambridge, dining every night in Hall for six weeks in January and February, and for a further four weeks in August.[35] This was an unusual departure from his normal practice of residing in Bury

36 Ibid., Mundum Book vol. VIII covering years 1483/4 – 1499. The books for years 1491/92, 94/95, and 97/98 appear to be missing.

37 Ibid., College Accounts, vol. V.

38 Day Book of Thomas Cliff.

and making only occasional visits to Cambridge. As Clerk doubtless shared the responsibility for the erection of the high roof, his unusually prolonged stay in Cambridge during the winter and spring of 1483 probably signifies that at least one section of the roof was under construction. In 1483/4, the King's glazier visited the Chapel[36] and on 6 August 1484, the great east window was scaffolded ready for glazing.[37] The erection of this scaffold, and the recorded glazing of the lateral windows in Bay 1 is the clearest indication that the roof over the east end was finished.[38]

Richard III issued his order of impressment on 26 August 1484 for the speedy completion of the Chapel. In June 1485 a further scaffold was erected for the building of a sixth window – from previous evidence the lateral window in Bay 6 N.[39] By August the King was dead and by Christmas the work had stopped. Attempts were made to continue the glazing, suggesting that a false wall had been erected to weatherproof the choir bays from the unbuilt antechapel. Glass with 'Antelloppes' was bought on 28 December 1485,[40] and at least one parent was approached to donate glass for the Chapel late in 1486.[41] The discreet introduction of antelopes into the glass was doubtless a subtle hint to the new Tudor King Henry VII, for the beasts had been the heraldic supporters of the founder, Henry VI, whose throne the Tudors had recaptured in the name of Lancaster. But Henry VII made no response and once again, the College found all Royal finances cut off. A partly glazed, partially built Chapel was of little use to them, and all that was done was to keep the rain out – on 24 January 1486, a plumber was paid for four days work 'about the church, and chapels of the new church'.[42]

39 Ibid. The window in Bay 6 N is the last on that side with Clerk's exterior cill moulding profile.

40 Willis and Clark, vol. I, p. 475.

41 Ibid., p. 474.

42 Ibid., p. 475.

The contribution of Simon Clerk

The major advance during the second campaign under Simon Clerk came in 1480/81, with the building of the lateral window bays from Bay 3 to Bay 6 S, and presumably also of Bays 3–5 N. This permitted the commencement of the roof over the five eastern bays. Hence Clerk's contribution to the fabric consists of the upper sections, from transom level, of Bays 3–6 S and 3–5 N, plus the mullions of Bay 2, together with the upper parts of the east wall and the east window tracery, and the uppermost walling of the choir bays from Bay 1 with its passages and square exterior openings. The upper walls of the choir represent a considerable change in both technique and building materials, for, above the apices of the lateral windows, King's College Chapel is built of red brick. The uppermost 9 ft 4 in. (2·84 m) of the elevation beneath the sixteenth-century battlements consists of two parallel brick walls flanking a longitudinal passage that runs unbroken from the eastern to the western stair turrets. The passage floor is some 69 ft 8 in. (21·21 m) above the choir

105 King's College Chapel: exterior Bays 1 to 6 S

floor. The exterior wall is faced in stone, and contains between the major buttresses three quatrefoil lights, each within a square frame. The inner wall is almost entirely of brick, and contains a door to the space above the vault in every bay, north and south. The quantity of doorways may have been connected with some difficulty envisaged in the vault construction, though all vaults were difficult to build, yet no other example seems to have been provided with such an abundance of access points. Possibly the doors were to admit air to 'quick-dry' the vault and to ventilate the main roof, the middle sections of which are nearly 145 ft (44 m) from the gable end openings.

The inner brick wall is 2 ft (0.62 m) thick, and is interrupted by right-angled wall piers that project a further 2 ft 2 in. (0.67 m) over every vault support in the Chapel below. The existing vault fill dating from the sixteenth century has obscured the junction between these internal piers

and the vault supports, so that their original interconnection can no longer be observed. Up to VS 5/6 N and S, the wall piers are made up of ashlar quoins with brick infill, and at the equivalent point within the adjoining passages, rough vertical breaks can be seen on the outer walls, denoting the extent of Clerk's westward progress by 1485. The break is also marked in the southern passage by a change in the material employed in the floor from rough stone to brick. This occurs partly over the lateral window in Bay 6 S.

The passages are a curious feature and would seem to be without parallel in English medieval vault construction. Their purpose is obscure, after *107* all most conventional vault spaces are entered directly from a stair turret through a single door. But there is ample evidence that the eastern stair turrets of King's College Chapel were altered substantially during construction so that they could provide access facing west into the passages and not north and south directly into the vault space. Major adjustments in the height and depth of the individual steps were made at some stage of the construction in order to turn the spirals so as to provide for the present access to the brick passages. The south-eastern turret was most affected, probably because it was constructionally in advance of the north-east turret during the 1450s and 1460s. The stairs from the original

106 King's College Chapel: interior, north vault passage

107 King's College Chapel: section through north wall (Mackenzie)

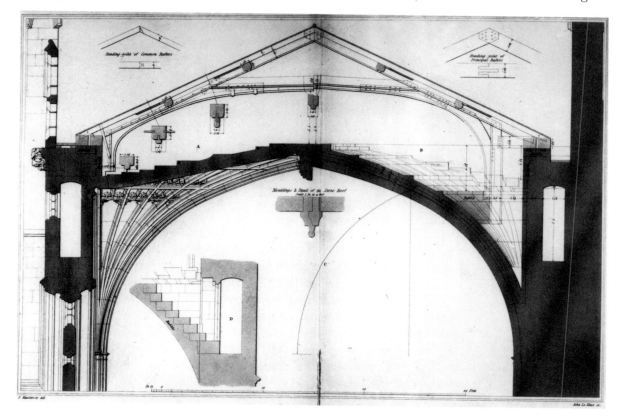

sanctuary floor level rise in a consistent sequence to a height of 45 ft (13·72 m) with an average step height of 0·20 m, though after the twenty-fifth step, the step height picks up to between 0·19 m and 0·25 m. At the 13·72 m height, roughly equal to the level of the head of the third window on the east face of the turret, the steps jump to between 0·29 m and 0·34 m with two final steps 1·37 m deep, more like platforms than stairs. The breakdown in the first regular sequence of steps coincides with the transom level of the lateral windows, and is also, notably, the level at which the smooth ashlar of the lower turret lining, much of it in brown oolitic limestone from Northamptonshire, gives way to a jig-sawed cutting similar to that on the exterior of the north-east turret at the same height. The alteration of the stair turret also occurs at the intended roof level of the east range of the great court, the junction of which could formerly be seen on the turret exterior. The great court project had certainly been abandoned by 1472. The adjoining lateral window in Bay 1 S was inserted by Wolryche in 1476/77. These two facts suggest therefore, that what we see within the upper sections of the stair turrets is further evidence of substantial alterations made to the elevations of the Chapel by Wolryche in the 1470s. But why should Wolryche have wished to rearrange the stairs and halt them in such an unconventional manner? And, what use was to be made of doors exiting westwards through the thickness of the lateral walls?

Wolryche had built Bays 1 and 2 up to apex level of the lateral windows. The exterior string course defining that height is 0·25 m below the present internal passage floor level – the depth of an average stone block. The relative heights of string course and passage floor would confirm that the existing passages are additions made during the master mason-ship of Simon Clerk as we have no evidence that Wolryche built any higher than the apex of the lateral windows in these bays. But the stair turrets had already been adjusted by Wolryche as low as transom level, the height at which Ely's work appears to stop, and it was clearly Wolryche's intention to provide the present exits above the lateral windows and within the thickness of the lateral walls – walls that in Wolryche's time stood to just below the level of the passage floors. Were the stair turret doors to be gutter walk exits on top of a lower Chapel? This would seem to be the only logical explanation for the tortuous attempt to break the stairs to face west – the Chapel was to be lower, the vaults abandoned and the battlements placed immediately above the lateral windows. We have already shown that many of the problems of the interior elevations of the choir bays may have resulted from the implementation of a lower, unvaulted compromise scheme by Wolryche in the 1470s, on which both Clerk and Wastell have attempted to reinstate a vault. The stair turrets seems to provide further evidence in support of this theory.

The financial restraints that had dictated such a drastic reduction in the scale of the Chapel did not change immediately upon the arrival of Simon Clerk in the summer of 1477, indeed, there is nothing to suggest that he enhanced the elevational height of the choir bays to their present level before 1480/81. The evidence, though retrospective, indicates that between 1477 and 1480, Clerk continued the lateral walls only to the apex height of the windows in Bays 3–6 S, and 3–5 N, and only then did he return to the east end and add the upper brick construction, the structure of which is continuous for the first five bays on both sides. By 1480 the financial prospects for the Chapel were very different than they had been three years earlier. Royal money assured steady progress and there would have been every hope that the original plan of 1448 could be revived. However, the reduced scheme of the 1470s had inflicted several structural problems for Simon Clerk. It was not now an easy task to reinstate the vault given that the 'vault supports' in the choir had been built at a level suitable for an open wooden roof but impracticable for a stone vault. In addition, the arcature of the lateral windows had been designed without any requirement to carry either additional upper walling nor a high stone vault. The result was that no conventional vault could have been built on to the choir elevations as altered by Wolryche and continued by Clerk up to 1480. The 'vault supports' would either have to be lowered and the windows strengthened, or the walls raised to provide abutment for a vault at a higher level. Any proposal *c.* 1480 to return to a vaulted interior for King's College Chapel must have been met with serious reservations – either demolish the vault supports already built to a level low enough to clamp a vault around the eleven existing windows, giving a vault crown of about 21 m above the choir floor or, raise the walls of the Chapel to accommodate the extra height forced upon any design for a vault springing from the support level as existing, but risk crushing the weak lateral window heads with the additional weight.

Fortunately Simon Clerk was experienced in just these problems – since 1466 he had supervised the complete high vaulting of the Romanesque Abbey church at Bury St Edmund's. The solution to that problem, the vaulting of a structure built without any provision for vaults was probably the key to the design at King's College Chapel. The lost Bury vaults doubtless reflected the identical and contemporary solution at Norwich Cathedral after 1463, where the great mass of the Romanesque clerestory, with its through passage within the thickness of the wall provides an internal buttress, which was utilised to resist the side thrust of a high stone vault. In order to bring the lateral thrust of the new vault as low as possible, to a level capable of being absorbed by the ancient structure, the masons of Norwich, and probably Bury, opted for a segmental barrel profile, whereby the vault crown rises higher than the lateral wall with the vault springing from a very low level. The cross-axial ridge rib is not level from north to south but forms an arc, sitting just above the *108*

108 Norwich Cathedral:
interior, nave vault

109 King's College Chapel: interior detail of panelling over east window

apex of the clerestory windows and rising up to the vault crown. This vaulting solution had been used for a similar 'Romanesque conversion' over the nave of Winchester Cathedral, but at Norwich, the segmental curve of the cross-axial ridge is concealed almost completely by the mass of secondary tieceron ribs. Of course, King's College Chapel was not a Romanesque structure, nor did it have a clerestory with passages but the solution adopted by Clerk is effectively just that – a double skin wall containing a through passage capable of absorbing much of the lateral thrust of a segmental profile rib vault. The profile of Clerk's intended vault project of the early 1480s can be seen clearly over the east window, which is Clerk's work from just above transom height. The window is wrapped up within an extension of the vertical blind panelling, a more elegant version of the east wall elevation of Eton, executed but not designed by Clerk. The uppermost wall rib against the east wall at King's indicates the segmental profile of the intended vault, barely pointed at the apex. The actual vault, as designed later by Wastell, is considerably *109* more pointed so that a noticeable gap develops at the top.[43]

The north-south profile of Clerk's vault design as indicated above the east window would place it with the high vaults of Norwich Cathedral, built after 1463. The complex lierne vaults gave ample scope for sculptured bosses and could easily have been adapted for the wide span of King's College Chapel. In all probability, the existing vault of the Ely Lady Chapel represents a fifteenth-century design imposed upon a previously unvaulted interior, *c.* 1485, and it may well reflect Clerk's current proposal for King's.[44] The Ely Lady Chapel vault plan is very lavish, with axial and cross-axial ridge ribs, six pairs of tiercerons to each cross-

43 The roof design of *c.* 1480 made provision for a thicker or higher vault crown than at present, probably in expectation of a thick rubble packing above a rib vault rather than the thin, all stone fan vault as existing. Presumably, the intended height of the packing *c.* 1480 led Prentice to construct his roof without base tie beams. For the roof design see Appendix III.

44 F. Woodman, The Vault of the Ely Lady Chapel. *Gesta*, 23, Pt 2, 1984. pp. 137–144

axial ridge and two pairs on each axial, all caught up in a mesh of liernes. The Ely vault is also very wide with a clear span of 43 ft 6 in. (13.26 m) approximately the span of King's. The master mason of Ely, Thomas Peyntour, may have been familiar with the new proposals at King's from *c.* 1480 and the Ely Lady Chapel vault may well be the nearest indication of Clerk's unbuilt design for Cambridge. Alternatively, the vaults of both the Ely Lady Chapel and Clerk's design for King's might be reflections of the vaults of Bury St Edmund's in progress since 1466.

It is no longer possible to determine what relationship Clerk intended between the profile of his vault scheme and the lateral window bays other than it was not to be as at present. Bonding interruptions and obvious insertions indicate that in Bays 1–6 S, and 1–5 N (the bays completed by Clerk to their full height) Wastell had to insert the existing wall ribs which determine the present profile. This was carried out in the sixteenth century as part of the introduction of blind vertical panelling immediately over the lateral windows, for it can be seen that in those bays where the upper walling was built by Wastell in the sixteenth century (Bays 7–12 S and 6–12 N) the background ashlar, panelling and the vault wall rib are integral and have even coursing. In contrast, in the preceding bays by Clerk, the vertical panelling and vault wall ribs have been smashed into a more haphazard background walling.

The inner brick passage wall in Bays 1 and 2 N contains what have been dubbed 'through stones' for an intended vault. The stones vary in size and are rather random in position, those in Bay 2 N, do not even form part of a curve. They are also very small, some as little as 0·25 m by 0·23 m, yet the wall through which they are supposed to penetrate and to emerge on the far side as sections of wall rib is 0·62 m thick. In reality, those stones available for a more complete inspection appear to terminate only 0·20 m into the bricks walls. This would render them structurally useless. Whatever their intended purpose, they were built by Clerk but rapidly abandoned after a few courses. They do not occur in the southern passage, an indication perhaps that the northern upper walling was begun first.

A further uncertain relationship hangs over the question of the square framing of the lateral window bays. This feature was first built by Wolryche and was maintained by Clerk, yet in all the bays built by 1480/81, the angles have been abbreviated by Wastell for the later insertion of the wall ribs and *tas de charge* base courses of his vault. Thus it is impossible to say if Clerk had changed this element of the design in 1477, or, whether he had built the square frames up to Bay 5 N and 6 S before the vault proposal was revived.

Clerk's major achievement at King's was to make possible the provision of the high vault, which he fully intended to build, and to press ahead with the completion and roofing of the five eastern bays, something that

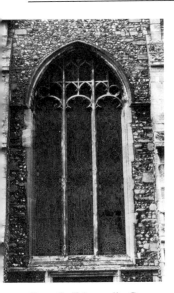

110 Bury St Edmund's, St Mary's: exterior, south chancel window

45 See p. 132.

would have seemed impossible in 1477. His contribution to the actual appearance of the Chapel is rather more limited. The basic bay elevation had been determined in Bays 1 and 2 before his arrival and the scheme was only open to discreet changes rather than any major overhaul. But changes there are and they are quite informative. The first, and most famous, is the change within the tracery heads from Bay 3 westwards, associated with the introduction of more vigorous mullion moulding profiles. Clerk continued the asymmetrical motifs – with four window heads built it was too late to eliminate so central a feature – but other elements were changed. The top lights became crisp gables, the uppermost lobe segments disappear in favour of hard triangles, the central top lobe is diminished, but most important of all, the odd, up-ended mouchettes within the heads of the outer lights were replaced by more standard 'Perp.' dagger lights accompanied by tiny quatrefoil circles (see Figure 4). This last motif was employed by Clerk in the chancel aisle windows of St Mary's Bury *c.* 1460,[45] while both dagger lights and quatrefoil circles *110* are major features of the lateral windows of Eton College Chapel erected by Clerk in the late 1450s. Their presence in the King's windows is a *111* reflection of the more regular Perpendicular design of the alternating tracery of the side closets, and are a clear announcement of Clerk's stylistic taste.

The elaboration of the mullion profiles also marks a return to a greater articulation and enrichment of surfaces avoided during the lean years under John Wolryche. Clerk also made a minor modification to the arch head moulding profile over the lateral windows in line with his additional roll moulding on the mullions. The result is that the arch head outer roll moulding sits uncomfortably on the square edge profile of the inherited jamb. Not only does this make it easy to spot the Clerk tracery heads, beginning with Bay 3 N and S, but also the Wastell tracery heads from the early sixteenth century as he reverted to the original square edged profile throughout his window campaign. Thus the last arch heads executed by Clerk in the second campaign up to 1485 are those in Bays 6 N and 7 S.

The east window tracery can be attributed to Simon Clerk by comparison with his alterations to the lateral window design. Here everything is sharply pointed, overlaid and filled with dagger lights – all asymmetrical elements have been eliminated. The whole ensemble is a three-part version of the bipart windows of Eton, though without the quatrefoil circles and super transoms. The arch head is extremely depressed, another indication of the segmental barrel profile that Clerk intended for his high *112* vault.

Simon Clerk also instigated the more regular sequence of window jamb niches, replacing the rather bizarre assortment that had hitherto been acceptable. From Bay 3 N west jamb and Bay 4 S west jamb, he intro-

111 Eton College Chapel: exterior, south windows

duced a two-sided canopy pierced by three trefoil circles, with projecting polygonal pilasters and top crenellations and a simple lierne vault without cusping. In Bay 4 N west jamb and Bay 5 S west jamb the canopy facades become two-tiered with four quatrefoil circles on two planes, and with an interior fan vault. This series continues until Bay 7 N east jamb and Bay 8 S east jamb – an antechapel bay and the first indication that Clerk intended to press on with the entire project of 1448. One other interior jamb niche appears to be by Clerk, the east window south niche, which follows the basic design of its earlier northern partner but contains an accomplished fan vault. It is made from a block of white magnesian limestone from Huddleston.

112 King's College Chapel: exterior, east window

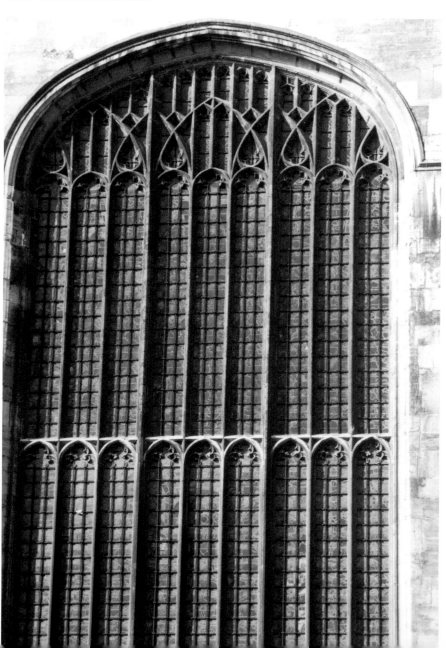

113 King's College Chapel: interior detail, vault lunette Bay 5 N

The upper brick walling added by Clerk to take his intended high vault was subjected to substantial alterations by Wastell after 1508. In Bays 1–6 N and 1–7 S, the interior elevations have been mutilated severely by the imposition of the existing wall ribs, and by the insertion of the blind panelling and the *tas de charge* courses of the fan vault and transverse arches. Nothing can now be recovered of Clerk's intentions *113* for this area save that above the square framing of the lateral windows a certain area of blank walling was provided to receive the high vault, and that it was evidently possible within Clerk's design to continue this square framing, now sliced off at its extremities. Whatever the means by which Clerk intended to place his vault against the lateral walls, it was apparently to have a slighter profile than the present fan vault, for there was every intention to utilise the passage doors for access above the vault fill, something that was only maintained by Wastell with the greatest difficulty due to the low placing of the doors *vis à vis* the vault springing and the sharper curvature of Wastell's vault.

The interior upper walling is in reality a veneer of stone cladding on the inner brick wall, but how and where this veneer stops is now hidden within the fill of the sixteenth-century vault. The walls, as seen now from above the vault in Bays 1–5 N and 1–6 S, were plastered over before the vault was erected. Presumably this was a temporary measure to mask

the areas of brick construction which otherwise would have remained visible from within the choir after the sudden halt to building operations brought about by the fall of Richard III in 1485.

The evidence for Clerk's proposal suggests a vault placed against blank walls and raised high above the lateral windows. This would recall the appearance of the late fourteenth century chapel of Winchester College. Perhaps this was the model suggested by Bishop Waynflete.

The exterior elevations of King's College Chapel were also changed fundamentally by the enhancement of the walls, though it is true that Clerk's additional upper brick section restored the overall height of the

Chapel to around the ninety feet specified in the Will and Intent. The blank upper walls, broken only by the passage lights, are strangely reminiscent of the aisles of the nave of Canterbury Cathedral, where the clerestory is so recessed and low as to be all but invisible. The parallel *114* must have been even stronger before the Brenchley Chapel at Canterbury was removed, for it was built 'closet style' between the buttresses with a flat roof beneath one of the south aisle windows. The additional upper walling at King's inevitably leads to the top-heavy feeling of the exterior aspect of the whole Chapel. Inside, it disappears within the vault, though the resulting lunette spaces are admittedly unhappy. On the outside, nothing can eliminate the heaviness and blandness of the addition, except perhaps the secret knowledge that it is all in reality, lightweight and rich rosy red.

The style of Simon Clerk

King's College Chapel is not the best building in which to study the architectural style of Simon Clerk. Hardly any element of the choir design was open to a new stylistic imput at so late a stage, save for the pattern of the east window tracery, and the only areas of the interior on which Clerk might have hoped to stamp his own mark were to be left unbuilt in his time – the completion of the antechapel and the building of his high vault scheme. Nevertheless, some stylistic pointers do emerge from his short campaign, like the desire for more angular 'Perpendicular' elements in the tracery and niche designs, a move away from the more wilful apsects of the work of his predecessor plus certain stylistic traits drawn from beyond the immediate Cambridge circle.

The earliest surviving work attributable to Simon Clerk occurs in the Chapel of Eton College. The project for the great church, recommenced in the late 1440s, had not progressed very far before the master mason, John Smyth, was transferred to Westminster Abbey. When Clerk took over as master mason, probably in 1453,[46] the plain lower socle walls of the choir were already built, together with the panelled socle walls of the first bay east, part of the east wall and the basic projection of the east window. Smyth's work includes a base type similar to those at Canterbury between 1432 and 1458,[47] hardly surprising as he had been a leading mason at Canterbury Cathedral since *c.* 1430. In contrast, the bases standing high up on the cill level of the lateral windows at Eton are of a different stepped design, and this change of profile may well indicate the height at which Clerk took control of the construction. The east window tracery at Eton contains several London/Canterbury forms from the first half of the century, with elevated transoms and regular lozenge lights. The lateral windows, executed by Clerk between 1458 and 1460, are more complex, with a twin, three-part design overlaid on

46 Oswald, pp. 61–62.

47 F. Woodman, *The Architectural History of Canterbury Cathedral*, London 1981, p. 162.

to only five main lights, with the central light common to both parts. The soft curves of the east window tracery are here replaced by hard gabled lights, while the central diamond lozenge immediately above the intersection of the subarcuation is curiously sliced in two by the upper vertical mullion. Clerk has also woven three dagger lights into the composition and this, and all the other elements were to reappear in the tracery of the east window at King's Cambridge, and some in the minor alterations that Clerk made to the design of the King's lateral windows.

Simon Clerk was also master mason of the Abbey of Bury St Edmund's, a post held by him since *c.* 1445. As an architectural centre, Bury was perhaps the most conservative in eastern England. The three principal works carried out by the Abbey in the course of the fifteenth century all contained work by Simon Clerk, though two, the rebuilding of the great western tower and the high vaults of the Abbey church, are quite lost.[48] The tower project dragged on for decades and may still have been incomplete at the time of its demolition after the Dissolution. The high vaults of the Abbey church were commenced after a serious fire in 1465.[49] Their loss is a particular blow, for the design would doubtless have thrown light upon Clerk's proposed high vault for King's College Chapel of *c.* 1480. The third project at Bury was the rebuilding of the parish church of St Mary, which survives almost intact. The plan of the new church originally consisted of an aisled nave and an unaisled chancel but this was blurred subsequently by the addition of chancel aisles. The new north aisle was added first sometime prior to 1463 and a matching south aisle by 1480.[50] In general, the chancel arcades built with their respective aisles follow the design of those in the nave with their curious triple shaft motif found in several other East Anglian works of the period.[51] In the north chancel aisle, pre-1463, the capital and base mouldings conform to those in the nave, but in the later south chancel aisle a stepped base design similar to the cill level bases at Eton was introduced. The tracery *II* of the aisle windows at Bury rejects the nave designs with their regular lozenges in favour of gabled upper lights, short transoms and quatrefoil circles, all elements drawn from Eton.

The identification of tracery elements employed by Clerk provides a vital clue in the attribution of a well-known tower drawing, now in the British Museum.[52] The design, headed 'Campanile Collegii Regalis Canterbrigae', has been identified as that made for Henry VI by Reginald Ely *c.* 1448.[53] More recently it has been pointed out that the paper on *II* which the drawing is made contains a 'watermark of the Lily pot type which is found in sixteenth century paper in England and France.'[54] This would suggest that the design was drawn by Wastell after the commencement of the last campaign at King's in 1508. However, no reference was ever made to such a free-standing tower during the Tudor period, which is comparatively well documented.

48 The tower was begun in 1430. See L. Saltzman, *Building in England down to 1540*, Oxford 1952, pp. 591–2.

49 James, pp. 204–12.

50 Bury Wills i.a. 95 and i.a. 304.

51 A feature of the nave arcades of Walpole St Andrew Norfolk of *c.* 1440. Also found in the Mancroft workshop Norwich and in the work of Reginald Ely at King's and Burwell.

52 B. M. Cotton MS. Aug.I.i.3.

53 J. Harvey, *The Perpendicular Style*, London 1978, p. 299, dates the design to *c.* 1450.

54 Colvin, vol. I, p. 272n.

15 Bury St Edmund's, St Mary's: interior detail, south chancel arcade base

Campanile collegij Regalis Cantebrigiæ.

Campanile . Collegij

16 King's College Chapel: drawing of proposed bell tower. BM Cotton Ms Aug. I.i.2

The King's Will and Intent of 1448 ordered that there should be 'a strong toure square, conteynyng xxxiiij fete within the walles, and in height Cxx fete vnto the corbel table, and iiij smale tourettis ouer that, fined with pynacles, and a dore in to the said cloistre ward and outward noon.' The tower drawing, if it is to any approximate scale, would be between 73 and 90 feet up to the corbel table, depending on where one chooses to fix the actual corners, whilst the turrets depicted could hardly be described as 'small'! The style is lavish and decorative, something generally frowned upon by Henry VI, and certain visible details would point to Simon Clerk as its designer. The tracery, though only sketched in, suggests overlaid patterns like those of Eton and the King's east window. Six of the tower windows have diamond lozenges split vertically by a central mullion, as happens at Eton and King's east window, and all of them contain elevated transoms, again pointing to Eton plus the chancel aisles of St Mary's Bury. The top windows have square-framed spandrels, used of course within King's College Chapel and again on the exterior of the south aisle of Saffron Walden Church, known to have been designed by Clerk and commenced in 1485.[55] The drip stones drawn over the arch mouldings terminate with spiral end stops, another unusual feature but one found in the cloisters and the north chapel door at Eton and on certain windows at St Neots.[56] The base and top of the tower design is decorated with a frieze of quatrefoils in square frames similar to those added by Clerk to the exterior upper walls at King's – all these stylistic points would suggest that if the tower drawing is by any of the four master masons of King's College Chapel, then it is most likely to be Simon Clerk.

There can have been no possibility of reviving such a secondary part of the original scheme for King's College Chapel prior to the patronage of Edward IV from late 1479, and even then, the financial support was hardly sufficient to encourage any unnecessary expenditure. Only with the accession of Richard III in 1483 did the Crown express the desire to complete the whole Chapel project – witness Clerk's inclusion of part of an antechapel bay, Bay 8 S, within his choir campaign. The new tower scheme fell with the King and it was not revived under Henry VII. On stylistic and historical evidence the drawing should be dated to *c.* 1484, even if that is somewhat early for the occurrence of the watermark.

55 King's College Muniments College Accounts, vol. V. For Saffron Walden see Lord Braybrooke, *The History of Audley End*, 1830, pp. 180–230; Oswald, p. 64; and F. Woodman, 'John Wastell of Bury, Master Mason', 1978, unpublished PhD, thesis, Courtauld Institute University of London.

56 Possibly this work and the fine tower is by Clerk.

CHAPTER 3

THE TUDOR CAMPAIGN

The architectural patronage of Henry VII – Windsor and Westminster

Henry Tudor stood victorious upon the battlefield of Bosworth. The battered crown retrieved from beneath a hawthorn bush was his by force more than by right. His claim to the throne of Lancaster was obscure and on the distaff side, others had stronger claim even through the rival House of York. Henry's proposal to marry Elizabeth, eldest child of Edward IV, had persuaded some of York's most powerful adherents to fight against the unpopular Richard III and the general pardon issued by the new King in September 1485 boded well for the peace, security and stability of the realm. The events of 1485 saw no revolution in the modern sense. The status quo was maintained, Parliament assembled and made legal what was already reality and the dynastic marriage was duly performed. The White Rose of York united with the Red Rose of Lancaster. Henry VII seemed more interested in the financial reform of the Crown than in retribution, though favourites and loyal supporters found their just rewards with high offices of Church and State. England settled down, or rather back, into the quiet domestic security that it had enjoyed before the dark days of the mid century. Trade and towns flourished. Foreign observers marvelled at the richness of the land, the prosperity of the people and the great display of wealth by clergy and nobility alike. The character of the new King is rather obscure. Traditionally he is a mean and austere figure, standing in stark contrast in his dashing and cavalier second son and heir, the future Henry VIII. However, Henry Tudor was a great patron of building, indeed it might be said that architecture was his one extravagance. It is to Henry VII that we owe the completion of King's College Chapel Cambridge, both in his lifetime and, through his executors, after his death. Thus we should investigate the main works of Tudor patronage that preceded the new campaign at King's for signs of Henry's personal taste and stylistic preference.

The two chapels directly associated with his patronage and munificence, St George's Windsor and the Henry VII Chapel, Westminster, both display something of his megalomania, with coats of arms, escutcheons and heraldic supporters disporting themselves amongst the stonework. The incessant dynastic struggles of the fifteenth century must lie behind the insecurity that led Henry to stamp his mark so blatantly around the country. His completion of St George's Windsor and the rebuilding of its axial Lady Chapel were not connected with any fondness for the memory of Edward IV who had begun the new work. Rather, it was to rival and exceed the work of the usurper of the throne of Lancaster, to twist an act of Yorkist piety and national pride into a glittering apotheosis of the 'martyred' Henry VI. In his second project, the new chapel at Westminster, the tomb of Henry VI was to be enshrined amid a fantastic frenzy of architecture extolling the glory of the lineage of the House of Tudor. Both royal chapels clang with a cacophony of architectural cadences, yet on first sight the styles of Windsor and Westminster appear to be different. At Windsor, the original appearance of the axial Lady Chapel has been lost in a lethal overdose of encaustic Victoriana and it is only in the nave of St George's and in the vaults of the choir that the style of the earliest Tudor work, and the architectural taste of Henry VII can still be appreciated.

117 Windsor, St George's Chapel: interior nave from west

From the start, St George's Windsor was a triumph of the minuscule. It marked not only the revival of ecclesiastical patronage after the turmoil of the Wars of the Roses but also a resurgence and notable victory for the 'Fantastic School' of architecture. The essential elements of the structure are treated with the same exquisiteness as one might expect to find on a tomb or an altarpiece. The architecture no longer inspires belief in its own strength or virility, rather the mass and weight of the whole is disguised, caught up in a finely spun mesh of minutiae. The pier bases *117* must be seen at close range in order to establish their design, while their mouldings are deliberately complex and asymmetrical. No opportunity to elaborate was overlooked and it is only the relative breadth of the Chapel that prevents the architecture from crowding out the spectator. The Windsor nave is a reworking, through Winchester, of the Gloucester choir, another Royal burial chapel of a murdered king, Edward II. At Windsor, however, the aisles take on more of the proportions of the Winchester intermediary. Verticality is everywhere stressed by the insistent presence of the oblong panel which appears beneath the aisle windows, across the spandrels, up the crossing arches and throughout the tracery. The only respite is the Angel frieze, a feature most happily inherited from the earlier elevations of the choir. The climax of the Windsor nave comes at the west end where no less than ninety-five oblong panels are crammed into the west window ensemble. The high vaults of St George's, under way in 1502, are the perfect complement to the richness of the interior facades. The inherited width of the nave, the relative narrowness of the bays and the flattish profile of the high roof determined

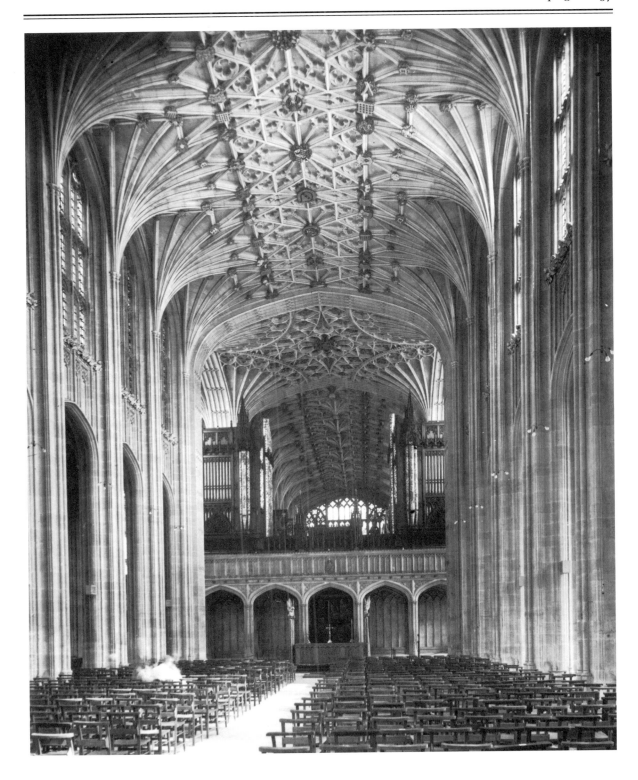

1 W. St John Hope, *Windsor Castle*, London 1913, vol. II, pp. 460–1.

that the high vaults should hardly rise from springing point to crown, indeed the arcature lifts only some 11 ft (3·35 m) across a span of some 40 ft (12·20 m). The oblong bays of the nave were quite unsuited to the fan vaulting that covers the aisles, and the architects Aylmer and Vertue skilfully adapted a lierne vault to this most difficult situation.[1] Cones of ribs burst forth from every point and fire off almost immediately into a myriad of stars, triangles and box shapes. The whole complex of ribs is saved from chaos by a rigid continuation of the three axial ridge ribs, a clear reference to the choir vault of Gloucester. The style of the Windsor nave vaults can be traced back to Oxford, where a similar system had been employed over the choir of St Frideswide's (now the cathedral) and another over the relatively flat vault space of the Divinity School. The Windsor vaults begin as serrated cones, a form much favoured since the nave vaults of Canterbury Cathedral of *c.* 1400. The cones are contained within transverse and secondary ridge ribs, the latter defining the central zone. The vault pattern is then syncopated so that a large hexagon is formed, centred on the transverse arches, while the axial junctions occur at the true intersections of each bay. Additional ribs create sixpoint stars within the hexagons, lozenges overlapping the junctions and series of triangular panels containing cusped circles. The geometry is intricate and angular, the only curved elements being the inset circles and the subcusping. The narrowness of the bays, however, and the excessive multiplication of the ribs creates a cluttered and wirey effect that contributes to the overall impression of brittleness.

The absence of pendant drops from the nave vaults is probably due to the flatness of the profile, otherwise the Windsor nave vault can be seen as an elaboration of St Frideswide's Oxford, with its serrated cones and interest in triangular forms. The nave vaults at Sherborne, *c.* 1490, would also appear to stem from the same tradition, for although they are fan vaults, the panels are allowed to break out into a harsh pattern of cusped triangles. Perhaps the closest parallel to the nave vault of St George's is the tiny vault of the Waynflete Chantry in Winchester, another Oxford work of *c.* 1480, where triangles and lozenges dominate the little vault to such an extent that there is no true rib pattern. This manner of vaulting can be traced back further to the Duke Humphrey Tomb in St Alban's, *c.* 1450, probably an Oxford or Eton work, and on back to the Wykham Chantry in Winchester, *c.* 1405, the Aerey porch at Windsor of *c.* 1355 and the Gloucester south transept vault of *c.* 1335–40.

The Henry VII Chapel at Westminster was the major new architectural project of the reign, and being entirely new, it best reflects the personal taste of its founder as well as displaying the complete repertoire of the Windsor–Westminster workshop. Thus it provides the most important comparison with the architecture and style of the antechapel of King's

College Chapel which, though paid for by Henry VII, was under the stylistic control of John Wastell, a man far removed from the frivolity of the official 'Court' style. Between the antechapel of King's and the Henry VII Chapel at Westminster we see the whole range of royal ecclesiastical patronage of the early sixteenth century. The Henry VII Chapel and the work at St George's Windsor are inexorably linked, and the original Oxford background of Windsor is made even more apparent

118 Westminster Abbey, the Henry VII Chapel: interior from west

2 J. Stowe, *Survey of London*, London 1633, p. 499.

3 Colvin, vol. III, 1975, pp. 210–22.

when the workshop moved on to Westminster. The first stone of the enlarged axial chapel was laid on 24 January 1503,[2] and it was intended that the Chapel should provide a burial place both for Henry VI and Henry VII, though the vagaries of history were to determine otherwise. The cost of the elaborate project soaked up the royal finances for several years, reaching a high point in 1505, with a second peak in 1508.[3] The structure was all but completed in 1512, the year that saw the commencement of the high vaults of King's College Chapel.

The arcade elevation of Windsor became the model for that of the Henry VII Chapel at Westminster, though one might be forgiven for thinking that Westminster has no elevation of substance whatsoever. Henry's eastern chapel at Westminster Abbey is the epitome of Tudor taste – extravagant, exuberant and fantastic. It combines architecture, sculpture, metal and woodwork in a way that is truly repellent yet it is not without a certain power. The only way to appreciate the finer points of the building is to think away the accumulation of stage effects and to get back to the design on paper. The chapel would remain rich, but at least its form and style could then be examined. The form is basilican, that is, it has side aisles, a fact hardly discernible in the interior today, yet behind the fretted barrier of the wooden stalls there are four bay aisles that, at least in the mind of the architect, opened directly from the nave. These are terminated with eastern altar walls, so that there is no true ambulatory. Instead, the polygonal main apse is constrained by five rectangular chapels. The plan is simple, the execution exotic. The most unusual and unnerving feature of the architecture is the treatment of the exterior aisle walls, if it is fair to call them walls at all, for they bulge and buckle like heavy damask curtains slung between the massive buttressing piers. The plan of the side aisle walls is polygonal below the window cills but round above, while each chapel in the apse formation has six canted sides forming three points, all perforated into a galaxy of window openings. Between these screens of glass stand great octagonal buttressing piers enmeshed in panelling that makes no distinction of interior or exterior. The idea behind the extraordinary design of the aisles at Westminster came from Henry VII's tower at Windsor Castle, a product of the same architectural workshop.[4] The design has the benefit of giving a larger area of glass than could be afforded by a flat wall.

4 Ibid, Pl. 22 and pp. 306–8.

The aisle vaults are not drawn into the irregular bays of the periphery walls but maintain a strict, rectangular fan-vaulted system. The springing of the vaults from the aisle responds ignores the vaulting requirements of the canted walls so completely that the aisle vaults seem to hang free of the exterior walls that would normally retain them. This results in the placing of independent vaults within each interior 'oriel' of the aisle, one of the many indications of the blending of ecclesiastical and domestic architecture so typical of the early sixteenth century.

The notion of the aisle wall as an independent screen was taken up

119 Westminster Abbey, the Henry VII Chapel: interior vault

within the east end of the Chapel. Until the nineteenth century, the openings into the last bays of the aisles and into the first of the apsidal chapels were shut off from the main interior by pierced stone screens standing on panelled socle walls. These trilobe plan screens bulged into the chapel proper and created tiny closet chapels quite divorced from the general interior. The screens were conceived as separate design features within the arcade, though their remaining scars prove that they were integral to the initial structure.

The most prominent feature of the elevational design of the Henry VII Chapel is the treatment of the 'triforium' level. The Windsor Angel frieze is employed immediately above the main arcade, providing a horizontal definition for the lower section of the design as well as a corbel base for a scheme of canopied niches containing free-standing figures. The niches run right around the main chapel interior, broken only by the upward rush of the vault responds. The gouging of sculpture niches into the wall marks the rejection of the surface clarity of the Windsor nave triforium, a design feature inherited from the earlier choir. Westminster shows a renewed interest in light and shade and the manipulation of the plastic possibilities of stonework. It most closely resembles the late Decorated choir of Wells Cathedral, though Westminster does display a greater regularity and rigidity that stems from the employment of an overall grid pattern. Sculpture plays an important role in the design of the Henry VII Chapel and is another indication of the contemporary interest in non-Perpendicular forms. The distillation of Gothic by the first architects of the Perpendicular style had led to a decline in the use of such architectural sculpture. Foliate capitals or integral figure sculpture would have been an unwarranted intrusion into the harmonious and transparent interiors of the late fourteenth century, but the rise of the Fantastic style in tombs and chantries in the fifteenth century led to a limited restoration of architectural sculpture. The Henry VII Chapel brought such sculpture back as a major design element by utilising standing figures in such dense groupings as to replace the wall itself.[5] It is tomb architecture expanded to giant proportions and a style quite alien to John Wastell who managed at King's to restrain such sculptural excesses. The clerestory windows of the Henry VII Chapel now provide a moment of relief in this noisy department store of architectural odds and ends but quite unintentionally, for the windows once contained great Biblical scenes that crashed their lurid way across the mullions. The tracery pattern of the clerestory is another development on from St George's Windsor, though inevitably the Westminster windows are fussier with their tiny foiled and cusped motifs crammed into the subarcuated spandrels.

The clerestory range finds itself caught up amid the most celebrated feature of the chapel – the pendant fan vaults. The sugar icing vaults of the Henry VII Chapel are clever rather than beautiful, their well-known structural system adding but a cerebral pleasure to what is undoubtedly a breathtaking scenic effect.[6] The great pendants that dollop from the filagreed vaults do appear to be suspended from the raking struts that reach out from the vault responds at an impossible angle, but it is all illusion, for above the traceried meringue, the struts continue as structural transverse arches of which the pendants are merely a downward extension of a single voussoir block. The three tiers of panelling of each fan cone that spring from the suspended pendants reach out so far that there is hardly any central spandrel space to fill. Nevertheless, more pendants force their way through as central bosses to provide some semblance of an axial line. The see-through effect of the vault panelling is enhanced by the pierced tracery above the exposed sections of the transverse arches. These in turn sprout segments of fans which add to the visual complexity of the whole. The climax comes, as it should, within

5 The design may also have been intended as a continuation of the adjoining Chantry chapel of Henry V.

6 For the construction of the Henry VII vaults see R. Willis, *On the Construction of the vaults of the Middle Ages, Transactions of the Royal Institute of British Architects*, vol. I, pt II, 1842, pp. 43–60; W. Leedy, *Fan Vaulting, a Study of Form, Technology and Meaning*, London 1980, pp. 214–17; and F. Mackenzie, *Observations of the construction of the roofs of King's College Chapel Cambridge*, London 1840, pp. 10–18 and pls I–IV.

the apse. Six pendant fan vaults collide around the polygonal apse like some aerial traffic jam, while a seventh hangs in the centre surrounded by the sculptured ciphers of the Tudor family. The ensemble has no parellel in English architecture, indeed the only comparable works would be the Chapel of the Constables in Burgos and the choir vaults of St Pierre in Caen.

Nevertheless, it is in England that the stylistic and structural traditions of the Westminster vault lie, representing the culmination of the Oxford–Windsor work of the last quarter of the fifteenth century. What was revolutionary about Westminster, and what sets it apart from all the other products of the workshop, was the decision to include the whole gamut of their architectural repertoire in just one design.

While the pendant vaults of Westminster are essentially a reworking of the Oxford Divinity School, the basic structural system has been changed slightly. At Oxford, the suspended fan cones appear to be supported directly by the exposed transverse arches rather than hanging free as at Westminster. The ethereal effect of the Henry VII vault is of course entirely due to the concealment of the upper section of the transverse arch. By utilising a sharper overall profile, the transverse arch can disappear happily above a fretwork of ribs, while the more acute intersection of the exposed arch and the pendant drop adds to the visual instability of the whole. This ploy had been used in the choir vaults at St Frideswide's Oxford, though there the dramatic potential was hardly exploited.

The pattern of both the Oxford examples is extremely simple when compared with Westminster where the vaulting shows the same concern with the rigid demarcation of each zone as at St George's, though in the body of the Henry VII Chapel there is no interpenetration of ribs from bay to bay or even from fan to fan. The complex interrelationship between the vault bays at Windsor is here abandoned for a more organised approach. Only in the apse does the central vault spandrel show any interest in the stellar forms of Windsor. Yet despite the differences between the organisation of the two vaults, the decorative repertoire is common to both: circles, triangles, gable-headed motifs and carved Tudor ciphers are pushed in with such density that they overwhelm the strict order of the bay design. Only one element at Westminster is allowed to ride through the swirl of endless units – the free-hanging cusping that traces the line of the concealed transverse arches, a flimsy indication of the essential structural order that lies hidden above the frantic turmoil.

One new decorative motif has entered the repertoire since Windsor, a band of cresting that defines the first tier of each fan. Its sudden appearance at Westminster is doubtless a reflection of Wastell's masterly vault high up within the central tower of Canterbury Cathedral, completed before April 1509.

The exterior of Henry VII Chapel has been subjected to extensive rebuilding and refacing. Some of the existing features are incorrect but the overall effect has not suffered unduly.[7] The chapel bristles with pinnacles, spirelets and finials. It is a building on which one would not like to fall from a great height. Originally, the pinnacles flashed with the revolutions of gilded metal wind vanes supported by fantastic beasts – their noisy pirouetting adding one final touch of absurdity. As with the interior, no opportunity has been lost to decorate, filagree and generally distort the structure. The design is dominated by the great buttressing piers that rise through the aisle walls to become polygonal turrets studded with canopied niches and topped by four-centred Tudor 'onion' domes. The angular turrets and the buckled aisle walls in between give a restless feeling to the whole lower zone, above which the clerestory rides like a ship through a storm. Even with the original fretted parapets, the external design of the clerestory level acts as a deliberate foil for the activity below.

7 For the restoration of the Chapel see J. Frew, The Destroyer Vindicated? James Wyatt and the restoration of the Henry VII's Chapel Westminster. *Journal of the British Archaeological Association*, CXXIV 1981, pp. 100–6.

120 Westminster Abbey, the Henry VII Chapel: exterior from south-east

The stylistic parallels of the Windsor–Westminster Workshop

The design of the Henry VII Chapel at Westminster is perhaps the most outrageous architectural indiscretion of the English Middle Ages, and one totally in keeping with the brash pretentions of the Tudor Court. The stylistic net of the Windsor–Westminster Workshop was cast wide across Europe. It may be that English architects had seen the exotic creations of Isabelline Spain or even the gorgious extravaganzas of Moorish Granada. There were also close links at this time between England and the Low Countries – Henry Tudor and other important architectural patrons like Sir Reginald Bray had spent their exile under Edward IV in Flanders.[8] But neither Spain nor the Low Countries offer such interesting comparisons with the products of Henry's 'Official Style' as can be seen in Northern France.

The Henry VII Chapel is by no means a French building but, equally, it cannot be explained wholly within the context of English Perpendicular alone. The basic elevation may be English and, of course, there are no fan vaults in France, but the architects of the chapel have incorporated a vast repertoire of architectural elements, some very English and others with French precedents. The niched wall above the main arcade of the chapel is the most insistent use of this motif in England since the early fourteenth-century choir at Wells. It is true that great screens composed almost entirely of niches began to appear from the mid fifteenth century, such as Winchester, Southwark and St Albans, but they tended to restrict and organise their niches and sculpture to one surface, the reredos. The Henry VII Chapel wraps the niche wall all around the building, inside and out. Only the Alcock Chantry in Ely Cathedral, another Windsor– *121* Westminster product, exhibits such a similar excess. The idea of the all-embracing niche wall probably came from the northern and western French churches which blossomed with spectacular west and transept *122*

8 The flow of architectural ideas between England and Flanders may have been two-way; see, for example, the choir elevation of St Pierre Louvain, completed in 1448, a Flamboyant exercise in Perp. The extension of the clerestory tracery down to the extrados of the arcades is reminiscent of Burwell, and of course the original design for the antechapel of King's from the same years as the completion of St Pierre.

121 Ely Cathedral, the Alcock Chantry: detail of south wall

122 Beauvais Cathedral: exterior detail of south transept portal

facades during the Flamboyant period: Abbeville, Toul, Sens, Vendome, Troyes, Senlis, Tours, Louviers, etc. One principal design feature of these was the dissolution of the buttresses and wall plane by means of deep niches clustered tightly together, staggered in height and twisted through odd angles. In essence it was a reworking of the early Gothic figure portal but now it was the niches and their disposition that counted more than the sculpture, the best example being perhaps the early sixteenth-century west portal of Rouen Cathedral. Many have lost or never received their intended figures so that the effect of the niches is heightened. The French admirably restricted such displays of exuberance to the exterior of the church; the Windsor Westminster masons exercised no such caution.

A number of other French buildings and ideas appear to be reflected in the design and decoration of the Henry VII Chapel. The use of carved stone heraldry and ciphers is one of the constant themes of the Windsor–Westminster Workshop and was of course common to late Gothic architecture across Europe. One favourite French motif was the Fleur dy Lys, employed in stonework as early as the 1440s,[9] and still much in evidence *12,* in the early sixteenth century – the Ste Chapelle west parapet, Troyes Cathedral, Senlis south transept, etc. Carved stone escutcheons also make their appearance early in France, for example on the 1440s section of the central tower of St Ouen, Rouen. Carved stone heraldry in England tends to be restricted to bosses until the reign of Henry VII. More specific reference to Rouen can be found on the exterior turrets of the Henry VII Chapel with their faceted niches and crocketed onion domes.

9 Fleur de Lys tracery occurs in the lower section of the central tower of St Ouen Rouen before 1441, in the Bourbon Chapel at Souvigny of 1448, in the Palais Jaques Coeur Bourges *c.* 1450, in the axial chapel of Evreux *c.* 1465 and in the Vielle Chateau at Moulins, amongst many other examples.

123 Evreux Cathedral: exterior detail, south window of axial chapel

10 The same workshop used this in
the Alcock Chantry in Ely.

11 Added to the south aisle of c. 1490
see Louviers *Dictionnaire des Eglise
de France*, vol. IV, p. 98. Cusped
vault ribs can be seen as early as
c. 1450 in the Chapel of the Palais
Jaques Coeur Bourges. See also
the side chapels of the Cathedrals
of Bourges and of Nevers, while in
Spain, the vault of the Miraflores
in Burgos, a design of John of
Cologne, incorporates similar
cusping. It was completed in 1488.
See G. Street, *Gothic Architecture
in Spain*, London 1814, vol. I,
p. 50.

12 Completed before 1535 when the
tower was built. See P. Signoret,
Mortagne au Perche. *Dictionnaire
des Eglise de France*, 1968, vol. IV,
p. 115. A similar combination of
cusped ribs and pendant drops can
be seen in the axial chapel of St
Gervais Paris from 1494 and in the
earliest part of the Hotel de Ville
Dreux from 1512.

13 The Jube of la Madelaine at
Troyes was begun in 1508 by
Jean Gailde, see F. Salet, 'La
Madelaine, Troyes' 'Dictionnaire
des Eglise de France' vol. V p. 127.

14 Dating from 1517, see C. Enlart,
'Architecture Religieuse' Paris
1902 p. 701.

15 It occurs as blind tracery on the
western turret.

They are virtually identical to the corner turrets of the upper section of the central tower of St Ouen from 1492. This part of the tower also has ogeed flyers with segmental underarches and pierced work infill, a Flamboyant form seen on many other French buildings but few in England except Westminster.

Another odd feature at Westminster is the use of fretted hanging cusps to 'outline' the transverse arch of the pendant vault. In England this motif appears to be unique to the Windsor–Westminster Workshop,[10] whereas decorative free-hanging cusps occur commonly in France, even sometimes framing pendant drop vaults: the south porch of St Ouen, Rouen, before 1441, and the south porch of Louviers, c. 1506.[11] The application 124 of hanging cusps directly on to the vault ribs in association with pendant drop vaults can also be found in French Flamboyant from the late 1490s: the choir of Mortagne, begun c. 1490,[12] beneath the fantastic Jubé at 125 La Madelaine at Troyes,[13] and in the Castle Chapel at Thouars.[14] There are no English parallels for this combination outside the Windsor–Westminster Workshop.

At St George's Windsor, the curious parapets added in the early sixteenth century appear to have only one English parallel, the same workshop's project at Canterbury, the Christ Church Gate, completed c. 1520.[15] Both designs are clearly English versions of perhaps the most common traceried parapet form of late Flamboyant architecture seen at Mont St Michel, Sens north facade, Vendome, Cherbourg, Tours, Abbeville, Evreux, etc.

The case for French stylistic intervention in the Windsor–Westminster Workshop must not be pushed too hard, but it cannot be denied that the Henry VII Chapel and its associated workshop products do stand apart from contemporary English architecture. This is not just because they contain elements of the French style, for we have seen that this was a fairly common trait in other major English workshops from *c.* 1420, but because the French and English elements of the Windsor–Westminster Workshop are thrown together and churned about with such reckless abandon as to become something alien. The Henry VII Chapel does seem more at home amid the final frenzied flurry of French Flamboyant. The architecture of the Chapel is indeed the ultimate triumph of the Fantastic style of Gothic and is its final manifestation in a major English building. Nothing is what it appears to be and everything is executed in the miniature scale of unreality. This virtuoso display of architectural fun and games stands in stark opposition to the products of the Perpendicular style of the fourteenth century with its rejection of exaggerated contrasts and its fidelity to the precepts of structure. It is almost as though the architects of Westminster were aware that they were designing what was to be the last great ecclesiastical monument of the English Middle Ages and that they made a conscious effort to incorporate into it the entire repertoire of architectural experience of the last three centuries.

Architecture in the Eastern Counties about the time of the Tudor campaign upon King's College Chapel

The Windsor–Westminster Workshop was the single most important architectural 'style' in England during the late fifteenth and early sixteenth centuries. This is due not just to its status as the 'Court' workshop of its day, but also to its stylistic cohesion and the sheer quantity and quality of its output. This is in great contrast with the remaining late Gothic workshops in the east, which, with one notable exception, produced large numbers of buildings but few of any great quality. The one exception is the Cambridge workshop of John Wastell, the last master mason of King's College Chapel. The Tudor campaign upon the Chapel is especially interesting as it was the only major project to receive the patronage of Henry VII that was not also under the direct stylistic control of the Windsor–Westminster Workshop. It will be interesting to see, therefore, what influence if any the royal workshop managed to exercise over the more traditional and sober Wastell style. There were also a number of other prominent workshops in the region that may be considered briefly in order to place the Wastell style at King's in its proper perspective.

The eastern counties of England are littered with late Perp. churches, especially Norfolk and Suffolk. Many of these have acquired lofty reputations though few can be regarded as first-rate works. The Lavenhams and Sheltons are thin on the ground. Some churches depend for their fame on fittings or spectacular feats of carpentry – Dennington would be unremarkable without its screens, whilst the Needham Market timber clerestory suspended high upon a dazzling hammerbeam roof covers little more than a box of rubble. Throughout the fifteenth century the parish churches of the region were rarely able to compete on equal architectural terms with the great cathedral and monastic workshops. This was partly due to financial constraints and to the problems of availability – the best masons could command the most prestigious and well-paid jobs. Some of the leading workshops did undertake outside projects, Bury St Edmund's, for example, seems to have been responsible for the elegant nave of Walpole St Andrew in Norfolk in the 1440s. The nave of Fotheringhay, on the other hand, represents no more than an elephantine pastiche of what must have been a refined 'London' style choir, now lost, whilst the remarkable church at Tattershall may be very well intentioned but it is hardly in the same quality league as Burwell. A connection

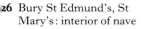

26 Bury St Edmund's, St Mary's: interior of nave

between the few top-quality parish churches and the great centres of architecture within the region is already discernible by 1450. During the latter part of the century it becomes more obvious still, and despite the countering of the slackened pace of cathedral and monastic building by the great expansion of parish church construction, the number of first-rate workshops within the Eastern counties appears actually to decline, or at least to concentrate.

The English are curiously fond of their parish churches, perhaps due to the appeal of an additive mish mash of styles and quality combined with a general sympathy towards the amateur and deep suspicion of the slick and the professional. This fondness has led to an interest and study of parish churches quite out of proportion to their artistic merits. If we were honest, the number of first-rate works of architecture amongst the parish churches of England is no more than a handful, and of those in the Eastern counties from the latter years of the fifteenth and early sixteenth centuries most can be attributed more or less directly to a very small number of important workshops. The rest are at best second-rate provincial copies.

One of the first major workshops of the period was an offshoot from King's College Chapel before *c.* 1470 – that of John Melford. A pupil of Reginald Ely, Melford continued to employ many of the stylistic motifs of his master.[16] His work includes the nave of Cavendish, the chancel aisles of Glemsford and of Lavenham, the north aisle of Boxford and

16 Oswald, p. 98.

127 Long Melford, Lady Chapel: interior south aisle

128 Long Melford: interior of nave

the Lady Chapel and Martin Chapel of Long Melford. The latter church *127* well illustrates how a wealthy parish grew impatient with its local rustic masoncraft and turned to someone a little more 'cosmopolitan' at least by Suffolk standards. The church rebuilding had begun at the west end and proceeded on its rather lumpy way towards the chancel whereupon a second hand took over, refined what elements he could from the earlier work and 'dressed' the clerestory and the intermediate zone with vertical tracery – Burwell style. The inclusion of this Reginald Ely motif as late *128* as *c.* 1480 suggests that the transition at Long Melford from rural to mainstream work was then under the direction of Melford. He was undoubtedly responsible for the unusual Lady Chapel and for the characteristic 'Ely' windows of the south chancel aisle. The remarkable Lady Chapel, finished in 1496, contains a series of vaulted niches, two of which contain miniature vaults copied from the vault of the Alcock Chantry in Ely Cathedral, a Windsor-Westminster design of *c.* 1490. Despite Melford's Cambridge background, his workshop products remain curiously local, strung out along the Suffolk/Essex border. This may relate to its centre of gravity, i.e. the home base for both men and equipment. Melford described himself in his will as 'of Sudbury', so it would seem that by the late fifteenth century, this small but wealthy Suffolk wool town had acquired its own Cambridge-trained architectural practice of some distinction.

Bury St Edmunds suffered something of an architectural eclipse from the mid fifteenth century and the principal work within the Abbey, the high vault, is quite lost. In addition, the Abbey's master mason, Simon Clerk, was engaged successively upon Eton and King's College Chapel, while his possible successor at Bury, John Wastell, worked almost exclusively outside the town. Hence Bury became absorbed into the Cambridge scene and disappeared as an independent architectural centre.

Norwich, on the other hand, blossomed in the late century, producing some of the finest parish churches in the region. No less than four of the major churches are products of a single workshop, with yet another by the same team out in the county. This workshop appears to have evolved from that of Robert Everard upon the arrival of the Auntell family from Cambridge, of whom John at least had worked King's College Chapel.[17] The new style first manifests itself at St Michael Coslany, rebuilt from *c.* 1490, a stunning design made all the more intriguing by its incomplete state. The work is extremely elegant, with clear-cut and well-formed mouldings, exceptional masonry and, of course, the famous flint flush-work exterior. The second product of the Michael Coslany workshop, Shelton, was built for Sir Ralph de Shelton and was 'unfinished' in 1497. Even without its intended roofs, the church stands out as a first-rate work with its red brick aisles and stone arcades and clerestory.[18] It is linked to St Michael Coslany by its mouldings, the

17 Harvey and Oswald, p. 21.

18 One doubts that the intended roofs were ever built.

pier, capital and base types and through its window tracery. Shelton also employs blind tracery descending Burwell style from clerestory to arcade and this is but one indication of a Cambridge origin for the workshop. *12* Other Cambridge elements include the use of the asymmetrical ogee tracery lights as at King's, plus the profusion of quatrefoils enclosed in circles. Other details and mouldings of the Michael Coslany workshop find parallels in the Wastell workshop, suggesting a common stylistic source. In any case, a Cambridge 'link' for the Norwich workshop is quite likely, as St Michael Coslany was given to Gonville College Cambridge by Sir Thomas Boleyn, master 1464–72. Once established in Norwich, the workshop went on to build St Andrew's Church, a fine *13*example of their style, the nave of St George Colegate and probably the first work upon St Stephen's, some fifty years in the making. The latter demonstrates that in the early sixteenth century we are dealing with a workshop rather than a single master mason, for the design incorporates some earlier Norwich elements such as the concave pier plan, whilst still conforming in other respects to the basic Michael Coslany style.

Finally, Cambridge emerged in the late fifteenth century as the single most important centre in eastern England, rivalling the Windsor–Westminster workshop both in quality and output. It was essentially conservative, and dominated by the Wastell workshop. The inventory of work produced by Wastell between *c.* 1490 and 1520 includes much of

129 Shelton: interior of nave
130 Norwich, St Andrew: interior of nave

the best architecture of the region – the central tower of Canterbury Cathedral, the antechapel of King's College Chapel, the naves of St James' Bury St Edmunds and of Lavenham, the nave arcade walls of Great St Mary's Cambridge and Saffron Walden, and the New Buildings at Peterborough. The geographic spread of the workshop is some measure of its success, matched only by the Windsor–Westminster work-shop, whose products range from Canterbury to Oxford to Ely. However, unlike the royal workshop, Wastell is not known to have produced any-thing for either a London or Westminster patron, and King's College Chapel was his only work to enjoy royal patronage. Nevertheless, Wastell's other patrons included Cardinal Morton, Archbishop Warham and the Duke of Norfolk, as well as the Abbots of Bury and Peterborough. Wastell's style will be discussed later with regard to his work at King's. Another Cambridge workshop was centred upon John Lee, master mason of King's College Cambridge and also of Ely Cathedral. He was responsible for several works in Cambridge – possibly he was the archi-tect of St John's College. Lee's work reveals that he trained with the Windsor–Westminster workshop, and at present he is the only known master in East Anglia active in the early sixteenth century to have come out of the royal workshop. He was employed at King's College before Wastell's arrival in 1508, and his appointment by the College may have formed some part in their attempt to interest Henry VII in the plight of their Chapel.

The last building campaign upon King's College Chapel

It is a curious fact that although Henry Tudor was the nephew of the deposed Henry VI, he appears to have been quite indifferent to the forlorn state of his uncle's college at Cambridge. In 1485, the Fellows of King's might well have held out hopes for the speedy completion of their Chapel and college buildings despite the fall of Richard III who had avowed in the last year of his life a strong desire to see the work finished. But the new King had other interests. Windsor lay at the fore-front of his mind despite its association with the usurper Edward IV. The new Lady Chapel that Henry VII added to the east end of St George's Windsor was intended to enshrine the remains of Henry VI, though this plan was frustrated in 1498 by the protests of the monks of Westminster, who claimed that the saintly King had requested burial in their Abbey church. It was during this period of claim and counter-claim that King's College attempted to attract at least some Royal patronage towards their own Lancastrian cause. The Provost prodded the regal conscience with a gentle reminder that his uncle's dearest project lay neglected for want of funds: 'Structura regiis sumptibus magnifice inchoata iam turpe in spectaculum deserta est.'[19] But the pleas of the

College fell on deaf ears as Henry shifted his attention from Windsor to Westminster.

Only when that new work was well under way did Henry VII show any interest in Cambridge. His first response was undoubtedly prompted by his mother, Lady Margaret Beaufort, who was a prominent figure in the resurgence of the intellectual life of the university. Her mentor was St John Fisher, her confessor, and President of Queens' College and himself a friend and supporter of the New Learning. In the early sixteenth century Cambridge burst forth with academic enterprise. The city boiled with ideas, particularly questions concerning the traditional role and content of Church teaching. Both inside and outside the Church the status of the clergy and their role in education was seriously challenged. Some bishops responded positively to the new situation by assisting the growth of the unversity and by founding new colleges. In turn, their patronage influenced the laity, particularly the nobility, so that whereas the fifteenth century had seen an enormous rise in ecclesiastical patronage from outside the hierarchy, the early sixteenth century witnessed a dramatic switch in patronage towards education. Even the pretentious Cardinal Wolsey founded colleges not churches. Lady Margaret Beaufort's attention was drawn to Godshouse, occupying a ramshackled series of properties along St Andrew's Street in Cambridge. The College had been moved by Henry VI from its old site to make room for the enlarged scheme for King's College Chapel.[20] Henry had made great promises of a larger site and substantial buildings, but as with so many of his good intentions, the reality fell far short of the will. With the encouragement of Fisher, Lady Margaret refounded the College as Christ's in 1505, and laid out sufficient funds for imposing buildings ranged around a planned court. She clearly intended to keep a watchful eye on her new foundation, for the upper floor of the Master's Lodge was reserved for her own personal use. The fulfilment of the promises made by Henry VI was plainly stated in the deed of foundation and, doubtless, King's College was able to take some satisfaction in this turn of events. Lady Margaret was assisted in her plans by her step-son, Robert Stanley, who was elevated to the wealthy Bishopric of Ely in 1505. The co-operation of the Bishop of Ely was a vital factor in assuring the growth of the intellectual life of Cambridge, which lay in his diocese, and it was thus fortunate for Lady Margaret, and for the university, that the see should fall vacant so conveniently. The rebuilding of the university church of Great St Mary that stands between King's College Chapel and the market was also encouraged and assisted by Lady Margaret, who gave liberally towards the work and persuaded the King to do likewise.[21] During her sojourn in the city, Lady Margaret cannot have failed to notice the great spectre provided by the unfinished Chapel of King's College. The east end must have towered over Tudor Cambridge as Beauvais Cathedral still rears unfinished above its urban skyline. King's stood as

20 H. Rackham, *Christ's College in Former Days*, Cambridge 1939, and Willis and Clark, vol. I, pp. 187–232.

21 W. D. Bushell, *The Church of St Mary the Great Cambridge*, Cambridge 1947; J. Foster, *The Churchwardens Accounts of St Mary the Great, Cambridge*, Cambridge 1905; J. Sanders, *Historical and Architectural notes of Great St Mary's Church Cambridge*, Cambridge 1869; F. Woodman, Great St Mary's – a Quincentenary? *Cambridge Review*, vol. C 1978; and John Wastell of Bury, Master Mason, PhD thesis, 1978, Courtauld Institute London.

a silent reminder of dynastic struggles, of divided families and broken promises.

The turning point in the fortunes of King's College Chapel came on 23 April 1506, when Henry VII kept the Feast of St George at King's Cambridge.[22] The ceremony surrounding this 'National Day' was more appropriately conducted at Windsor, but the great castle Chapel was quite simply in a mess. Scaffolding filled the nave, the west block was unfinished and the choir had doubtless been cleared ready for the commencement of the vault construction in June. Henry could have transferred the ceremony across the river to Eton but, instead, he chose to come to Cambridge, partly no doubt to see his mother. The St George's Day festivities were performed as uncomfortably as possible in the old, small chapel of King's College – the Provost and Fellows making sure that the conditions were very tight in order to impress upon the King the urgency of completing their great Chapel next door. Fortunately, the visit in 1506 bore fruit and twenty-one years of Royal neglect turned into regal munificence on a scale hitherto unimagined. True, the initial gift of £100 was small, but the indenture drawn up between the Royal Clerk of the Works and the Provost 'towards the bildings of the church of the said college' signified Henry's commitment to the completion of the Chapel.[23] On this same day, another gift was bestowed to 'one John Wastell, a scoler of Cambridge for his exebucion for one half yere, begynnyng ye ix day of may.'[24] This John Wastell had entered Cambridge in 1503/04 to read civil law and was undoubtedly one of the sons of John Wastell, the great Tudor architect.

22 Colvin, vol. III, p. 188.

23 Ibid.

24 PRO E 36–214 p. 60 King's Book of Payments, 9 May 1506. See also Oswald, p. 286.

John Wastell and Cambridge

Henry VII probably met John Wastell on the occasion of the St George's festivities at King's Cambridge, if the reference to the exhibition is interpreted correctly. Possibly, the King already knew the great master mason from his previous visits to Canterbury, particularly that in 1498 when Henry stayed with Cardinal Morton for six days, Wastell was then in Canterbury completing the pinnacles and battlements of the new central tower, Bell Harry. The King cannot have failed to take note of so outstanding a talent. The magnificent central tower of Canterbury Cathedral, with its sheer lines and elegant proportions, must have become a familiar and much-loved sight to all who travelled the Pilgrim's Way to the Shrine of St Thomas. Nothing could recommend an architect more than this sublime steeple. Wastell was also well known in Cambridge. *131* He was master mason of King's Hall, now Trinity College,[25] and undoubtedly architect of the nave interior of Great St Mary's, the university church. This work probably brought him into contact with Lady

25 Trinity College Cambridge, King's Hall Accounts Vol. XIX. See also Oswald, p. 281.

131 Canterbury Cathedral,
central tower from
north-west

Margaret Beaufort, whose own foundation, Christ's College, appears to have been executed by members of the Wastell workshop. John Wastell was also a familiar figure at King's College, having been entertained by the Fellows on many occasions since 1490. There is no known architectural connection between Wastell and King's College Chapel prior to 1508, but the first known reference to Wastell anywhere does come from King's College. On 14 June 1485 Wastell is mentioned as being in the company of Simon Clerk during negotiations with the Church Wardens of Saffron Walden. Wastell's position in these early years may have been subsidiary to Clerk, the third master mason of King's College Chapel and this single reference has led many to speculate upon a senior-junior partnership between the two men.

Wastell's appointment as master mason of King's College Chapel may have been the result of pressure from the College who knew him well but it was clearly acceptable to Henry VII, whose own architects were engaged upon the completion of the projects at Westminster and Windsor.

The initial grant from Henry was followed by a year of apparent inactivity. The next reference to the Chapel project comes on 1 May 1507, when the Royal Clerk of the Works, Henry Smyth, the master mason of St George's Windsor, William Vertue, and John Lee, the 'chief mason' of King's College held a meeting in Cambridge, evidently without Wastell.[26] The exact topic for discussion is unknown but the outcome was a further grant from the Crown for the Chapel of £350, paid over in the following June.[27] Almost another year passed before the first of a series of royal grants, commencing in the spring of 1508, provided some £1,400 total for the work.[28] Building had certainly begun by July 1508, when ironwork was purchased for 'great windows' and 'four great hooks for the (west?) door of the Chapel'.[29] What reason lay behind the two-year delay in the recommencement of the Chapel is unclear. Possibly the lodges were totally empty of both men and materials but the formation of a new team, if that was actually necessary, and the purchase of fresh supplies could be resolved quickly, given that the necessary cash was forthcoming. But Wastell appears to have brought most of his own team with him and perhaps the delay was caused simply by their unavailability. The final work at Canterbury, the crossing vault, is not precisely dated – only the heraldry provides evidence indicating that the bosses were made after November 1504 but prior to the death of Henry VII in April 1509.[30] Might we suppose that the commencement of the last campaign at Cambridge under Wastell's direction from about July 1508 marks the end of his workshop commitment at Canterbury?

But why delay at all? King's College already employed their own 'chief mason' John Lee, who had attended the meeting with Smyth and Vertue in 1507. Yet despite enjoying the confidence of the College, Lee was

26 King's College Muniments
Mundum Book, Vol. IX 1506–07.

27 PRO E 36–214, pp. 157–79.

28 Ibid., pp. 274, 302, 325.

29 King's College Muniments
Building Accounts vol. I. 1508–09.

30 The former date fixed by the
enthronement of Archbishop
Warham.

passed over by Henry VII and by King's College for the post of master mason of the Chapel – that was clearly going to Wastell, even, so it would appear, if this involved some delay in building operations. Lee certainly stayed on at King's and within a year of the start of the work, his position changed fundamentally. His exact role within the Chapel project from this date will be discussed later.

The documents

A few weeks before Henry VII died, he took measures to settle the financial arrangements of his various building projects. Towards the end of March 1509 he again visited Canterbury and was doubtless impressed by Wastell's splendid crossing vaults. On the 24th of that month Henry had instructed that £5,000 be paid to King's College for 'the bilding and making of the said church'.[31] The indenture is worth quoting in its entirety for its considerable detail and the mention of more money if the initial £5,000 'shal not suffice'.[32]

31 Colvin, vol. III, p. 188.

32 Willis and Clark, vol. I, pp. 476–8.

This Indenture made the last day of March the xxiiij yere of the Reigne of the most christan Prince oure soueraigne naturall liege lorde Henry the xijth king of England and of Fraunce and lorde of Ireland, betwene the same our soueraigne lorde on thone partye, and Richard Hatton Clerke, Provost of the College of our blissed lady and seint Nicholas called the kinges College otherwise the new College in Cambridge in the countie of Cambridge and the scolers of the same College on thodre partye, witnessith

  That where our said soueraigne lorde is noble Progenitours is and vncle of blissed memorye king Henry the sext founded and endowed the said College and in the same beganne a greate Churche and a large for diuine seruice to be said and doone therin by the Provost and scolers of the same which Churche as yet restith vnperfited and not finisshed litle or no thinge wrought or done therupon sens the deceasse of his said Vncle, but that now of late our saide soueraigne lorde of vertuous disposicion for the wealle of his soule and the singuler truste he hath to the Prayers of his said blissed Vncle for the great holynes and vertue that he was in his life, Oure saide soueraigne lorde at his awne propre costes and charges hath fremasons and other werkemen in greate noumbre dayly werkinge and laboring of and vpon the bilding and making of the said Churche and so intendith by the grace of Almight godd incessauntly to persever and contenue till it be fully fynisshed and accomplished after like fourme and entent as it was ordered and devised by his said vncle, And because the same shuld be surely doon and executed in maner and fourme aforesaid, And that his hignes calleth to his gracious remembrance that therby shuld not be onely a notable Acte and a meritorious werke perfited, whiche els were like to grow to desolacion and never to haue ben done and accomplisshed, but also diuine seruice there hereafter mayntened and supported to thonour and laude of almighty god thencrese of Cunnyng and doctrine of his lawes in Edifying and encrese of our faithe; And for that deed of charite done in life of man and wilful departure and refusall from the possession of proprete of goodes to suche and other gode vses and intentes be moche more meritorious and avaieleable for the wealle of mannys soule then to be done after deth, And for the sure perfourmance and finisshing of the premisses and the more redy payment of the money necessarie in that behalue, his said highnes hath deliuered and by thies presentes indentures deliuereth the day of the making herof vnto the saide Provost and scolers the somme of fyve thousand poundes of good and lawfull money of England whiche fyve thousand poundes they knowledge themselfe to haue receyued the day of the date of thies Indentures the proprete wherof his highnes clerely vtterly and absolutely forsaketh refuseth and renounceth euermore. And the said somme of v.M1.li Oure saide soueraigne lorde geveth and graunteth to the saide Provost and scolers to the oonly vses and intentes heraftre ensuyng that is to saye that the saem v.M1.li and euery parcell therof shalbe truly spent ordered and employed by the saide Provost and other Provostes of the said College for the tyme being and to and for the bilding and finisshing of the said Churche.

And the saide Provost and Scolers covenaunteth and graunteth and bindeth theym and their successours by thies presentes to our saide soueraigne lorde And his Executoures that the said v.M1.li and euery parcell therof with all diligence and spede shalbe truly employed and spent for and aboute the costes charges and expenses of the making and finisshinge of the said Churche as far as the somme shall extend vnto, by and aftre the ouersight, aduise, and the comptrollement of suche persones as therunto shalbe assigned and appoynted by our saide soueraigne lorde in his life, And aftre his deceasse by his Executors.

And for the sauegarde and sure kepinge of the said somme of v.M1.li in the mean season, and to the tyme it shalbe so expended, a stronge Chest bounded with Iron having iiij lockes and iiij keyes to shete and open the same, shalbe prouided by the saide Provost and scolers and sett in the Treasure house of the said College wherin shalbe put and remayne the saide somme of v.M1.li. And of the same iiij keyes oon of theym to be in thandes and keping of the saide Provost of the same College. A nother key in the keping of the Vicechaunceler of the saide Vniuersite for the tyme being. The thirde key in the keping of theldest Burser of the saide College for the tyme being. And the fourth key in thandes and keping of the Master and ouerseer of the werkes of the side Churche for the tyme being. Thies foure persones their deputies or assignes in that behalue with the saide keyes to be to giddre at euery openyng and shitting of the saide Chest and at suche tyme as often and when ony parte of the said somme of v.M1.li shalbe taken out of the same for the vse and intente aforesaide.

And ouerthat the saide Provost and scolers covenaunteth and bindeth theym and their successours by thies presentes thet the same some of v.M1.li and euery parcell therof shalbe truly and with diligence employed spent and bestowed for, aboute, and vpon, the werkes and charges for the bilding of the saide Churche from tyme to tyme by thaduise comptrollement and ouersight of the persones aforesaide, with out discontennuying or cesing of the saide werkes or only parte of theym till they be fully perfourmed finisshed and accomplished as fer as the said somme of money of v.M1.li woll extend vnto.

And that the saide Provost and his successours for the tyme being shalbe accomptable and yeve a true accompte and rekenyng with out concelement of themploying expensis, and bestowing, of the said somme of v.M1.li vpon the werkes of the saide Churche and other the premisses of oure soueraigne lorde in his life and of such parcelles therof to his Executours as after his deceasse shall rest vnbestowed and employed and before that not accompted, As aften and whensoeuer he or they shall call him of his successours therunto.

And in case of the saide v.M1.li shalnot suffice for thole perfourmance and accomplisshement of the saide building and werkes and euery parcell of theym, and that there be not perfitely Finisshed by oure saide soueraigne lorde in his life, That than his Executours after his deseasse ffrom tyme to tyme as necessite requireth shal delieur to the saide Provost for the tyme being asmuche money ouer and above the saide v.M1.li as shall suffice for the perfite finisshing and perfourmynge of the same werkes and euery parte of theim in maner and fourme abouesaide. And the said Provost and scolers covenaunteth and graunteth and bindeth theym and their successours by thies presentes to oure said soueraigne lorde and his Executourss that the saide money and euery parcell therof so to theim deliuered by his saide Executours as aforesaide shalbe trule with all diligence employed and bestowed for, aboute, and vpon, the werkes and bildings of the saide Churche from tyme to tyme by thaduise comptrollement and ouresight of his saide Executours or suche other as they or more part of theim shall depute and assigne to the same without desisting or discontennuyng the bilding of the saide werkes in only wise till they and euery parcell of theym be fully and perfitely accomplished and perfourmed in maner and fourme aforesaide. And that the saide Provost and his successours for the tyme beinge shalbe accomptable and yeve a true accompte and rekenyng without cocelement vnto the said Executors of the more parte of theim how and in what maner the same money and euery parcell therof is spent employed and bestowed vpon the same werkes and bildinge when and as often the saide Executours of the most parte of theim shall call the saide Provost or any his successours therunto.

In witnesse wherof to the one part of theis Indentures with the saide Provost and scolers remaynynge the king oure soueraigne lorde hathe caused his private seale to be putt. And to the other part of the same Indentures, remaynyng with oure saide soueraigne lorde, the foresaide Provost and scolers haue putt their Common Seale the day and yere abouesaide.

The £5,000 did not suffice, it was all spent by 1512 and the executors of Henry VII were called upon for more – another £5,000. This they duly paid on 8 February 1512, on condition that:[33]

33 Ibid., pp. 478–9.

as hastily as they can or may resonabyll without delaye vawte the chirch of the said college after the fourme of a platte therfor devised and subscribed with the handes of the said executors; Ande cause dowble deskes to be maid in the qwere of the said chirch; glase all the windowes in the same chirch with such Images, storis, armys, bagis, and other devises as it shalbe devised by the said executors; And also clerly and holy fynyshe perfourme and end all the warkes that is not yet doon in the said chirche in all thinges aswel within as withowt.

Unlike Henry VI, the Tudor kings fulfilled their promises, and between 1506 and 1512 a total of £11,850 was given to King's College for the completion of the Chapel fabric. How was all this money spent? One of the most interesting aspects of the last campaign upon King's College Chapel is the degree of surviving documentation.

Despite the loss of sixteen of the seventeen account books handed over to the Provost in 1529, the one surviving account plus the remarkable series of contracts form perhaps the most complete picture of any large-scale English building work of the late Middle Ages. The one surviving acount is totalled in fortnights and covers the whole last campaign from 1508 to 1515. It includes all the major purchases, as well as personal payments to members of the building team. The accounts run from Easter to Easter.[34]

In the first year of active operations, 1508/09, the major purchases were of stone, iron and wood. The amount of stone totalled less than 500 tons, being approximately 222 tons of Weldon from Northamptonshire, 210 tons of Clipsham, Leicestershire and 50 tons of Hampole from Yorkshire. The delivered price per ton at the site was Weldon, 5/4d Clipsham, 5/6d and Hampole 6/- the latter being 4/10d to Lynn plus 1/2d barge fee to Cambridge. In the account to 23 July 1508, ironwork was purchased for the 'great windows', i.e. the lateral windows of the antechapel. This included 270 crossbars, 88 standards and 10 staybars, together with four great hooks for the chapel door, the unspecified sum being paid to Robert Olyver, the Royal Smith. Later, on 10 December more ironwork was bought comprising 240 crossbars for 'great windows', 63 for 'low windows' that is those of the side closets, and 96 standards for both great and low, and 6 staybars. New moulding profiles were also being prepared during the autumn of 1508, with wainscot to the value of 16/8d purchased on 1 October plus elm board at 18/10d, poplar board at 10/9d, oak board at 2/8d, and paper and ink for the tracing house.

At the beginning of 1509 a new scaffolding was prepared, with 80 great nails for this purpose bought for John Monday on 21 January and 102 elms for scaffolding valued at £1 9s 2d entered under 18 February, with a further 68 'loads' of elm on 4 March. For the rest of 1509 there are three further purchases of board for the tracing house, on 5 and 14 August and 28 October and two purchases of ironwork for the 'great windows', this time specifying their numbers – 'four great windows' on 16 September and 'two great windows' on 23 December.

The acquisition of stone increased dramatically during the account year Easter to Easter 1509/10, with 1,396 tons of Clipsham and 1,439·6 tons of Weldon. In the next account, under the fortnight to 23 June 1510, further ironwork was bought for another six of the lateral windows and in the same year the purchase of lead soared from just over £80 in 1509/10 to £342 9s 8¼d, falling back to under £150 in the following year, 1511/12. This expense must denote the preparation of the antechapel roof con-

34 Unless stated otherwise, the majority of these references were extracted from the notes of J. Saltmarsh who does not appear to have made use of this great wealth of material. He did, I believe, supply the RCHM with employment figures in quarter years, see *Cambridge* RCHM, vol. I, p. 102.

struction. Considerable quantities of board were purchased for the tracing house to make moulding patterns – 21 July, 4 August, 15 September (£1 15s 2d a large order) and a further 12/3d on 27 October 1509. Substantial amounts of wood arrived at the site in March 1510, when 1,518 feet was paid for. Stone deliveries in the account year 1510/11 reached 1,601 tons of Clipsham and 1,651 tons of Weldon, with high points for delivery in the fortnights to 17 March and 15 September 1510. It will be seen that Huddleston is never mentioned in the accounts of the last campaign and we should therefore not expect to find any more than the odd block in the antechapel, perhaps left over from the earlier campaigns. The only Yorkshire stone known to be employed by Wastell was from Hampole. The last reference to ironwork for the making of the lateral windows of the antechapel comes in the account to 27 April 1511, when 'two great windows' were paid for. Between 25 May and 31 August 1511 a number of major deliveries of brick arrived, to the value of £30 13s or the equivalent of about 128,500 bricks.

At the same time, board for the tracing house was paid for on 22 June, 6 July and 28 September 1511. Stone deliveries from Weldon reached 1,903·5 tons in the year 1511/12, with the high point during the fortnight to 20 July 1511. However, there are no payments for Clipsham in this, nor any of the years from 1511.

The first in a series of contracts and agreements between the College and Wastell, and Wastell and others occurred between 22 April and 7 June 1512, under which Wastell agreed to build the high vault of the Chapel.[35] In August £6 6s 8d was paid for wainscot, presumably for moulding patterns, and stone purchases from Weldon rose to 2,859 tons during the account year 1512/13 – reaching a peak around 12 September 1512. Lead purchases continued at a fairly high level, with £117 11s 9d spent in the same year. At the begining of January 1513 another contract was drawn up for the building of the pinnacles and one trial tower design.[36] This contract appears to have prompted the purchase of yet more wainscot for moulding patterns in February. One final brick purchase was recorded, 31 July 1513, when £1 1s 4d was expended, or approximately 4,250 bricks at the going rate, together with 1,418 feet of wood, presumably for new scaffolding. Some of this material may have been intended for the vaulting of the side closets and porches, for which a contract was agreed with Wastell on 4 August 1513. Yet more board went to the tracing house on 13 July and 23 October 1513, while paper and wainscot were bought in the fortnight to 9 October. Stone supplies show a decline during the account year 1513/14, with only 1,761 tons of Weldon, whilst lead totals drop to the value of a mere £5 6s 8d. The gradual fall in the expenditure on supplies continued throughout 1514/15 and indicates the reduced level of activity and the advanced state of the fabric. Weldon deliveries in 1514/15 drop to 1,363·1 tons and in the fol-

35 Willis and Clark, vol. I, p. 608.

36 Ibid., pp. 609–11.

lowing half-year account for 1515, only 153·6 tons entered the College for use at the Chapel. Surprisingly, a considerably amount of board was still being bought for the tracing house at a time when there can have been few moulding details to make – elm board was bought during the fortnights to 9 and 23 April and 24 September 1514, wainscot and paper 30 July 1514, and 'board' on 2 and 16 July and 30 September and 9 November 1514. There is no surviving record of payments for any ironwork, brick, new scaffolding or lead in this period, though a few plumbers were still at work. The Chapel fabric was completed before 29 July 1515, when the accounts were closed.

There exist, in addition to these accounts and contracts, detailed lists of the numbers of workmen employed upon the Chapel, once again totalled in fortnights, and covering almost the whole period of the last campaign. From these it can be shown that the high point in employment came during the summer of 1511 when over 200 men of various skills *132* were at work. This dropped to just over 50 at the end of the campaign. *133*

Such a comparative welter of documentary material almost obviates the need to study the fabric at first hand, but the wealth of purchases and other payments must be regarded with some caution, for example; the ironwork payments refer to at least eighteen 'great windows' between 1508 and 1511, yet by 1508 only the west window (which is never referred to specifically) and eleven of the lateral windows actually remained to be built, and possibly the mullions for the windows of Bays 6 N and 7 S. Thus a payment for six great windows does not necessarily involve all the ironwork for six entire lateral windows but may possibly refer only to the tracery heads which were an integral part of the elevation, plus additional ironwork for the mullions of other lateral windows with tracery heads already built. The cash amounts paid are no help, for there would appear to be no consistency between the quantity and value.[37] Despite these reservations, it is possible to propose the following schedule for the building of the antechapel and high vaults between 1508 and 1515.

The stone purchases of the first year, 1508/09, are relatively minor, suggesting that the major supplies had only just been ordered and had not yet arrived. The work at this time was undoubtedly concentrated upon Bays 6 and 7 N and Bays 7 and 8 S – the point where the last campaign had tailed away in 1485. Some materials intended for these bays may have remained stored in the lodges. The earliest payment for ironwork for the 'great windows' probably refers to the mullions and transoms of Bays 6 N and 7 S whereas the four large hooks for the 'great doors of the Chapel' can only refer to either one of the porch doors or, given the wording, to the great west door. This suggests that at least some construction was in progress upon the main elevations on several bays at once and distributed around the antechapel.

The considerable purchase of materials for the tracing house in the

37 The ironwork for a single window in 1476/7 cost £12 10s. 2¼d. The same for four of the great windows in Sept. 1510 cost £12 2s. 4½d while on Dec. 1510 ironwork for only two windows cost £34 10s. 6d.

132 King's College Chapel:
graph of Building
Accounts and employment
1508–11

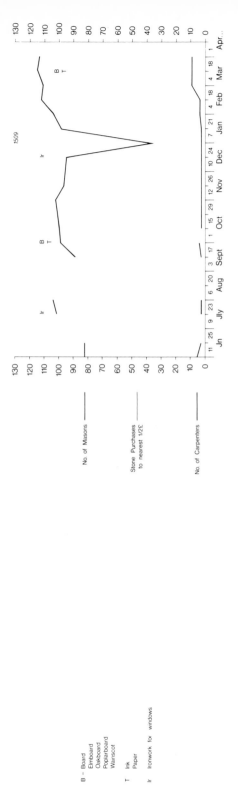

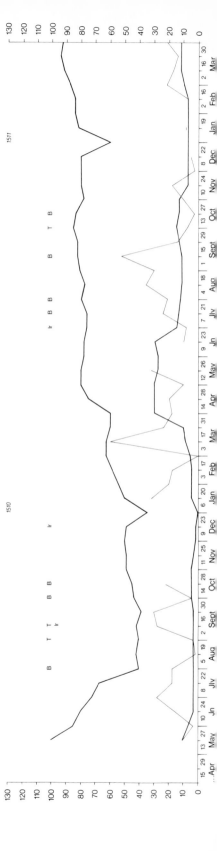

No. of Masons ——————

Stone Purchases ——————
to nearest 1/2£

No. of Carpenters ——————

B – Board
Elmboard
Oakboard
Poplarboard
Wainscot

T Ink
    Paper

Ir Ironwork for windows

33 King's College Chapel;
graph of Building
Accounts and employment
1511–15

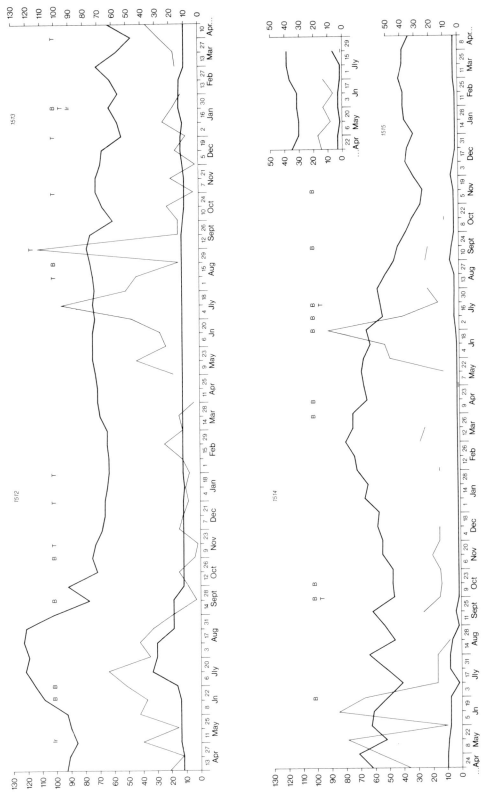

October of 1508 implies that a new phase of work was about to commence, one requiring new mouldings and new plans. The window mullion moulding for example, changes for the last time in Bays 7 N and 8 S and it was probably for these windows that ironwork was bought in the following December. This would also pinpoint the precise date for the final design of the antechapel elevations. The erection of Bays 7 N and 8 S required a new scaffolding, the materials for which were required in January and February 1509. The rapid increase in stone deliveries from the following April, rising from under 500 tons to nearly 3,000 signifies the determined effort to build the antechapel socle walls, the vault supports and the side closets as quickly as possible, no doubt hastened by the death of Henry VII in that month and the consequent uncertainty the event must have caused for the whole future of the project. The construction of the antechapel appears to have been as uniform as possible in each bay, for example, in September 1509 ironwork was purchased for four of the lateral windows, followed by two more at Christmas. The speed at which up to six of the lateral window bays could be put in hand suggests that, as in the earlier choir campaigns, several window jambs were built at once, thus enabling the erection of the tracery heads in series rather than one at a time.

The preparation of the seven bays of the antechapel roof in the summer of 1510 denotes that the elevations were approaching completion with the window tracery in place. Only two 'great windows' are referred to in the accounts of 1511/12, during the fortnight to 27 April 1511. There are no specific references to the building of the west window, which was presumably included as just another great window. The amounts of lead supplied increased dramatically towards the end of the summer that saw the making of the high roof, with nearly £350 spent between 15 September and 27 October 1510. This compares with only £80 spent in the whole previous year. By an agreement made prior to the death of Henry VII and ratified by Henry VIII on 31 July 1509, Thomas Larke, the Provost of King's College who was acting as the surveyor of the work, was permitted to choose 144 oaks from the royal forest at Wethersfield in Essex, which probably met nearly all the main timber requirements for the antechapel roof. However, despite all the references in the accounts to the timber and lead, the completed timber structure of the roof cannot have been erected finally until the building of the inner brick wall at the top of the elevation on which the roof sits. No substantial payment for brick occurs before 25 May 1511. Between then and the end of August, more than 128,000 bricks arrived with carriage from the river to the Chapel recorded on 8 and 22 June, 6 and 20 July, and 17 August, with later deliveries on 26 October and 23 November. Assuming that the brick walls were commenced in Bay 6 where the fifteenth-century walls break off, then the final roof assembly could have followed the building of the brick walls from bay to bay, beginning in the late summer of 1511. Large stocks of lead had been in store since September 1510, but another order to the value of £100 was necessary in November 1511, possibly to cover the final western bays.

The year 1511 was clearly crucial for the constructional history of King's College Chapel. It saw the completion of the antechapel walls and vault supports, the building of the double skin upper brick section and the completion of the high roof. The leading of the completed sections of the roof began after 3 August 1511, when a large amount of firewood was bought for the plumber. In February 1512, the College received £5,000 from the estate of Henry VII, thus assuring the completion of all the outstanding work. The conditions attached to the grant confirm that the structure of the Chapel was complete and the roof built. The Chapel wanted only a vault and its exterior trimmings, fittings and glazing.[38]

38 Willis and Clark, vol. I, pp. 478–9.

The building of the great vault of King's College Chapel was subject to a series of contracts covering the period May 1512 to August 1513. *134* Some, including the initial contract, survive in the Muniments only in draft form while another is known solely through a copy made in the eighteenth century. The vault contract, known as Contract A, was drawn up sometime in May 1512, between Thomas Larke, acting as surveyor of the works, John Wastell, master mason of the Chapel, and Henry Semark, one of Wastell's wardens.[39] It was agreed that Wastell and Semark 'shall make and set up, or cause to be made and set up at their cost and charge, a great vault of twelve bays'. The phrase 'or cause to be made . . .' suggests that Wastell and Semark could subcontract the actual building work if they so wished. The vault was to be 'good sure and sufficient. . . . be workmanly wrought and set upp after the best handlyng and fourme of good workmanship according to a platt therof made and signed with the hands of the Lordes executors unto the King.' The 'platt' would have been a design drawn in sufficient detail and agreed between Wastell, Larke and the King's executors such that Larke as surveyor could check during construction that the design had not been embellished or restructured in any way that would increase or decrease the cost, it being a fixed price contract. Under the contract Wastell and Semark agreed to select the Weldon stone and to organise the supply of 'lyme, sand, scaffolding, cynctours, mouldes, ordinaces', etc, as well as the necessary workforce. In return, they could keep two bays of the great scaffold employed for the building of the vault upon completion and could use the existing building material within the Chapel – 'gynnes, wheles, cables', etc. The whole vault project was to be completed in three years, that is by May 1515, a time scale that would allow for the construction of approximately four bays per year with a slight delay for the initial

39 Ibid., p. 608. See also Appendix IV.

134 King's College Chapel:
interior, great vault

period of scaffolding. The financing was at a fixed price of £100 per bay. Wastell and Semark were also responsible for negotiating the price of materials, which would be paid for upon arrival by the surveyor, Thomas Larke, and the individual sums deducted from the £100 upon the completion of each bay. Wastell and Semark would then receive the balance, if any. This system encouraged Wastell to use the materials sparingly and to drive hard bargains. He evidently considered that these terms were advantageous for on 7 June 1512 a second agreement was drawn up, known as Contract B, between Wastell and Semark, under which Wastell who is styled as 'Master Mason of the King's Works within the College Royal' took over sole responsibility for the vault contract, whilst Semark agreed to accept 20 marks a year instead.[40] It is not clear why Semark should have agreed to this, especially as it also bound him to attend to the work 'hourly and daily', taking only such leave as Wastell permitted.

Contract B contains a number of references to Wastell's health, rather more than might be expected. It was agreed that Wastell should accept all responsibility and profit as long as he shall 'lyve and have his helth to ruele the werke'. This may seem a common safeguard but it is one of no less that three clauses directly related to Wastell's health, including one that stipulates that if Wastell should die or fall sick, then Semark and Wastell's son Thomas should share the contract and profits equally. Both the early contracts make it clear that Wastell alone was master mason and that he did indeed 'reule the werke'. There is no reference in any of the contracts to John Lee, former chief mason of King's College Chapel, who was appointed as joint master mason with the same salary as Wastell in 1509.

A third Contract, C, drawn up between Larke and Wastell on 4 January 1513, dealt with the pinnacles and exterior buttresses and with the construction of one corner tower.[41] Contract C evidently succeeded a lost agreement for the building of one trial pinnacle, for it contains a reference to the one pinnacle already made. Equally, there is no surviving contract concerning the high battlements. Under Contract C, the remaining twenty-one pinnacles were to follow the 'platts conceyved' and the one already built except that they were to be 'sumwhat larger in certeyn places . . . according to the mouldings made'. In addition, Wastell was to build one corner tower, from later evidence that at the north-west angle, so that a decision could be taken on its appearance before the three others were erected. The tower was to have 'fynyalles, ryfant gables, batelments, orbys or cross quaters'. Both the pinnacle and tower experiments point up the inability of the medieval master mason to put over to his client the exact physical appearance of his paper design, or at least the patron's inexperience in these matters in the absence of a prototype or an example already built elsewhere that could be copied. It is little wonder therefore that patrons in general should have based so much of their architectural endeavours and requirements upon the pattern of

40 Ibid., p. 609.

41 Ibid., pp. 609–11.

existing named buildings, with the usual rider of 'only better'.

As before, under the terms of Contract C Wastell was to find all the materials and workforce. The stone was to be Weldon. The College would lend him existing scaffolding and all the usual lifting tackle – the 'gynnes and wheles', etc. The work was to be finished by 25 March 1513, that is in approximately eleven and a half weeks. Payment was again fixed price: £6 13s 4d for each pinnacle and £100 for the trial tower, the money to be paid out as required and the profit going entirely to Wastell. A workforce of at least sixty men had to be maintained, to be found as soon as Wastell had received his 'commission' from Larke. The agreement also included an 'industrial relations' clause whereby Larke shouldered the responsibility for admonishing 'errant' masons and labourers, despite the fact that they were technically employed by Wastell. The College also agreed to supply ironwork to the cost of 5/- per pinnacle, any more than that would have to be paid by Wastell from his profit. The contract concludes with an unusual indemnity clause, whereby each party agreed to give the other £300 on the following Easter Sunday, 27 April 1513. This arrangement was in order to bind the College to their part and Wastell to his, though, as the contract was due to be completed by 25 March, its termination would presumably nullify the clause. This insurance may be another indication that the College feared that Wastell would not live long enough to finish the work.

Another contract, known as D, survives only as an eighteenth-century copy in the library of King's College.[42] It is dated 24 January 1513, with an additional memo extending it to May 1514. By this agreement, Thomas Larke, surveyor, was to keep a record of all monies paid to Wastell and his suppliers as part of the preceding contracts. The payments entered cover materials and other expenses from several contracts, including some which no longer survive, i.e. the material for the side closet corbel tables. Between 4 and 24 January 1513, Larke paid Wastell £71 12s 5d for the pinnacles, entered as 'money and stone delivered, plus 192 tons 3 feet of Weldon at 3/- per ton, £57 12s 10d totalling £129 5s 3d.' In addition, Larke paid for 10 tons 2 feet of Weldon for the 'corbel tables of the chapells' at 6/- per ton, making a total of 60/9d. On the same day, 24 January 1513, the 'stone remaynyng after 2 parcels' equalled 331 tons 5 feet of Weldon, 68 tons 13 feet of Yorkshire (presumably Hampole stone, mentioned in the contract to vault the side closets) plus 27 tons 5 feet of Clipsham and refuse stones and 'sawyngs' from all three sources and 'moulded stones of sondry sorts' all totalling 427 tons 3 feet.

The next entry in Contract D covers the remaining period of the pinnacles contract, 24 January to 25 March 1513, and records that Larke paid Wastell £164 via the hand of John Ray, who was one of the churchwardens responsible for the rebuilding of Great St Mary's Church. Between 25 March and 13 April 1513, Wastell received another £100,

42 Ibid., pp. 611–12.

43 'Prest' = on account.

while between then and 24 May John Ray delivered £126 10s 10d to Wastell for 'pay days', that is to pay the mason's wages, as well as to pay for the carriage of stone by land and water. A sum of £20 was paid 'prest to Chikley and his felowes', evidently a payment to the quarryman and his team.[43]

During the summer of 1513, between May and June, work continued on the great vault and on the three remaining corner towers, built by a contract of 4 March 1513. Larke paid Wastell, through John Ray, £147 including 'pay days' and certain 'prests delyvered to the quarrymen as appereth in the fourtnyght bokes'. Within the next two weeks, 8 to 17 July, Wastell received £56 18s 3d for stone, 'werkmanship prests', etc., while between then and 26 September 1513, he received a further £113 10s from John Ray 'at sondry times'. These payments cover the initial work on the porch and side closet vaults built by an agreement of 4 August 1513.

On 26 September 1513, Thomas Larke paid a certain Master Kyrkeham £20 3s 1d for 142 tons 4½ feet of Weldon at 2/4d per ton, received by Wastell by land, and totalling £18 19s 9d, plus another 4 tons 19 feet arriving by water at £1 3s 4d. The whole entry is most curious. Clearly stone that normally cost 6/- per ton delivered to King's by water could not suddenly drop in price to 2/4d per ton when carried by more expensive land transport. In addition, the sums do not add up. The Weldon delivered by land should not have come to more than £17 15s 2½d and the price per ton of Weldon delivered by water appears to be 4/9d per ton. The larger payment more probably covers only the cost of land carriage for the stone, but why then was the amount of stone brought by the cheaper water transport so small? The last entry in the memo is mathematically still more curious, recording that Larke paid to Wastell, through John Ray, the sum of £380 72s 6d (that is £383 12s 6d) between 27 September 1513 and 12 May 1514. No details are provided.

Two further contracts were drawn up during the period of the above memo. Contract E, of 4 March 1513, covered the building of the three remaining corner towers which were to follow the example of the north-west tower already built, and which were to be finished by Midsummer's Day, 24 June.[44] This suggests that the first tower was built in less than sixty days. The indemnity clause was raised in value on either side to £400. Contract F followed on 4 August 1513 and concerned the vaults of the side closets and of the two porches.[45] Wastell was to make and set up, or cause to be made and set up, two porches of Yorkshire stone and vaults for seven chapels 'in the body of the same chirch' out of Weldon stone. Vaults for the nine other remaining closets 'behynd the quere' were also to be of Weldon but 'of a more coarse worke' that is, they were to be plain rib vaults and not fan vaults. Wastell was also to *135* build the battlements of the porches and closets, and to find all the Hampole (Yorkshire), Weldon and the tackle himself. He must keep at

44 Willis and Clark, vol. I, pp. 612–13.

45 Ibid., pp. 613–14.

135 King's College Chapel: interior detail, a 'coarse work' closet vault

46 Ibid., pp. 614–15.

least sixty freemasons at work and finish the whole by the feast of the Nativity of St John the Baptist next, that is 24 June 1514. This last may be a mistake, for the contract was dated 4 August 1513, and the indemnity clause was to come into effect on 2 February 1514, the Feast of the Purification of the Virgin. Possibly the completion date was to be on the Feast of St John the Evangelist, 27 December 1513, especially as 24 June was referred to in Contract E not as the Nativity of St John the Baptist but as Midsummer's Day. However, a mistake such as this would seem unlikely. Payment under Contract F was £25 for each porch vault, £20 for each closet 'in the body of the chirch' and £12 each for the more 'coarse vaults' lying 'behynd the quere'. The battlements for twenty bays would total £100.

One further record, known as Contract G, is an annual summary of all expenditure covering the period from 13 May 1509 to 29 July 1515.[46] The highest expenditure was incurred during 1510/11 with £2,139 8s 6¾d. The lowest was in 1514/15 at £983 15s 9¼d not including the two- or three-month period from April 1515 to the close of work when expenditure ran at approximately the same monthly rate as in the whole year 1514/15. The summary was signed by Larke as surveyor, Wastell and Lee as master masons, Richard Russell, the master carpenter, John Burwell, the master plumber and Thomas Stockton, the master carver. The total expenditure was given as £10,026 3s 9d. This represents amounts paid not only to Wastell but to many others, for example, the entry for 1513/14 is £225 13s 9d more than the highest calculation that could have been paid to Wastell alone in that year.

Wastell's contribution to the design of King's College Chapel

The antechapel of King's College Chapel was built in a remarkably short time. Work commenced during the summer of 1508 yet the upper walls of stone-clad brickwork were already under construction in the late May of 1511. The rapid speed of the building is explained partly by the relatively small amount of actual structure – the foundations and some lower sections of the exterior walls had been built to an uneven height prior to 1472 while the greater part of the antechapel elevations that remained to be built consisted of large window openings. The main work of the *136* last elevational campaign involved the building of the socle walls beneath the lateral windows, the vault supports, window jambs and buttresses, the window spandrels and vault lunettes and the continuation of the double-skin brick wall to support the roof. An examination of the antechapel reveals that the fine white magnesian limestone from Huddleston in Yorkshire, associated with the earlier work completed in 1485, is present only in the lowest courses of some of the side closet walls, in some of the pier bases of the vault supports, in the base courses of the

136 King's College Chapel:
interior of antechapel Bays
9 to 12 N

north and south porches and in some of the side closet window tracery.
The Wastell parts of the elevations are executed in Clipsham, Weldon
and Caen, and while odd blocks of Huddleston can be found they are
very scarce and their use haphazard.

The lowest sections of the antechapel must be examined in some detail
before any assessment can be made of Wastell's contribution to the built
fabric and, more importantly, to the overall design.

One detail, used by Willis to determine the attribution of the side closet
construction, is particularly revealing in quite other respects. The side

closet behind Bay 8 S adjoins the most crucial section in the architectural
history of the Chapel – vault support VS 7/8 S. The vault support stands
at the junction of the choir and antechapel and represents a curious combination of the two different designs; the one corbelled out at cill level,
the other rising directly from the floor. The vault support was built to
a considerable height by Reginal Ely in the first stage of the Chapel's
history. Its design denotes that Ely had determined the general arrangement of the mouldings of the antechapel bases before *c.* 1461. The north-
east angle of the side closet behind Bay 8 S forms the reverse side of
VS 7/8 S. The angle within the closet is filled with a vault respond that
rises directly from a plain glacis base, and the whole unit is made of evenly
coursed white Huddleston. The mouldings of the respond consist of
wedges, mostly accompanied by half or three-quarter rolls. The respond
has been altered subsequent to its original construction by the removal
of two intermediate wedges, leaving slight, but detectable scars. Their
removal has reduced the number of vault rib springing points originally
provided from two wall ribs and four ribs down to two wall ribs and
two ribs.[47] This alteration was made to enable Wastell to plant the present
fan vault over the side closet rather than a rib and lierne vault like those
by Reginald Ely prior to 1461. Therefore, all the closet responds in which *137*
the 'cut back' evidence occurs should denote work executed before the
last campaign under Wastell from 1508. The wall rib in the side closet
of Bay 8 S also marks a change from those preceding, e.g. those in Bay
7 S which have a half bracket, raised fillet and quarter roll moulding
whereas that in Bay 8 S has a hollow chamfer, half bracket and quarter
roll. Thus the respond in the north-east angle of side closet Bay 8 S is
by Ely while the wall ribs are by Wastell.

   The side closets are divided from the antechapel proper by pierced
stone screens standing upon panelled socle walls, with doorways at their
western ends. From the interior of closet Bay 8 S the screen can be seen
set back within a moulded jamb that is drawn as an extension of the

47 Willis and Clark, vol. I, p. 493.

137 King's College Chapel:
   diagram of Wastell
   alteration to closet vault
   respond (left), before,
   (right), after. (Willis)

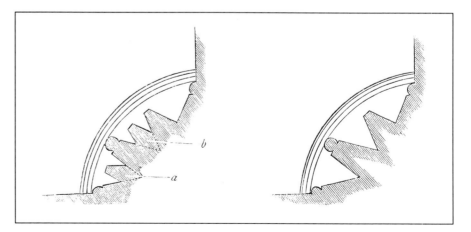

angled responds. The moulded jamb has a hollow chamfer, half bracket, hollow chamfer and deep casement profile, the whole of which is carried over the screen as an overarch. The springing block at the north-east angle was built as part of the Huddleston vault respond, whereas the rest of the overarch is of Weldon, the material used by Wastell for the adjoining vault. Thus the whole of the north-east angle of side closet Bay 8 S up to the level of the vault springing and on to the first block of the screen overarch existed prior to 1508 and, in fact, forms part of the Ely construction of VS 7/8 S. The closet respond shows not only the type of vault that Ely proposed for the side closets – rib and lierne – but also that he intended the closets to have substantial overarches into the antechapel interior. But what of the stone screens? At floor level within the closet, the double chamfered plinth of the vault respond swings westwards and sets out along the screen socle wall as far as the first glazed opening, but there it changes. The junction between the Huddleston work of the first section and the Clipsham second section is marked by a simplification of the plinth moulding from a double to a single chamfer, as well as the obvious change in the colour of the material. Nevertheless, the Huddleston section passes sufficiently far beneath the screen to indicate that Reginald Ely intended some form of low wall beneath the present opening. Three courses above the plinth the Huddleston angle has been cut away to allow for the cill of the present screen – the junction is again clearly visible in the change of stone and of coursing. It is immediately above this point that it can be seen that the north-east vault respond of the side closet Bay 8 S and the antechapel vault support VS 7/8 S are part of one uniform build, for above the cill two courses of the Huddleston pass straight through the glazed screen light and on into the antechapel to become part of the vault support. Unless the Huddleston jamb *138* of the easternmost light of the screen has been recut by Wastell, which does not seem to be the case, then the moulded jamb opening into the antechapel formed part of the Ely's design – Reginald Ely decided that the closets should have low arched openings into the antechapel and that they should be partially blocked by low retaining walls if not exactly by pierced screens. The evidence of the existing stone screens makes it very difficult to assess the original design of *c.* 1448, as the upper traceried sections of the existing screen could not be coursed evenly into the jambs due to the different size of the blocks required. Hence whatever the sequence, the tracery will always look inserted. It is the use of materials and the cutting of the earlier jamb for the cill, evidently not provided by Ely, that reveals that the existing screen is Wastell's. Furthermore, in the opposite north-west angle of the side closet Bay 8 S there is evidence that the opening now occupied by the door of the present screen was also prefigured by Ely – the base course of the angle vault respond is of Huddleston, and the coursing continues through the present screen door jamb at floor level and out into the antechapel where it forms part

138 King's College Chapel: interior detail of closet Bay 8 S, the Ely through jamb behind VS 7/8 S

of the vault support VS 8/9 S. But higher up at the screen door head, there is an abrupt junction between the earlier jamb and Wastell's door head, which also springs with a different moulding than that of the jamb. This is perhaps the clearest indication that Reginald Ely's antechapel design did not include pierced stone screens but just simple openings and retaining walls.

The north-west angle vault respond of the closet Bay 8 S also shows signs that Wastell removed two unwanted springing points plus the unexpected occurrence of either Clipsham or Weldon within that section of the respond. The lowest course of the moulded section is of Huddleston, but the next five courses are made of a beige Northamptonshire oolite, yet they too show the 'cut back' evidence associated with Wastell's alterations of Ely's work. Either this respond is entirely by Ely, mixing the two materials as he did in the early closets Bays 2 and 3 N or Simon Clerk recommended this angle in closet Bay 8 S prior to 1485.

The evidence of the side closet Bay 8 S reveals that the concept of the through arches from closet to antechapel with low retaining walls was Ely's, while the execution of the stone screens was by Wastell. The only other contribution made by Wastell to the design of the side closets is the vault and the alterations necessary to the vault responds to fit the fan vault. The side closet against Bay 9 S confirms the evidence of its neighbour. The north-east angle respond is made of a brown oolite, except for the base course which is of Huddleston. The vault respond has evidence that two of the original ribs have been cut away and the springing block of the screen overarch again forms part of the first build of the respond. In the north-west angle, only the lowest courses of the vault respond show any evidence of the cutting back of the extra unwanted elements, but these courses do include the base of the screen door jamb. Thus the relationship between at least two of the southern side closets and the antechapel had been established before Wastell came to work at King's in 1508.

The noticeable intrusion of some of the other closet screens can be used as a pointer to the extent of the fabric of the antechapel already built prior to the last campaign. The cill of the screen in Bay 9 S has been cut into both VS 8/9 S and VS 9/10 S. This also applies to the screen in Bay 10 S which adds yet another southern bay to the situation that existed in 1508. On the northern side of the antechapel, side closet Bay 8 N contains no evidence of the cutting away of unwanted sections of the vault responds. The south-east angle should, therefore, post-date Wastell's arrival in 1508 and, due to its relationship with the adjoining antechapel vault support, this date should also apply to VS 7/8 N. Yet the south-east angle within the side closet Bay 8 N also contains random blocks of Huddleston but cut to Wastell's respond design. This would appear to be the latest use of this material at King's and probably represents the use of stone found in the lodges left over from earlier campaigns.

The evidence of the side closet Bay 8 N would confirm the known advancement of the southern side of the Chapel by 1485.[48] At the northern end of the present pulpitum screen, VS 7/8 N appears to have suffered the later intrusion of the closet screen though in fact it is the same problem as on the south side, the springing of the tracery section cannot be coursed neatly into the horizontal layers of the vault support and there is in fact no clear evidence to suggest that any of the northern tracery screens have been inserted into fabric already in existence in 1508.

The earliest antechapel vault support, the southern pier VS 7/8 S, provides yet more information regarding Ely's intentions for the antechapel elevation, and its influence upon Wastell. Apart from the closet openings and retaining walls, the early Huddleston section of the vault support contains the springing of the socle panelling beneath the lateral window. The colour contrast between the white Huddleston half arch and the answering Clipsham is particularly obvious, as is the hacking back of the upper surface of the Huddleston to make room for Wastell's diamond fleuron frieze along the window cill. Clearly, Ely intended to overlay the socle walls with blind panelling as at present, though exactly how he intended to stop the mullions at the closet openings we can no longer determine. Thus the relationship between the lateral window, the panelled socle and the open arch into the side closet as intended by Ely would have resembled the interior elevations of Burwell, though with vastly different proportions and emphasis. Only Bay 12 N has evidence to suggest that the panelled socle mullions were, in that bay, to reach straight down to the wall bench at floor level, for the lower sections of the bench and the feet of the mullions are made of Huddleston. However, Bay 12 N was always intended to be 'blind', that is, it was not have a side closet and therefore, no arched opening.[49] In this respect there is a curious *139* resemblance between the Ely design and that of Eton College Chapel, where the first bay east has blind panelling beneath the lateral windows, while the Lupton Chantry in the next bay breaks through the panelling with a low four-centred entrance arch leading into the adjoining side closet. What a pity that the Lupton Chantry represents a sixteenth-century alteration!

The design of the side closet traceried screen is definitely not by Reginald Ely, though drawn from the downward extension of the lateral window mullions. The inherited screen overarch profile is four-centred and relatively flat sided. The outer lights of the screen are treated differently from the central three. All the lights are subdivided except that at the western end which contains the doorway, above which are three quatrefoil cirles arranged within the head, the uppermost being elongated into a 'teardrop' lobe. The three central lights are crossed by a mid-height *140* transom with uncusped heads below and staggered cusped lights above, each one supporting a quatrefoil circle. The screens are made of Weldon

139 King's College Chapel: interior, the blind screen of Bay 12 N

140 King's College Chapel: interior antechapel closet screen

50 For the original design see D. Loggan, *Cantabrigia Illustrata*, Cambridge 1690. The tracery was removed by Essex in the eighteenth century.

and Clipsham. The most notable feature of the screen tracery is the use of foiled motifs contained within circles. Circular motifs occur in Clerk's design for the east window and are a favourite motif in other windows that can be attributed to him: the lateral windows of Eton College Chapel and the side chancel windows of St Mary's Bury St Edmunds. On the other hand, they do not feature in work by, or attributed to John Wastell. The nearest approximation to the design of the closet screens is that of the former aisle windows of Great St Mary's in Cambridge, a design possibly as early as 1478, and very possibly by Simon Clerk.[50]

The cill level of the lateral windows is marked by a frieze of sculptured diamond fleurons. Beneath are the great heraldic beasts and ciphers relating to Henry VII. These sculptural ensembles, together with the crowned ciphers clambering up the wall piers that flank the vault supports, are the most obvious decorative feature of the antechapel elevations. All the sculpture beneath cill level appears to be cut from Caen stone, though there is no record of any purchase from this French source. The immediate model for such use of heraldry was the Henry VII Chapel at Westminster, begun in 1502, where smaller carved ciphers similarly

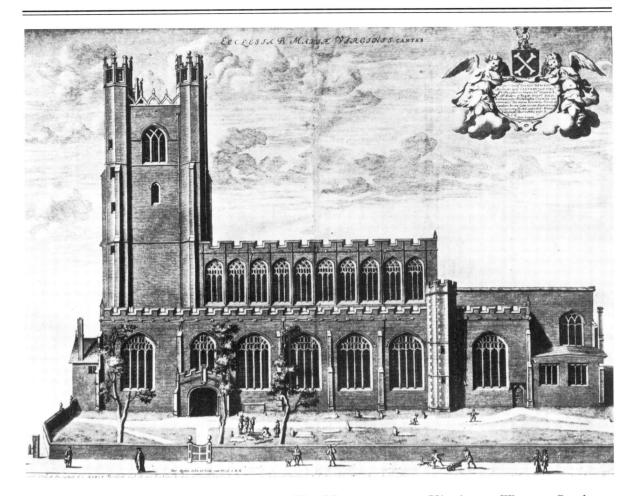

ECCLESIA B. MARIÆ VIRGINIS CANTAB.

141 Cambridge, Gt. St Mary's: exterior south side with original tracery (Loggan 1690)

51 *City of Cambridge*, RCHM, vol. I, pp. 102–3.

52 Willis and Clark, vol. I, p. 475. Four 'intaylers' were paid.

53 Discovered by Ratee and Kett during cleaning operations.

decorate the piers. The Master carver at King's was Thomas Stockton, who was paid at a rate of a shilling a day from 1509.[51] The earliest mention of carvers at work at King's College Chapel occurs as early as July 1508, rather soon to be working on the elevations unless the fine carved work was made and stored in the workshop to be placed only after the completion of the high vault.[52] The lowest of the Tudor ciphers are certainly inserted into their 'host' piers, sometimes into remarkably shallow slots, but their added appearance may be misleading, for being additions in a different material they may yet be contemporary with the construction of the elevation. Possibly, the lowest work arrived 'ready made' from *142* Westminster where Caen was in plentiful supply, it being the major material in the interior of the Henry VII Chapel. The emblems and beasts above the side closets at King's are also made in Caen and the different material and the need to employ massive blocks makes them also appear to be 'added'.[53] Yet the uppermost registers of Tudor and Beaufort ciphers do not appear added, nor do they appear to be made

142 King's College Chapel: interior detail of Tudor Rose emblem in Caen set into Clipsham

54 This is also a feature of the Ely niche on VS 7/8 S and of the chancel niches at Burwell.

of Caen. Quite obviously, the carved ciphers and beasts were not part of Reginald Ely's conception of the antechapel, nor, possibly, were they originally part of Wastell's. The contrast between the setting of the lower and upper registers raises the possibility that Henry VII did not order their inclusion but Henry VIII did. Hence they might have been included in the construction of the upper sections of the antechapel, built after the death of Henry VII in April 1509, and added subsequently to the lower sections already constructed.

As shewn in Chapter One, the introduction of additional jamb niches flanking the cill of the lateral windows occurred during the earliest campaign. The three-sided canopy against VS 7/8 S has hanging ogee gables supported by demi-angels, and a tall crocketed spirelet in four tiers. The finial and top course represent a Wastell completion in Clipsham. Wastell adapted this earlier design for his own lower niches, with only minor variations. Once again, it can be demonstrated that this additional decorative element within the antechapel was intended by Ely from 1448. *14*

Wastell's upper niches are extremely curious, repeating the canted gables of the lower design but topping them with a flat canopy, almost a vandalised version of the niche in Bay 3 S west jamb. Some, but not *14* all, of Wastell's upper niches have fan vaults, which spring from tiny human heads of the 'back' wall plane, a motif lifted from the first Ely niche.[54]

The Tudor Roses and the Beaufort Portcullis are marvellously realised in high relief, topped by crowns of exquisite execution. Finer still are the incredible chains that collect and buckle beneath the Beaufort arms. The centrepiece of each bay is taken up by the Griffin and Greyhound *145* supporters of Henry VII, holding the 'dented' shield of the first Tudor King. The west wall interior is an enlarged version of the lateral bay design – a nine-part division drawn from the window and filled with spectacular sculpture. The whole conception is so Spanish that it is difficult not to propose some influence, especially with the growing connections between the English and Spanish courts after 1500.[55]

55 For example, the marriage of Arthur and Catherine of Aragon. Such architectural heraldry in Spain reflects the strong German influence post-1445. The most notable example, the Chapel of the Constables in Burgos, was built by Simon of Cologne between 1482–87, though probably designed by his father John of Cologne before 1466. The other notable example is the transept of St Juan de los Reyes Toledo, begun after 1480 and still unfinished in 1491. See also D. Watkin, *The Virtue of Magnificence. Architectural Review*, vol. CXLV, Feb. 1969, pp. 139–40 and Colvin, vol. III, p. 125 and n.

In the west wall interior several of the base courses of the descending mullions and of the small turret doorways are made of Huddleston, a material not purchased during the Wastell campaign, and are probably therefore features dating from the initial laying out of the ground courses. Thus, Henry VI intended the present arrangement and enrichment of the west wall from the outset. Wastell also followed the Will and Intent in giving the west window nine lights. The tracery of the great west window is based upon that in the lateral windows with tiers of asymmetrical 'Yorkshire' ogees and some remarkably long subdivided panels in lights three and seven. The arch head profile conforms with that of the *146* present vault (unlike the earlier east window) so that at least is to Wastell's

43 King's College Chapel:
interior detail of Wastell
window jamb lower niche

44 King's College Chapel:
interior detail of Wastell
window jamb upper niche

45 King's College Chapel:
interior detail, the west
door sculpture

56 Seen earlier on Mapilton's SW
porch at Canterbury, see
F. Woodman, *The Architectural
History of Canterbury Cathedral*,
London 1981, p. 174.

57 Restored 1785–87.

58 W. St. John Hope, *Windsor Castle*,
London 1913, vol. II, p. 481.

design. The whole interior arrangement of the west wall recalls that of
St George's Windsor, though the early base walling at King's would
make the Cambridge design the earlier.

The sculptural elaboration of the antechapel facades had not formed
part of the original scheme of Henry VI and is the one major elevational
departure from the strict adherence to the 1448 plan. Reginald Ely had,
however, intended the overlay of blind tracery and the multiplication
of the window niches.

The tracery in the lateral windows of the antechapel continues Clerk's
compromise design of 1478/79, with a slight variation in the mullion _147_
moulding profile. The porches were also completed according to the
moulded base courses laid down by a previous master mason, either
Reginald Ely or John Wolryche. The porch exteriors, now heavily
restored, have early plinth courses up to the level of the niche bases. The
Ely mouldings include the sharp triangular pilasters and the overlaid
plinth mouldings, all typical of the Fantastic style of his day.[56] The _148_
general design of the porch facades is a reworking of the choir doors in
Bay 3: an ogee arch over a four-centred opening. The spandrels are infil-
led with large circles and ogee lobes, now with poorly restored Tudor
ciphers.[57] The entries are flanked by tall niches topped with two-tier
canopies resembling Wastell's pinnacles of the central tower of Canterbury Cathedral designed _c._ 1493. Inside, the canopies have intricate fan _149_
vaults.

On the exterior of the side closets, Wastell opted for only one repeated
tracery pattern – the flowing 'Flamboyant' rather than the strictly Perp.
Beasts and ciphers also attack the great buttresses, here perhaps a reflection of the exterior of the choir of St George's Windsor as decorated from
1506.[58] The decoration of the exterior buttresses at Kings, from Bay
7 N and Bay 8 S westwards is the most obvious external indication of
the extent of the last campaign upon the elevations.

Wastell's contribution to both the interior and exterior elevations of
King's College Chapel might best then be summed up as 'decorative'
– perhaps not all of it to his own taste. But there is one large area of
the Chapel where his inventiveness and architectural talents were

146 King's College Chapel: exterior, west window

stretched to the limits – the great vault. The design of the fan vault and its relationship with the lateral walls of the Chapel presents the major problem for all those who study the building. It cannot be said the vault sits happily on the vault supports, nor does the elevation within the vault lunette space assist in unifying the horizontal and vertical planes. In short, the Wastell vaults, magnificent as they are, do not fit on at all well.

There have been a number of pointers suggesting that Clerk did not intend to build a fan vault over the Chapel. Firstly, from the surviving evidence, the fashion in eastern England during the second half of the fifteenth century was for rib and lierne vaults such as those in Norwich Cathedral. These vaults tend to be very thick, with a considerable use of 'top packing'. They were designed to be segmental cross-axially, so that the springing point and wall ribs stayed low against the lateral walls, while the crown could rise to a height well above that of the adjoining lateral wall plate. The present gap between the panelling above the east window at King's, by Clerk, and the Wastell fan vault certainly suggests that Clerk's proposed vault of *c.* 1480 was to be segmental. In addition, the roof over the five eastern bays of the choir, designed and erected from 1480, has no base ties, a factor that led to structural weakness rectified only in the nineteenth century.[59] The absence of horizontal trusses crossing from wall plate to wall plate was undoubtedly to allow the upper surface of an intended vault to rise above the level of the lateral wall plates. When, for example, it was decided to erect a roof with horizontal base trusses over the Ely Lady Chapel in the eighteenth century, it was necessary to raise the lateral walls in order to clear the crown of the segmental profile vault. The Wastell fan vault at King's is remarkably thin, but despite the fact that its profile is sharper than that intended by Clerk,

59 See pp. 221–2.

147 King's College Chapel: exterior of Bays 8 and 9 N

148 King's College Chapel: exterior of south porch

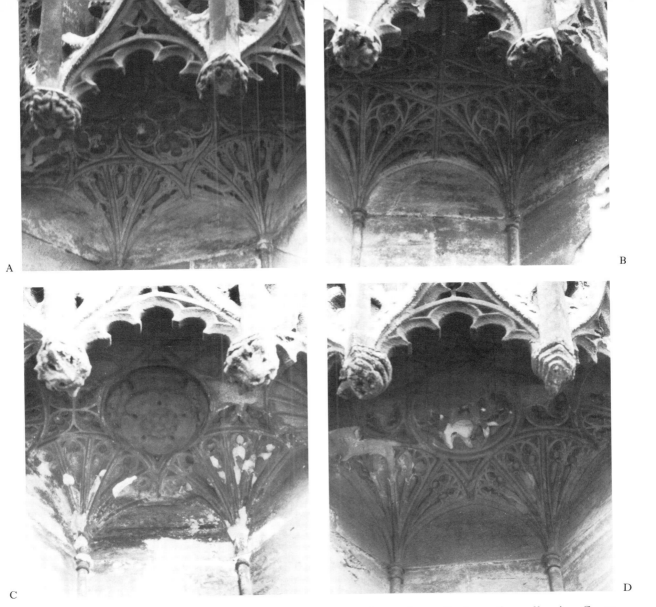

A

B

C

D

149 King's College Chapel: exterior details of niche vaults on the porches, A: N porch, E niche, B: N porch W niche, C: S porch W niche, D: S porch E niche

the crown rises a bare 0·15 m above the wall plate, thus allowing Scott to insert the existing iron tie bars in lieu of trusses in the nineteenth century.

But the most extensive and convincing evidence that Wastell imposed the existing vault solution upon Clerk's finished work can be seen in the vault lunette spaces – the triangular areas above the lateral window 'unit' and enclosed within the vault wall ribs. The present lunette design commences above the horizontal string course which defines the apex and spandrels of the lateral windows. Each lunette space is divided into seven vertical units of equal width. The outermost, being severely curtailed by the angle of the wall rib, are left as plain triangles whereas the others have cusped triangular arch heads – the resulting upper triangles left empty. The background walling is left plain. In section it will be seen that the lunette tracery covers the inner surface of the brick wall that supports the roof – the inner brick wall of the vault passage.[60] The tracery simply fills the space forced upon the elevation by the high level of the vault springing against the low level of the window apex, plus the inevitable geometry of the fan vault. The vault lunettes contain the most important structural evidence for the history of the great vault of King's College Chapel, bearing on the exact process by which the existing vault design was chosen and erected. The lunettes in Bays 1–6 N and 1–7 S share a number of structural features not found in the remaining bays. The spandrels of the lateral windows completed by 1485 have been subjected to a degree of recutting and stone replacement that has obscured their original design – for example, the outer rib of the lower cusped lobe has had a small block removed and replaced for no apparent reason. The lunette tracery in each of these bays has been inserted into pre-existing stone facing of a very haphazard build. In most of the bays, there appears to be a slight horizontal bonding break between the tracery base and the lower half of the string course that defines the apex level of the lateral window, a break made more obvious in some bays by a slight change in the colour of the stone. The lunette tracery in Bays 1–6 N and 1–7 S appears to have formed an integral part of the construction of the vault wall rib, that is, the inserted lunette tracery and the wall rib of the present vault appear to be bonded together.[61] The lunettes in Bays 7–12 N and 8–12 S display different structural evidence altogether. The spandrels of the lateral windows are constructed in a more regular fashion, allowing for the structural progression of the vault. The lunette tracery is bonded uniformly into regularly coursed background stonework and the whole lunette forms an integral part of the lateral window bay construction rather than being bonded to the vault wall ribs.

The important structural evidence within the vault lunette spaces indicates two phases of work. The vault lunettes of Bays 7–12 N and 8–12 S were built as integral parts of the lateral window bays, indicating that the profile of the present vault had been determined by the summer of 1508 when work began. It was, however, necessary to go back and alter every lunette space in Bays 1–6 N and 1–7 S in order to insert the blind tracery and this work was carried out only when the vault was under construction from 1512. In Bays 7–12 N and 8–12 S the vault lunettes were ready and waiting by the time the vault campaign commenced. The main structural evidence in favour of an attribution of the design of the present fan vault to Wastell and not to Clerk is the substantial alteration that was necessary in order to convert those bays completed by 1485 under Clerk to accept the existing vault scheme.

Why, though, was it thought necessary to alter the lunettes within the choir bays already completed simply in order to match those of the ante-

60   See F. Mackenzie, '*Observations on the Construction. . . .* Mackenzie's cross-section is a little distorted.

61   Without the benefit of scaffolding to the apex of every bay it is impossible to be dogmatic on this point.

150 King's College Chapel: interior detail, vault lunette Bay 3 N

151 King's College Chapel: interior detail, vault lunette Bay 8 N

chapel? After all, the provision of blind tracery beneath and partly obscured by the swell of the vault cones could hardly have been expected to inject any visual unity into the two separate parts of the building. The choir bays as far as Bay 7 are different in many respects from those in the antechapel and the lunette tracery can only regularize the relationship between the vault and the top-most section of the elevation. But there is the possibility that the provision of tracery within the vault lunettes had formed part of Reginald Ely's first design of *c.* 1448 and that it was revived by Wastell after its total abandonment in the 1470s. The fact that it might now have to be blind tracery and not glazed may be one of the many accidents of the architectural history of the Chapel, though had the original elevational 'platt' survived merely as an ink drawing the difference between glazed and unglazed tracery might have been indistinct by 1508.

Wastell's instructions were explicit. He was to complete the Chapel 'after like fourme and entent as it was ordered and devised' by Henry VI. We have already seen how Wastell complied with the overlaid socle tracery scheme predicted by the Ely vault support VS 7/8 S and the original elevational arrangement of the west wall. Of course, the Will and Intent of 1448 makes no mention of the upper parts of the elevation and certainly has no reference to a clerestory. Thereagain, many of the features of the Chapel as begun by Reginald Ely departed from the instructions from the outset – the number of side closets, the abandonment of the two-storey vestry and the provision of porches, etc. It is quite possible that Ely intended clerestories beneath his original vault scheme and that they were eliminated by Wolryche along with the vault. Clerk had made provision only to reinstate the vault. Perhaps Wastell made a token attempt to restore the clerestory.

Whatever may have led Wastell to the final elevational design of King's College Chapel, it bears a remarkable resemblance to three earlier buildings. The overall panelled effect of an interior rising through several storeys recalls the choir of Gloucester in the most general way. More specifically, the antechapel elevation with its pierced screen socle, tall windows, horizontal stress at apex level and upper tracery within the vault must have looked like a more up-to-date version of the interior of St Stephen's Chapel Westminster, where the socle wall was set back and seen through an open arcade, the windows were tall and square-framed and surmounted by a strong horizontal cornice, above which a glazed clerestory filled the lunette space created by the high springing level of the vault – there even higher up the elevation than at King's. Wastell's addition of blind upper tracery to the choir bays of King's added a third tier to a more severe elevation, with a blank socle and tall window, recalling the side view across the nave of Canterbury Cathedral, conflated to only one dimension. When seen sideways, each bay of the aisle of Canterbury with its blank socle and tall window can be seen framed by the moulded piers and decorated spandrels of the main arcade. Above rises the blank vertical tracery that only becomes a glazed clerestory high up within the vault lunette – indeed three of the nave bays of Canterbury have no glazing at all. It could be that Wastell merely compressed this design for the elevations of King's. Wastell knew the nave at Canterbury extremely well, having worked at the Cathedral since *c.* 1490 and being master mason of the Cathedral Priory from *c.* 1496. Certainly the sharp contrast between the austerity of the aisles of Canterbury seen against the richness of the main arcades was to become a frequent ploy in many of Wastell's later buildings.

152 King's College Chapel:
interior, the great vault

153 King's College Chapel:
interior detail, a Wastell
vault support, VS 7/8 N

If Wastell's elevational scheme marks a return to the Will and Intent of 1448, the design of the high vault certainly does not. The great vault of King's College Chapel is twelve bays long, each 7·37 by 12·6 m. The bays are divided by moulded transverse arches, with roll mouldings responding to the central group of vault shafts on each support. The *152* transverse arches have the same profile as the vault and define the geometry of each bay, that is, the fan cones do not continue 'geometrically' through the transverse arches and into the next bay. The transverse arches were evidently executed before the cones, there being a filling of cement between them and the vault where the two constructions have parted company. At the vault springing level, however, the first four or five courses of the transverse arches and their accompanying vault cones appear to be constructed together in the horizontal corbelling technique known as *tas de charge*. The vault structure is a combination of ribs with *153* rebates for panelled infilling, and cut masonry bands providing the cusped traceried sections. This was a fairly common structural technique and one not only associated with fan vaults; for example, the high lierne vaults of St George's Windsor. Each cone of the fan vault at King's has ribs on major planes – the major ribs define the principal panels, the bounding ribs and the cross axial and axial ridges, whilst the minor ribs define the first panelled tier and the subsequent subdivided tiers. The design is strictly geometrical and contains no ogee curves. Six square-headed panels emerge from every springing point, each with a cusped four-centred arch head. The second tier is a subdivision of the first and every panel contains brattishing as decoration – one foliate unit per panel.

The bounding rib of the second tier is also decorated with brattishing, as are each of the successive bounding ribs. Altogether there are four tiers of panels in every cone, though there is no further subdivision after the first. The cones are separated from each other by cross axial and axial ridges and at no point is the strict geometry of each cone allowed to flow directly into its neighbour. The centre of each bay consists of a spectacular giant boss, resembling some enormous upturned wedding cake. Five-deck Tudor Roses decorated with vertical brattishing alternate with Beaufort Portcullis on a bed of leaves and chains. Both designs are surrounded by a variety of diamond fleurons. *154*

155

The construction of the vault has been examined in great detail over the last century.[62] It is undoubtedly the best-planned, best-cut and best-executed stone vault in England. Like timber roofs of the period, every unit is numbered and given an exact place mark, though, unlike timber roofs, there is unlikely to have been any opportunity for a 'dry run' assembly in the workshop. Any slight deformity of fit or moulding would have to be corrected *in situ* and before the removal of the scaffolding in that bay. Seen from above, the upper surface of the great vault recalls some lunar landscape. If the view from below is striking then the upper aspect is breathtaking. The tiers of blocks step up between the sloping panelled *156* stages and there is remarkably little filling in the vault pockets. The most notable feature is the rise and fall of the cross axial ridges compared with the flatness of the axial ridge. This was partly determined by the geometry necessary in order to cover a rectangular space with a fan vault but it also allowed the vault to be built beneath the earlier roof already existing over the five eastern bays. The rise and fall of the cross axial ridges also allows the crown of the vault to be 0.15 m above the level of the lateral walls. One particular advantage resulting from this form of fan vault *157* structure is that the vault has little lateral thrust, the cones being self butting against each other – it is the inward tension directed towards the central boss ring that ensures the stability, not the external counter buttressing.

The great vault at King's immediately recalls Wastell's earlier crossing vault at Canterbury. The arrangement is slightly different due to the square space to be covered at Canterbury and the consequent employment of eight cones springing from the angles and from the mid points of each wall. The cone pattern is identical in both examples for the first *158* two tiers, two being sufficient for Canterbury. Similarly, the cross axial ridges that separate the cones rise towards the central spandrel, here a belfry trap-door. The decorative motifs are common to both vaults, though the function of the central spandrel at Canterbury eliminates the possibility of a central boss. The Canterbury vault had to be kept as light as possible, there being great concern for the stability of the tower, and this apprehension, coupled with the very different scale of the vault, probably accounts for the slight constructional variations between the two;

62 Mackenzie etc.; Leedy, pp. 140–44, Willis, On the Construction of the vaults. . . ., pp. 43–60.

154 King's College Chapel: interior detail, great vault boss of Tudor Rose

155 King's College Chapel: interior detail, great vault boss of Beaufort Portcullis

156 King's College Chapel: interior above the great vault from west

157 King's College Chapel: interior above the great vault, the vault pocket above Bay 10 N

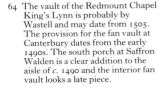

63 F. Woodman, *Canterbury Cathedral*, pp. 187–8.

64 The vault of the Redmount Chapel King's Lynn is probably by Wastell and may date from 1505. The provision for the fan vault at Canterbury dates from the early 1490s. The south porch at Saffron Walden is a clear addition to the aisle of *c.* 1490 and the interior fan vault looks a late piece.

for example, the use of the lighter, brick packing above the webbing at Canterbury. The design of Wastell's vault at Canterbury appears to have been taken directly from that in the south-west tower, designed by Richard Beke *c.* 1458.[63] The crossing vault is larger, with additional cones, and is also highly decorated but the stylistic and organisational parallels are immediately obvious. We know of no other fan vault designed by Wastell before Canterbury, nor are there any other earlier vaults that look particularly like it.[64] The existence of the south-west tower vault in Canterbury and the likelihood that it was chosen by the Cathedral as the model for their new central tower vault would eliminate the need to search for other Wastell 'prototypes'. *159*

The Wastell vaults at King's and Canterbury form a marked contrast with the other great school of fan vaulting in the early sixteenth century – the Windsor–Westminster workshop – and especially with the vault of the Henry VII Chapel at Westminster which is almost an exact contemporary. Structurally, the Westminster vault is built entirely of jointed masonry rather than the mixed rib and panel plus jointed masonry at King's. One result of the construction of the Westminster vault, with the pendants suspended from the overarches, is the degree of lateral thrust created, one requiring significant external buttressing which has had to be augmented by iron tie-bars. The Cambridge vault has little if any lateral thrust. In organisation, the Westminster vault cones crash one into the other the whole length of the straight bays of the chapel – the visual confusion being multiplied by the protruding pendants and

158 Canterbury Cathedral, the central tower: interior vault

159 Canterbury Cathedral, the south-west tower: interior vault

their associated struts. Wastell's vaults are more obviously organised and restrained, with strict bay divisions provided by the transverse arches. *160* The rib pattern at Westminster, being merely incised on the underside of the masonry, was capable of greater adventurism than in the more structural origin of the Cambridge design, and it was probably the desire for richness of pattern at Westminster that determined the choice of constructional technique rather than the other way around. Wastell's Cambridge high vault also consciously avoids the ogee curve, or any of the irregular and angular shapes that form the common vocabulary at Westminster.

The total absence of ogee curves in the high vaults at King's makes the design of the side closet fan vaults very puzzling. The whole of the first tier of panels consists of a series of ogees. The organisation of the small vaults is much as the others except that the central boss is directly in contact with the cross axial and axial ridges. The main deviation from the Wastell 'norm' is the use of ogee main panels in order to achieve the transition from one to two panels within the first tier. From then on, the arrangement returns to the strict geometry expected in a Wastell vault. The occurrence of the ogee panels appears to relate to the lack of springing points available for the ribs – two wall ribs plus one diagonal and one other. Wastell increased this number to seven by means of ogee subdivision. Yet it was Wastell who determined that there should be only four springers to begin with – he consistently cut back the original provision of six responds in all the closets begun prior to 1508 that were now to be fan vaulted rather than covered with rib and lierne. Six springing points would avoid a diagonal, and this omission may have been the reason for Wastell's action. The geometry of the existing fan vault works better, though the first tier does require subdividing to avoid becoming oversized.

160 King's College Chapel: interior detail, the south porch vault

161 King's College Chapel: interior detail, side closet fan vault

The decoration of the side closet fan vaults also moves away from the standard foliate brattishing of the Canterbury example and of the high vault at King's. The side closets have bands of Fleur de Lys and crisply sculptured crosses, which also occur in the more 'regular' fan vaults of *161* the north and south porches.

The side closets 'behind the choir' have simple tierceron vaults with sculptured bosses. These were described in the contract of 1512 as 'coarse work', a distinction drawn between them and the more elaborate and expensive fan vaulting. All the side closet vaults with the exception of those behind Bays 2 and 3 N were erected by Wastell, though those as far west as Bays 6 N and 7 S have wall ribs and half bosses from the earliest campaign by Reginald Ely.

By the beginning of the year 1513 Wastell had turned his attention to the exterior of the Chapel. At least one contract for the external details appears to be missing, that for the upper battlements and for one trial pinnacle, with perhaps a second contract governing the design of the side closet corbel tables. These contracts must have been signed by the Christmas of 1512, for in the Building Accounts dating fortnight to 24 January 1513, payments were made for the corbel tables and in the same month Contract D was signed. The latter related to the building of the remaining pinnacles and to one trial corner tower. The 'battlements' of the side closets and of the porches were included in Contract F of August 1513. The upper battlements were probably built in 1512. They are made up of repeated openwork lozenges, some doubled in height to form merlins. *162* The design is a straightforward reworking of Wastell's battlements on the central tower of Canterbury Cathedral. These had been projected in 1493 but were only built in 1498.[65] The side closet parapets consist of a frieze of diamond lozenges, again some are doubled to form rhythmic 'peaks'. The design calls to mind the minor strainers in the east end of

65 Woodman, pp. 201–8.

162 King's College Chapel: exterior detail, the high battlements

the nave of Canterbury, inserted by Wastell after 1495.

The pinnacles of the major buttresses are panelled on their show side, and have ogee gables and crocketed spirelets. They have been so extensively restored and rebuilt that it is no longer possible to determine which was the pilot considered unsatisfactory. The trial and error system of design was also applied to the corner towers, which are in many ways the oddest feature of the whole Chapel. The Will and Intent of 1448 had laid down precise instructions for the building of a great bell tower as part of the projected cloister to the west of the Chapel. The College certainly possessed a set of bells, some had formed part of the initial gift to the Chapel by Henry VI, and the tower project appears to have been revived in the 1480s, perhaps under Richard III. But in the sixteenth century, no reference was ever made to the possibility of building such a belfry, and its seems to have been accepted by the College that the bells should be housed somewhere within the fabric of the Chapel itself. For this purpose, each of the corner stair turrets was extended in the form of a slim belfry and it is this requirement that has determined their extreme height and fretted design. Contract C details that the towers are to have finials, 'ryfant' or ogee gables, battlements, and 'orbys' or 'cross quaters'. The last two details are clearly alternatives between diamond lozenges and quatrefoils in circles. In the event, both fretted designs were employed; 'cross quaters' in the lower section, with 'orbys' in the upper

163

63 King's College Chapel:
exterior, the north-east
corner stair turret
64 King's College Chapel:
exterior from west

register beneath the 'Tudor' domes. There is therefore some reason to
suggest that the intention in January 1513 was to build the towers only
to the level of their battlements, for all the details referred to in Contract
C occur below that level. Only in the later Contract E, signed in the
following March, is reference made to both 'orbys' and 'cross quaters',
together with 'badges and euery other thyng belongynge to the same . . .'.
The strong implication is that the first tower design was approved and
built without the existing top stage. Once seen, it was decided to make
them higher by the addition of the domed upper stage, which had been
added to the first tower before the March 1513 contract. Once again,
we see the *ad hoc* nature of medieval design and the slow evolution of
major architectural features. The 'Tudor' domes form a curious finial *164*
for such a crocketed and gabled ensemble. They probably owe their
origin to the similar domes of St George's Windsor and to the buttresses
of the Henry VII Chapel at Westminster.

The completion of King's College Chapel

The final additions to the exterior of King's College Chapel were the
two niches flanking the west door. The western entrance to the Chapel
had been planned from the start, though not intended as a major feature

68 King's College Chapel:
sixteenth-century drawing
of exterior north side BM
Cotton MS. Aug. I.i.3

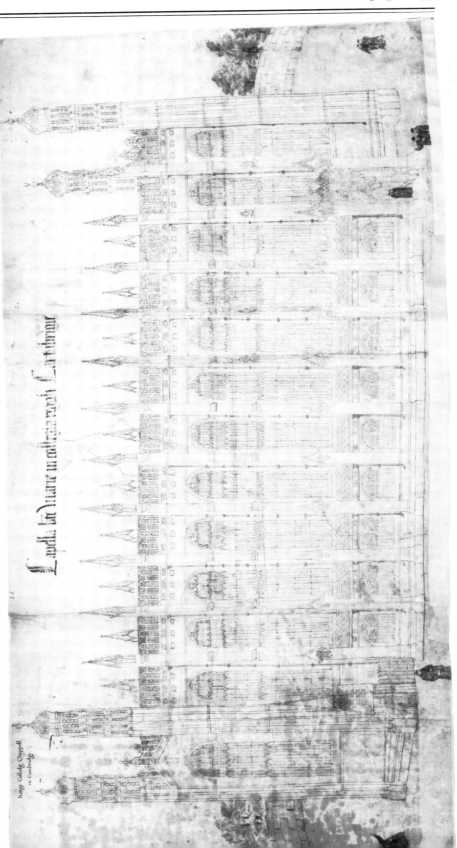

King's College Chapel was in full swing with Richard III eagerly promoting the completion of the entire project as envisaged by Henry VI. Clerk can have had little prospect of sparing time and energy for Walden, and the whole project may have been subcontracted out to Wastell from the start. Whatever happened, work at Walden began at once, and between 1485 and 1490/91 the present south aisle was built and roofed, despite the death of Simon Clerk in *c.* 1489.[75] The nave arcade walls of Saffron Walden were not commenced until 1497, some seven years after the roofing of the south aisle.[76] The elevations show a marked shift *16* away from the austere design of the south aisle, itself a reworking of the north aisle of the 1460s.

Wastell's move to Bury St Edmunds in about 1489 might appear to confirm that a professional link had been forged between him and Clerk over the previous four years.[77] Clerk had been master mason of the great Abbey of St Edmundsbury since *c.* 1445 and Wastell's shift from Cambridge to Bury may denote his appointment to the vacant post. It might equally suggest no more than Wastell taking advantage of a professional gap left by the death of Clerk, whose architectural practice was extensive and whose death must have created something of a commercial vacuum in the town. Wastell's connection with Bury remained strong, despite his extensive commitments in Canterbury and Cambridge, and his continued domicile in Suffolk throughout the rest of his life may have been dictated by some residence clause had he in fact signed a life contract as master mason of the Abbey.[78]

Throughout the 1490s Wastell had been building the central tower of Canterbury Cathedral where he had become master mason for the Priory in 1496. The Canterbury work was probably under way by *c.* 1490 for in a letter of 1493 the Prior, William Sellinge, could write to Cardinal Morton speaking in terms of the completion of the exterior of the tower in the summer of 1494. The Cardinal evidently had second thoughts on the project and caused Wastell to double the height of the tower at a very late stage and this extra work may have prevented Wastell from returning to Walden until 1497.[79]

The central tower of Canterbury Cathedral is Wastell's finest work and the interior vault has many points of comparison with his later vault at King's. The tower vault is supported on capitals decorated with a most unusual motif – a band of diamond fleurons in high relief. Foliate and decorated capitals are rare indeed in late Perpendicular architecture but Wastell consistently employed such forms at Canterbury and in the lower stage of the gate of King's Hall, now Trinity College Cambridge. On considerable stylistic grounds, Wastell can be attributed with the north arcade of Great Barton, Suffolk from *c.* 1490,[80] with the nave arcade walls of Great St Mary's Cambridge, begun after 1494, and of Saffron Walden after 1497, the nave arcade walls of Lavenham begun after 1502 and with *17* the nave of St James' in Bury St Edmunds from 1504. To these may

75　Churchwardens Accounts of Saffron Walden, ff. 136v. 137. 140v. See also Oswald p. 64.

76　*Transactions of the Essex Archaeological Society*, N.S. vol. II 1884, p. 298.

77　Book of John Swaffham Sacrist B.M. Harl. 58 f.97.

78　Recently a single reference to John Wastell has been published in connection with the Abbey but this still does not provide any conclusive evidence as to Wastell's position at Bury St Edmund's. See R. Thompson, The Archives of the Abbey of Bury St Edmund's, *The Suffolk Record Society*, vol. XXI 1980, p. 70.

79　F. Woodman, *Canterbury Cathedral*, pp. 199–211.

80　An estate of the Abbey of Bury St Edmund's.

169 Saffron Walden: interior of nave

170 Lavenham: interior of nave

171 Peterborough Cathedral, the New Buildings: exterior north side

172 King's Lynn, Redmount
Chapel: interior

173 Peterborough Cathedral,
the New Buildings:
interior from south

81 By comparison with the Warham
tomb in Canterbury of 1507,
though the Redmond tomb is
somewhat vulgar in execution.

be added the inner stone chapel of Our Lady Redmount in King's Lynn, possibly in use by 1506, the Redmond tomb in Ely Cathedral between 1501 and 1505,[81] the Warham tomb in Canterbury of 1507 and the New Buildings at Peterborough completed by *c.* 1518, though in this case, Wastell may only have provided the designs for another mason's shop to execute. The Redmount Chapel at Lynn includes a small but significant fan vault, perhaps the earliest actually executed by the Wastell workshop, though the Canterbury fan vault appears to have been conceived as part of the earliest work there from *c.* 1490.

The Wastell style is best seen at Canterbury and Peterborough, where the bare and uncluttered walls form a marked contrast with the richly spreading fan vault. Wastell's work is always sober and thoughtful – the arcades of Walden achieve a cathedralesque grandeur far beyond the 'norm' of parish church architecture. His work is marked by a surface clarity and uncomplicated design. The arrangement and decoration of the various elements is always correct and architectonic and his characteristic restraint is more reminiscent of the Perpendicular style of the fourteenth century than of the fads and fancies of his own day. In this context, Wastell's work at King's stands apart from his usual style. The decision to revive the elaborate antechapel scheme of the 1440s and to decorate further the elevations with heraldry and sculpture must have posed a difficult problem for Wastell. In all his known and attributed buildings, he employed the sharp contrast between decorated and organised surfaces against almost blank areas to great effect; either vaults against blank ashlar as at Canterbury and Peterborough, or elaborate arcade walls seen against blank aisles as at Great St Mary's, Saffron Walden and Lavenham. This is a lesson he appears to have learnt from the nave of Canterbury Cathedral. King's College Chapel was to present no such opportunities – the walls were to be strongly articulated, niches and canopies would introduce arresting detail and diagonal sightlines and the vault was to be arranged and decorated lavishly. Add to that the requirement for furuncular and clambering sculpture and the whole project must have seemed totally alien to a man of Wastell's architectural sensitivity. It is only through his sheer genius and firm hand that the interior of King's did not degenerate into the architectural pantomime of the Henry VII Chapel. By keeping the surfaces as thin and flat as possible, by maintaining the strictest regularity of panelling and vault supports and most of all by the 'banning' of any ogee elements from the interior space, Wastell was able to compensate somewhat for the sheer amount of 'architecture' involved. He may have consoled himself with an elevation and vault relationship that in some way recalled the fourteenth-century interior of the Gloucester choir or the Canterbury nave but was he personally pleased with the result?

Wastell could at least be contented with the certain knowledge that had he not finished the Chapel then it would have been handed over to a Royal mason from the Windsor–Westminster workshop and the outcome would have been very different. In compromising his own style with something of the Court taste as expressed at both Windsor and Westminster, Wastell created what was the most restrained and conservative interior that was possible under the auspices of the Tudor Crown.

Wastell was the leading master mason outside the Royal workshop and manifestly the upholder of an earlier tradition, one hardly touched by the fantastic elaboration of his day. There have been suggestions that, at King's, Wastell was somehow under the artistic control of a group of advisory masons from the Royal shop.[82] Certainly, Henry Redmond and William Vertue visited Wastell and saw the progress of the work and they were undoubtedly well qualified to report back to Henry VII and later to his executors. But neither man can be regarded as Wastell's superior or even his equal. By 1508, Wastell was a well-established architect in his own right, being already master mason of two Cambridge projects and of Canterbury Cathedral, the most important architectural position outside the offices of the King's master masons. He was experienced in many architectural disciplines from parish churches to complicated feats of engineering. Henry Redmond, on the other hand, was still an ordinary working mason at Westminster in 1496 and William Vertue was first named as a master mason only in the early sixteenth century.

82 Harvey pp. 271–72.

While Wastell undoubtedly benefited from his discussions with the younger men (Vertue was at that time building the choir vaults of Windsor), it is difficult to accept that Vertue exercised any practical or aesthetic control over him. The design of the King's vault goes back to 1508 for it is pre-empted in the antechapel elevation while the similar vault at Canterbury may have been designed as early as *c.* 1490. In contrast, the Windsor choir vault from 1506 was to be a mere copy of the earlier nave vault by Robert Janyns while the Henry VII Chapel, on which both men worked, was begun only in 1502. Indeed, it may have been that both royal masters came to Cambridge to seek the advice of Wastell. But even if Vertue and Redmond were junior to Wastell, what of John Lee, the other 'master mason of King's College Chapel' sometimes mentioned in the Building Accounts but never in the contracts? What role, if any, did he play in the architectural history of the Chapel?

John Lee, master mason of King's College Chapel

John Lee, or Alee, first appears as chief mason of King's College in May 1507.[83] No work was then in progress upon the Chapel so his position must have been related to the repair and additions to the College Buildings of the Old Court and to College properties elsewhere. On 1 May 1507, Lee dined in College with Henry Smyth, the Crown agent, and William Vertue, master mason in the service of Henry VII. Conversation doubtless revolved around the King's intention to complete the construction of the great Chapel but Lee's attendance at this dinner may have been more than a polite deference to his evident position in the College, it may also have reflected a personal or professional relationship between the three men. However, when the Chapel project did restart in 1508, it was John Wastell who was appointed as master mason, not John Lee, whilst the important position of Comptroller went to William Swayn, who had worked previously for Wastell at King's Hall in the 1490s and who may have been a permanent member of the Wastell workshop.[84] In the next year, 1509, Swayn was transferred to the new building at Christ's College, where he appears to have been at least the chief mason, perhaps carrying out designs 'bought in' from Wastell. In May 1509, John Lee was paid for the first time as joint master mason with Wastell on the King's College Chapel payroll, receiving the same annual salary. As a master mason, Lee was obviously considered capable of designing fabric and of organising its construction, but the Building Accounts for the Chapel reveal that his services, such as they were, were connected entirely with the purchasing of supplies. Between August 1509 and March 1512 Lee was paid on eleven occasions for purveyor's costs and once as a reward. Until February 1512, he was always called John Alee, whereas from that month onwards he was called simply Mr Lee. On

83 King's College Muniments Mundum Book, vol. IX, 1506/07.

84 For the career of Swayn see Oswald, pp. 258–9.

seven occasions, the purveyor's costs were to Lee alone and the sums never exceeded £2 5s. On the other four he was paid along with others, including £5 shared between Lee and Thomas Larke the master surveyor, on 16 March 1511. Lee was never paid purveyor's costs in association with Wastell. He received at least one reward, £1 18s on 11 May 1511. On the other hand, Henry Semark, Wastell's warden of the masons at King's and another member of the workshop, received purveyor's costs and rewards on at least fifteen occasions between 12 May 1510 and 1 July 1515, twice sharing £7 reward with Thomas Larke and Robert Worlyche. Wastell was also paid purveyor's cost seven times between 7 December 1511 and 30 July 1514; in the latter instance the money was shared with his son Thomas. Although John Lee's payments cease after mid-March 1512, his annual salary of £13 6s 8d continued to be paid until July 1515 and his name occurs on the list of expenditure drawn up on the twentieth of that month. However, Lee was not included in any of the contracts for the completion of the building at King's nor was he to share in any of the profits. In the agreement between Wastell and Semark regarding the building of the high vault, it was Semark and Wastell's son Thomas who were to complete the vault if necessary and to divide the profit in the event of Wastell's death. It is in this agreement that we are left in no doubt that it is John Wastell who alone did 'rule the work'. Why then was Lee employed upon the project? Almost certainly Lee owed his position as joint master mason to two factors; Wastell's age and the death of Henry VII. Wastell was old, perhaps in his sixties, and from the deep and unusual concern expressed repeatedly in the various contracts, he was unwell. If anything happened to Wastell after the decision to recommence the Chapel project in 1508, the King, and later his executors, would want some guarantee that a capable master mason would take over and finish the job. It may have been the death of Henry VII in April 1509 that eventually prompted his executors, now responsible for the project, to insist upon the appointment of a joint master mason which occurred just a few weeks later. However, once all the designs were agreed, Wastell was free to appoint his own warden, Semark, and in one case his own son as personal guarantors, thus keeping the whole project and its anticipated profits within his workshop and family. Lee was excluded from all these agreements and, apart from his annual salary, he was not paid purveyor's costs after March 1512. Lee was not present when Wastell dined with William Vertue in College a few months later on 30 July.

John Lee does not appear to have taken any active part in the building of King's College Chapel after March 1512, though the payment of his salary in each of the subsequent years does suggest that he was still 'available' in Cambridge.[85] Perhaps he had received the permission of the College to attend to another, more profitable, project – possibly the overall plan and some of the detailed design work for the new college of St John's.

85 Between 1511 and 1515 Lee was given commons on three occasions; Wastell on eleven including once with his son.

174 Cambridge, St John's
College: drawing of the
Fisher tomb from Willis
and Clark

Lee disappears from the King's accounts after July 1515 and next appears
in Cambridge in association with the building of the Fisher tomb and
Chantry Chapel at St John's in 1524. St John's College was the second
foundation of Lady Margaret Beaufort and the 'brain child' of her Confessor, St John Fisher. The College buildings had been under way from
1510 and the Chapel was completed in 1516.[86] In 1524, Fisher decided
to build a small Chantry on the north side of the Chapel to contain a
tomb for himself. The 'Master Mason of Ely' was paid for drawing a
'draught of the tomb and for his advice on the chapel'.[87] Later, the master
mason is referred to as 'Master Lee, the freemason'.[88] Thus we find Lee
in the process of designing the Fisher monument and, as suggested by
the wording, the chapel as well. The monument was finally set up in
1532/3, when Lee was paid for the work.[89] The tomb was of course never
occupied – St John Fisher went to the block in 1535 – and the tomb
was stored in sections until 1733 when it as thrown out. Fortunately,
the noted architect James Essex spotted the rejected fragments and made
a pencil sketch of them, which he sent to the Cambridge Antiquarian,
William Cole. Unfortunately, Cole inked over the sketch in order to pre-
serve it and the result is somewhat inept. Nevertheless, the monument   *17*
can be seen to have been fully Renaissance in character, with antique
pilasters at the angles, egg and dart borders, wreaths and classical figures
supporting memorial plaques.[90] This monument was designed by Lee
in 1524 and is therefore amongst the earliest Renaissance works in this
country. More significant still, it is perhaps the first work in the new
style that can be attributed definitely to an Englishman, the earlier works
at Westminster and Hampton Court being by Italians. The Fisher tomb
is fully fledged Renaissance and Lee must have spent a considerable time

86 For the history of St John's see
Willis and Clark, vol. II,
pp. 231–350.

87 Ibid., p. 282.
88 Ibid., p. 283.

89 Ibid.

90 Ibid., p. 286. and B.M. Add. MS.
5846.

175 Canterbury Cathedral, the
Christ Church Gate:
exterior detail

studying the new style and may even have travelled to France or Italy
in order to do so.

The Fisher Chapel designed to house the tomb was totally Gothic and
from the one remaining arch reset in the present Victorian chapel, the
style and complicated mouldings mark it as a product of the Windsor–
Westminster workshop.[91] There can be little doubt that John Lee
designed both works, which would provide him with a court workshop
background to add to his thorough knowledge of the new Italian style.
The juxtaposition of Renaissance and Gothic that would have been
evident within the Fisher Chantry recalls the still existing state of the
Henry VII Chapel at Westminster, but there, two workshops with totally
different backgrounds, nationalities and training were responsible for the
cultural clash, whereas Lee clearly wished to combine the two traditions.
The only contemporary comparable combination would be the Christ
Church Gate in Canterbury, completed *c.* 1519, where a frantically Perpendicular facade is treated to antique pilasters, capitals and bases.[92]

175

91 The central arch from the Chantry
is now in the Victorian Antechapel
of St John's.

92 A product of the Windsor–
Westminster workshop, see
Woodman, *Canterbury Cathedral*,
pp. 211–19.

The mouldings of the Fisher Chapel link Lee directly with the Windsor–Westminster workshop of Henry VII. The tomb suggests that his links with the Court continued till at least 1520 when the Torrigiano fittings were all complete. The mouldings at St John's may also provide some further information on the previous work of John Lee, for the south transept of Holy Trinity Cambridge combines identifiable Westminster mouldings with tracery patterns directly related to the lateral windows of King's College Chapel. The transept was built between *c.* 1504 and 1508, a time when Lee was chief mason of King's College. He is the only master mason known to have been working in Cambridge at that time with connections both at King's and Westminster, and Holy Trinity may now represent his earliest surviving work.

Ely Cathedral provides the remaining evidence for the life and work of John Lee. From the St John's accounts of 1524 we see that Master Lee was master mason for the cathedral, a post he still held in 1532. He is always referred to as Master Lee, as indeed he was in the later references at King's. [93] Ely Cathedral saw two major projects during the 1520s and 1530s – the cloister was rebuilt, though perhaps never finished, and the West Chantry was constructed within the eastern bay of the south aisle of the retrochoir. Little is known of the cloister other than what can be seen today. The remains suggest a Windsor–Westminster product. The West Chantry is relatively complete and is usually dated *c.* 1520–30, though the inscription over the door is dated 1534. In many ways, the West Chantry is the offspring of the exotic Alcock Chantry opposite. It employs the same idea of creating walls from tiers of niches and of using their canted sides to conjure a chaotic confusion of surfaces and shadows. All the minuscule mouldings are tiny versions of favourite   17 Windsor–Westminster profiles. The vault is a mesh of diamonds and triangles, a crystallised pattern drawn from the Spätgothic vaults of northern Germany.[94] This extraordinary design has only one English   17 parallel, the south niche vault of the west door of King's College Chapel, inserted after July 1515, and it is this link that confirms that the Master Lee of Ely is the same Master Lee who was joint master mason of King's College Chapel with John Wastell.

The whole feeling of the West Chantry in Ely Cathedral may be late Gothic at its most bizarre, but the decoration is pure Renaissance. Inscriptions in antique Roman letters, putti, swags, urns and all the fashionable motifs of the early Renaissance are stuck in between the vault ribs and the wall canopies. Unlike the Fisher Chantry of 1524/25, Lee has integrated the two opposing decorative traditions at Ely into a style that is recognisably that of the early English Renaissance. True, as the Reformation broke, the more 'Gothic' elements began to fade along with medieval Catholicism, and the 'new' ideas became more dominant, but

93 Lee should not be confused with John a Lee, Yeoman to the King *c.* 1526 nor with Richard Lee, Clerk of the Star Chamber in 1527, nor with Richard Lee, Page of the King's Cup in 1528, nor Ric Lee, a clerk in Wolsey's household in 1529, nor with Richard Lee, master mason for Wolsey in 1529 and for Cromwell in 1535.

94 Triradial vaults occur as early as *c.* 1350 in the Aerey Porch at Windsor. See also the west tower of St Michael Coslany Norwich, in building in 1424 and the pulpitum of Canterbury Cathedral *c.* 1452.

the Perpendicular content of English design throughout the sixteenth century never disappeared completely, and even managed something of a revival in the seventeenth century. It might be argued that the Perpendicular of Tudor England assimilated the 'new' and together they were to create an English style set apart from the mainstream of the Northern European Renaissance.

The dawn of the English Renaissance

Lee's work at St John's and at Ely is of enormous significance to the tracing of the origins of the English Renaissance style. Unlike Wastell, who died *c.* 1518, Lee was confronted increasingly by clients demanding works in a new and alien style. The whole concept of art and architecture was changing rapidly and Lee, and doubtless many others, was forced to accommodate these changes or go out of business. The only way to prevent a flood of foreign artists and architects was to take them on at their own game, though the artificers of London scored a victory by getting an act of Parliament in 1529, limiting the privileges of 'alien' craftsmen in the capital city.[95] English artists and architects were therefore forced to study and copy the existing Renaissance work in England and possibly, to travel abroad to see others. Torrigiano and company had built a few tombs, an altarpiece and some decorative roundels. Modern patrons, many of whom had been to France and Italy in the service of the Court, now required houses and palaces with walls and ceilings in the new style, but notably not churches. The quantity of Renaissance design available for inspection in England *c.* 1520 was still limited, and clearly other sources were considered. As early as *c.* 1507 Italian terra-

95 21 Henry VIII *c.* 16. See S. Lehmberg, *The Reformation Parliament*, Cambridge 1970, p. 97.

96 A fragment of a Renaissance terracotta figurine was recovered from a Norwich house site burnt in 1507. See A. Carter *et al.*, Excavations in Norwich 1973, Norwich Survey, Third Interim Report *Norfolk Archaeology* 36, 1973, p. 47 and n. The figurine is thought to be north Italian and *c.* 1490.

97 F. Woodman, *Canterbury Cathedral*, pp. 216–17.

cotta figurines were imported into England[96] and from 1511, new Brussels tapestries were set up in Canterbury Cathedral – late Gothic scenes in Renaissance architectural frames.[97] Undoubtedly, tapestries account for a considerable importation of Renaissance decorative motifs as well as providing illustrations of whole buildings, including some highly improbable ones that were not at all Italian but usually Flemish 'versions' often misunderstood and naïve. The second-hand nature of this vital source material is of considerable importance in the development of English Renaissance design and may explain something of its peculiarity. As in the West Chantry at Ely, where a 'German' late Gothic vault could be decorated with 'antique' designs within a Perpendicular chapel, the English show a remarkable propensity to mix styles, sometimes with little or no discretion. The desire was for novelty and not particularly for the Italianate. True, patrons of great sophistication and education, such as the King, may have developed a taste for things specifically Florentine, but for the rest, the key-word was variety. Just as the late Gothic style in England had turned ever more fantastic, so the Renaissance, albeit from a garbled Flemish recipe, could provide an extra zest to the mixture. It was the proverbial English diet of 'Spaghetti and Chips'.

The West Chantry is hardly a real building. Its architecture is almost entirely non-structural and its belongs to that long list of 'fantastic' overgrown ornaments that once littered the churches of England. Such closet chapels were being built right up to the end of the Middle Ages – some never to be occupied by tombs nor used for Chantry purposes.[98] The continuing fashion for such structures is in sharp contrast with the state of major church building. The completion of the fabric of King's College Chapel marks not just the end of that important project but, in a wider sense, the termination of major church building in medieval England. All the great royal church buildings had drawn to a close – the Henry VII Chapel at Westminster was finished, Windsor had abandoned its central tower, only Bath Abbey continued tinkering away at their interminable rebuilding.[99] This is not to suggest that all areas of construction came to a standstill but the architecture of England post-1515 takes a remarkable turn away from the ecclesiastical and towards the domestic. The great patrons of the new reign were not interested in founding friaries or rebuilding abbeys. Even ecclesiastics like Wolsey built colleges and palaces, but not churches. The shift away from church patronage is demonstrated in the Henry VII Chapel, an act of political expediency as much as religious piety. The architecture of the Windsor–Westminster workshop speaks a domestic language and it was a style capable of almost every use. The whole concept of the 'buckled wall' employed in the aisles of the Chapel originated in a domestic building.[100] Wastell's style, on the other hand, is hardly conceivable in a domestic context.

Other forces came into play. Many of the great English churches had been rebuilt and revamped recently and were not in need of any further

98 For example, the Longland Chantry, Lincoln.

99 Finished only in the nineteenth century.

100 The Henry VII Tower at Windsor.

rebuilding. The sheer cost of such work had also passed beyond the means of all but the richest patrons and institutions – costs doubled due to inflation during the reign of Henry VIII prior to 1540. Even the building of more modest parish churches was grinding down, except that is in the wool-rich eastern counties and over in the west, where bourgeois patronage was pumped into great glass-house churches. Yet even in these cases, the level of patronage wavered and fell after 1515 and many of the grandoise schemes held fire for decades before their final completion.

The decline in ecclesiastical patronage is especially noticeable amongst the hierarchy. The bishops and abbots of the late fifteenth and early sixteenth centuries now set about their own comfort with a vigour once reserved for loftier aspirations. Morton and Alcock of Ely rebuilt all their palaces and the latter founded a college in Cambridge by suppressing a nunnery.[101] Neither added much to their cathedral church save for Alcock's showy tomb chapel. By the reign of Henry VIII all the palaces of the archbishops of Canterbury had been rebuilt or greatly extended and refurbished at enormous expense, while the major additions to the monasteries of England at this time were the spacious abbot's houses like Castle Acre, Thame Park and Forde Abbey. Lady Margaret Beaufort felt no compunction in suppressing Creake Abbey in Norfolk to form part of her endowment of Christ's College Cambridge, and Wolsey suppressed several more in order to finance his colleges at Ipswich and Oxford. Thus the pattern of dissolution for financial gain, albeit philanthropic to begin with, was well established long before the major onslaught upon the English monasteries began. But it was not the Dissolution that brought about the end of major church building in England, it was the change of taste amongst the great patrons and their shift in interest towards education and investment in their own private luxury, all of which can be observed from the earliest years of the Tudor dynasty.

In the last quarter of the fifteenth century there had been a notable rise in domestic architecture. The Wars of the Roses had acted as a restraint upon such spending but the peace following the death of Henry VI and, more particularly, the arrival of the Tudors in 1485 had encouraged the building of new houses that were recognisably more 'modern' than their predecessors. True, many were still castle-like in appearance with gatehouses, turrets, and moats but few could have withstood a siege, particularly against artillery. The major revolutionary factor in the new wave of building was brick, though there were other influences at work that denote changes of taste, living standards and social expectations. We might for example contrast two great houses; Penshurst Place from the fourteenth century and Sutton Place from *c.* 1525. Penshurst is a sprawl, apparently unplanned, where rooms and wings were stuck on as and when required. The core is the hall range, the central living space for the whole household. Thus the hall is large and lofty and consequently cold, the only heating being an open central hearth. Immediately to the *178*

101 For the history of Jesus College see Willis and Clark, vol. II, pp. 115–83.

178 Penshurst Place
179 Sutton Place

east lies the service range, kitchen, buttery and pantry, separated from the hall only by the screens passage that traverses the block. To the west and beyond the high table is an upper chamber or solar, the only private room of note for the family. The central core block is eccentrically planned and the elevations differ from room to room as appropriate. The living arrangements were as unsophisticated as they were uncomfortable and all the architectural details were derived from contemporary ecclesiastical models.

Sutton Place belongs to a different world. The building is rigidly symmetrical. The original entrance facade balanced matching end blocks with stepped gables and identical windows either side of a great axial gatehouse, now lost. Within the regular courtyard, all the elements were balanced from side to side and the main axial line extended straight through the hall range. All the facades are two storeyed despite the fact that the hall remains as a single space the full internal height of the block. *17*
Thus from within the hall, one sees two tiers of windows superimposed. The insistent axial line causes the main entrance to the hall to be placed some way along the side wall and not at one end of the service screens. Immediately, we see that the hall has lost its pre-eminence as the principal living space. The screens passage has become no more than a vestibule to a magnificent stair and, with a special dining chamber, the service relationship between the screens passage and the hall is redundant. The hall and many of the additional rooms are heated by brick fireplaces and stacks. By the sixteenth century specialised rooms for dining, sleeping and sitting were making their appearance, due largely to the introduction of more efficient heating and draft-proof panelling. The multiplication of small, specialised rooms led to the development of living space on several floors, with the advantage of the maximum use of each chimney stack. The shift towards smaller, more private rooms occurred coincidentally with, or was perhaps propelled by, the new ideas and living standards emanating from France and Italy.

Attitudes were changing rapidly amongst most of the English 'building classes'. Many people were becoming richer, particularly those in the

102   From Wool merchants in the
fifteenth century the Springs
achieved great wealth and were
granted arms in 1525. They
married into the de Vere family,
the Earls of Oxford. In the
Subsidy Returns of 1528 the
Springs were the wealthiest
burgers outside London.

wool trade, and one-time small families began to buy themselves up the social ladder – the Springs of Lavenham are an often quoted example.[102] Suddenly, many families had a lot of money and much of this cash was devoted to the building of town and country houses. Yet more went on the new fashion for collecting. The Italian Renaissance saw a great revival in the collecting of objects for their own sake; Classical bronzes and marbles, books, paintings, and contemporary sculpture. England's Classical inheritance was long spent but patrons eagerly bought contemporary art objects such as tapestries, books, paintings and terracottas. The early sixteenth century also saw a marked rise in the number of London booksellers encouraged by the recent introduction of the printing press, while artists like Holbein were fully booked painting the members of the English Court. The mania for collecting and displaying newly acquired objects itself prompted a change in house design. 'Galleries', some of them 'long', became fashionable after the manner of Wolsey's Hampton Court and sometimes whole rooms were decked out as art objects in themselves; e.g. the Wolsey Closet in the same Palace. Nothing could have been further from the sparse wilderness presented by the great houses of an earlier epoch.

Many of these new ideas are reflected in the architecture of Sutton Place. The tracery, jamb mouldings and some of the panelled decoration on the exterior may look back to the High Middle Ages, but the facades are also littered with Renaissance scrolls and strapwork patterns, putti in terracotta and classical base mouldings. By 1525, English domestic architecture was developing fast – symmetrical planning and often symmetrical elevations, a more specialised room use which led to the employment of several storeys and hence led to the development of the great stair, the acceptance of brick as an architectural mode and the intermingling of Italianate details with a native but increasingly sterile repertoire. Such 'combination' buildings occur widely before the Dissolution – Hampton Court, Layer Marney, Hengrave, etc. When the total Dissolution of the monasteries finally came late in the 1530s, prompting the great house building boom for those lucky or wealthy enough to benefit, the style and planning for these houses was already available and in current use. It was not a style born of the event.

Education was the other main beneficiary of the change in patronage during the early decades of the sixteenth century. Many of the generation educated at Oxford and Cambridge in the new colleges of the fifteenth century now held major offices of church and state and they wished to devote their financial resources to the founding of yet more colleges. The principal motive still appears to have been religious, though not necessarily strictly orthodox. The period saw a rash of new colleges at both centres; Magdalen Oxford 1458, St Catherine's Cambridge 1473, Jesus Cambridge 1497, Christ's Cambridge 1505, Brasenose Oxford 1509, St

John's Cambridge 1510, Corpus Christi Oxford 1516 and Christ Church Oxford, originally Cardinal College, founded in 1517. All were founded by bishops of clergy, or in the case of Christ's and John's, by Lady Margaret Beaufort at the instigation of St John Fisher. The architecture of these foundations differs little from the great houses of the period, though the plan and elevations are more formal architecturally, and for community reasons the great hall and chapel remain dominant features. This group of colleges was just too early, or perhaps in the case of Oxford too conservative, to feel the full impact of the new 'antique'. The quasi-monastic origin of such foundations continued to be expressed particularly through a central cloister as at Jesus Cambridge[103] and at Magdalen and Christ Church Oxford. St John's Cambridge, however, foreshadows the great Elizabethan houses still to come – brick built and consequently vernacular in spirit, formally laid out yet homely in scale. More notably, and rare amongst foundations of the time, John's converted a modest existing building for their Chapel and placed upon it no special architectural emphasis.

Oxbridge College building was the one element of medieval patronage that was to survive and indeed flourish in Post-Reformation England; at Cambridge Magdalen refounded 1542, Trinity amalgamated in 1546, Caius 1557, Emmanuel 1584 and Sidney Sussex in 1594, at Oxford St John's and Trinity 1555, Jesus 1571, Wadham 1610 and Pembroke 1624.

The building projects prior to the Reformation, the colleges, chantries and the country houses that began to dot the English landscape, all required master masons or architects. As far as is known, John Wastell did not design anything domestic, he belonged to a generation old enough to enjoy a purely ecclesiastical career. John Lee, however, living at least into the 1530s, probably found himself faced with the problems of transferring from one discipline to another. Possibly he had been the initial designer of St John's Cambridge.[104] Nearby, Hengrave Hall, built between 1525 and 1538, illustrates how quickly things changed, becoming as it does more Renaissance as it progressed, though still displaying direct quotes from the last campaign at King's College Chapel. It shows *180* the same combination of Perp. and Renaissance as the Fisher tomb and chantry of John's, and at the same date. It is another building by Lee?[105] The great mansions of the pre-Dissolution era point to the inevitable. The grabbing of the vast monastic estates for financial and political gain led eventually to a mass emigration of the 'new gentry' out of the towns and into the healthier and more profitable countryside. The Court had always combined town and country, originally out of necessity, and this was emphasised by the extensive Palace building programmes of both Henry VII and Henry VIII.[106] The cessation of the civil turmoil in 1485 had also encouraged the great landowners to adapt or rebuild their existing castles into splendid houses, each surveying their extensive domains.

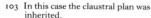
103 In this case the claustral plan was inherited.

180 Hengrave Hall, main entrance

104 The Gatehouse vault of St John's is often attributed to Wastell, indeed it does have a general similarity. The closest parallel would be the fan vault in the west tower of Fotheringhay of 1529. In view of Lee's later association with the design work at St John's it might be safely assumed that it was he who provided the original plan and some of the detailed work.

105 Such as the blind tracery on the turrets and the Tudor domes. For Hengrave see Sir J. Summerson, *Architecture in Britain 1530–1830*, Harmondsworth 1953, pp. 39–42.

106 Greenwich and Richmond by Henry VII, Bridewell, Nonsuch, Hampton Court, Whitehall and the post-Reformation Manors such as York and Canterbury by Henry VIII.

As private wealth grew and more of the bourgeoisie were elevated into the minor gentry, pressure for land in the country escalated. Kitson, the builder of Hengrave, was a London banker; the Westons of Sutton Place were very minor gentry promoted by the Duke of Suffolk; while the Marney's of Layer Marney were 'first generation nobility'.

The Dissolution of the monasteries may have been the greatest act of vandalism in the nation's history but it was not the decisive blow that put an end to major church building after more than five centuries – that had already been brought about by more peaceful and mundane circumstances. Instead, the Dissolution unleashed land and capital that created a new wave of architectural enterprise and patrons who would carry English building into the Elizabethan Renaissance and beyond. The completion of King's College Chapel in 1515 marked the pivotal point in this transformation. It was the end of medieval architecture as dominated by the Church. Never again would King or prelate embark upon such acts of religious devotion. It was as if the entire nation breathed a great sigh of relief that it was finally all over. The 'New men' of the sixteenth century were more interested in providing for their immediate comfort and for the intellectual advancement of their offspring. King's College Chapel reaches across this historic divide – the fabric, the stone, bricks and mortar belong the medieval traditions of building for the repose of souls. But the sixteenth-century glass and fittings that brought the Chapel to life are a glorification of the living and belong to a new humanistic age that had little time for priests and none for Purgatory.

REPAIRS TO THE FABRIC
POST-1515

All references pre-1885 from Willis and Clark. Post-1885 by courtesy of Rattee and Kett, Cambridge.

1579/80 3 pinnacles repaired.

1591/2 Bay 12 N window mullions replaced in Weldon. Clock and pinnacles repaired.

1606/7 General repair to exterior stonework.

1611 Bay 1 paved in tile.

1613/14 General repair of window mullions.

1614/15 New west door (existing). Marble and Ragg floor laid in a strip from Bay 11 to west door.

1634 New screen in Bay 2 (lost).

1636/7 General repair to battlements.

1661 Battlements at west end repaired in Ketton.

1669 Repairs to towers at west end.

1702 New marble floor laid in choir bays, except in Bay 1. Old choir floor relaid in antechapel.

1754–57 £400 on repairs to four corner towers and battlements.

1757–65 General repair and some replacement of window mullions.

1770 £300 for new antechapel floor.

1774 £400 from Lord Godolphin for Portland floor in antechapel.

1775 Paving of Bays 1 to 3. New altar set against east wall. Gothic panelling of sanctuary by James Essex.

1785–87 Repairs to porch battlements. £275 spent on 'repairing', that is replacing the porch heraldry.

1811 Battlements repaired by Wilkins.

1817 Clock removed from NE tower. Passage removed from east window of closet Bay 2 N and tracery restored 'in statu quo'.

1828 Bay 1 S exterior repaired and scar of intended east range of old court removed at a cost of £750.

1841 Bay 1 S window extended to full length.

1860–63 Repair to roof timbers, replacement of some, iron tie rods introduced. All under direction of G. G. Scott.

1875/6 14 pinnacles replaced. Battlements of Bays 7 and 8 S rebuilt. West door jambs renewed. All by Scott.

1885–93 Battlements repaired and renewed under J. L. Pearson.

1889 Eastern choir bays panelled by T. Garner (lost).

1910 Eastern choir bays panelled by Detmar Blow (lost).

1930-?   Battlements and pinnacles repaired with artificial stone.
1939   Attempt to clean Chapel thwarted by War. Glass removed.
1948   Corner towers repaired.
1964   Panelling removed from sanctuary bays.
1968   Chapel interior cleaned. Repairs to heraldic beasts and ciphers in
         Caen. Lowering of sanctuary floor and return to 1702 paving design
         within choir bays. Rubens altarpiece introduced.
1973-   Semi-complete replacement of battlements and pinnacles in Clip-
         sham. Corbel tables repaired and replaced in Weldon.

OCCURRENCE OF YORKSHIRE OGEE TRACERY IN ENGLAND

Bedfordshire
  Leighton Buzzard

Cambridgeshire
  Cambridge: King's College Chapel from 1476
             Holy Trinity Church *c.* 1505
             Trinity College Chapel *c.* 1547
  Marholm *c.* 1530
  Peterborough Cathedral, *c.* 1478 and 1515
  Thriplow

Essex
  Dedham *c.* 1492

Gloucestershire
  Northleach

Hertfordshire
  Possibly old west front of St Alban's Cathedral

Lincolnshire
  Addlethorpe
  Boston *c.* 1428
  Burgh le Marsh
  Croyland *c.* 1430
  Folkingham
  Glentham
  Lincoln Cathedral *c.* 1480 and 1540
  Moulton
  Spalding
  Tattershall *c.* 1450

Norfolk
  Belaugh
  Blofield *c.* 1440
  Broome
  Cawston *c.* 1440
  Cressingham, Great *c.* 1460–1500
  Dunham, Great
  Fakenham *c.* 1447/9

Feltwell
Foulsham *c.* 1460–70
Griston *c.* 1447
Heydon *c.* 1469
Hingham
Ingham *c.* 1456
Kimberly *c.* 1536–1631
King's Lynn, St Margaret *c.* 1460
Martham
Mattishall *c.* 1445
Norwich: St Andrew's *c.*1500
            St Clement *c.* 1475
            St George Colegate *c.* 1475
            St Michael Coslany *c.* 1500
            St Peter Mancroft *c.* 1445
            St Stephen's *c.* 1500–50
            Blackfriars *c.* 1440–50
Overstrand
Pickerton, North
Repps, North *c.* 1475
Repps, South *c.* 1450
Roughton
Saham Toney
Stradsett
Swaffham *c.* 1460
Walpole St Andrew *c.* 1430–63
Walpole St Peter *c.* 1423–30
Wiveton *c.* 1430–90

Northamptonshire
   Buckby, Long
   Newnham
   Watford
   Welton

Oxfordshire
   Oxford, Merton College Chapel *c.* 1418–24
   Sutton Courtenay *c.* 1450 (was in Berks.)

Shropshire
   Battlefield east window as rebuilt after 1550

Suffolk
   Bury St Edmunds, St James, *c.* 1504
   Barton, Great *c.* 1520
   Eye *c.* 1470
   Herringfleet
   Hollesley
   Lowestoft
   Sudbury, St Gregory

Yorkshire

York: Minster *c.* 1400

St Crux *c.* 1402 (lost)

St Denys *c.* 1450

St Martin le Grand *c.* 1416–37

Old East Riding:

Beverly, St Mary *c.* 1445

Bridlington

Driffield, Great

Hull, *c.* 1417

Patrington

Old West Riding:

Aldborough

Bradford St Peter (lost) *c.* 1430–58

Hatfield

Ripon Minster *c.* 1512

Rotherham *c.* 1480

Others

The west window of Kingsbury Episcopi, Somerset, appears to be the only example of this tracery type in the West Country. It was built *c.* 1470–90 by Bishop Stillington of Bath and Wells (a Yorkshireman), and Keeper of the Privy Seal for Edward IV. The east window of Northleach Gloucestershire, occurs in the group almost by accident. The design called for mouchettes within the apex which has coincidentally created an unresolved ogee coupling of the two central tracery lights below. Possibly it is drawn from Merton College Chapel example as Northleach is close to Oxford. The east window of St Mary on the Hill, Chester, appears to be a totally nineteenth-century invention. The church at Battlefield, Shropshire, fell into decay after the Reformation and was extensively rebuilt as a parish church after *c.* 1550.

THE ROOF

The roof of King's College Chapel is divided into twelve bays by pairs of principals with collars and arch braces. Secondary pairs subdivide each bay. The design employs double butt purlins each provided with slight wind braces which spring from both the major and minor principals. The braces are not pegged into the purlins but are merely 'slipped in' from above. There are seven common rafters between each principal. There is no ridge piece. The major wall posts are lodged on stone buttress piers, their bases now buried in the fan vault fill. The minor wall posts sit directly against the walls.

The design, with pairs of principals but no connecting base tie beams, has caused some considerable structural problems as the feet have tended to spread. The omission of ties from the original construction of *c.* 1480 probably indicates that the vault proposal then current required a thickness of packing above the webbing such that the apex would rise above the level of the lateral wall plates. The actual fan vault as built in the sixteenth century is flat enough to allow for the provision of base ties.

The roof was constructed in two phases: the first eleven pairs from the east

181 King's College Chapel: interior of roof Bays 11 and 12

1 See p. 119.

2 Ibid.

3 See p. 166.

end up to and including those in Bay 5, were built from 1480 as part of the 'second campaign' of the Chapel. In April of that year, a parchment was bought for Martin Prentice, master carpenter, on which to draw the roof.[1] By this time, the vault proposal appears to have been reinstated. From May onwards, timber was selected and felled in Stanstead Park and Walden.[2] Tree felling for the roof was still in progress during the spring of 1483, whilst Simon Clerk's continuous attendance at King's from January to May of that year probably covers the period of its erection *in situ*. The roof over the five eastern bays of the Chapel was finished before August 1484 when glazing work began at the east end.

The early design set out the guidelines that were followed in the later Tudor campaign, though the 1480s roof is slightly more decorative. The principals have double order chamfers, while the shoulders for the butt purlins are mitred. The wind braces are tiny and can have little practical value. The wall plates were replaced in 1860.

The common rafters of both periods of the work have curious 'open' tenons at their apices, giving the appearance of mortice and tenons made for a roof of steeper pitch, cut out and repegged for re-use within the flatter profile of the present roof. Similarly, the third major pair from the east has mortices for a far larger arch brace design than that actually employed.

The second period of roof construction was projected in the summer of 1509 and 144 oaks were felled in Wetherfield Park in the year following.[3] The plumbers' costs reach a peak in September 1510 and the lead purchases for that year alone represent half the total expenditure upon lead for the entire Tudor campaign. The brick employed in the supporting walls was paid for from May 1511, which suggests that a great deal of preparatory work was necessary before the final placement of the roof.

The 'second' roof was constructed by Richard Russell, the King's master carpenter at Westminster. The design follows the earlier construction, though the principals are plainer and more robust, having abandoned the double chamfers. Despite restorations in the nineteenth century under Scott, the roof of King's College Chapel remains one of the finest and largest late medieval roofs in England.

THE LAST CAMPAIGN – CONTRACTS

Contract A. *Draft contract for building the stone roof of King's College Chapel. 4 Henry* viij*, about May,* 1512

This indenture made the   day of   in the iiij[th] yere of the Regn of our souerain lord kyng Herry the viij[t] betwyne M' Robert Hacumblen provost of the Kynges College Royall at Cambryge and the scolers of the same with the advise and agrement of M' Thomas Larke surveyour of the kynges workes there on the oon partye, And John Wastell M' Mason of the said workes and Herry Semerk oon of the wardens of the same on the other partye witnesseth

that hit is couenaunted bargayned and agreed betwyn the partyes aforsaid that the said John Wastell and Herry Semerk shall make and sett vpp or cawse to be made and sett vpp at ther costes and charges a good suer and sufficient vawte for the grete churche ther to be workmanly wrought made and set vpp after the best handlyng and fourme of good workmanship accordyng to a platt therof made and signed with the handes of the lordes executours vnto the kyng of most famous memorye Herry the vij[th] whos sowle god pardon.

And the said John Wastell and Herry Semerk shall provide and fynde at their costes and charges asmoche good sufficyent and able ston of Weldon quarryes as shall suffise for the perfourmyng of all the said vawte together with lyme, sand, scaffoldyng, cynctours, moldes, ordynaunces, and euery other thyng concernyng the same vawtyng, aswell workmen and laborers as all maner stuff and ordenaunces that shalbe required or necessary for the perfourmaunce of the same.

Except the seid M' provost and scolers with thassent of the said surveyour graunten to the said John Wastell and Herry Semerk for the great cost and charge that they shalbe at in remevyng the great scaffold there to haue therfore in recompence at the end and perfourmyng of the saide vawte the tymber of ij seuereys of the said grete scaffold by them remeved to their own vse and profight.

And over that the said provost scolers and Surveyour graunten that the said John Wastell and Herry Semerk shall haue duryng the tyme of the said vawtyng the vse of certeyn stuffes and necessaryes there as Gynnes, wheles, cables, robynettes, sawes and such other as shalbe delyuered vnto them by indenture. And they to delyuere the same agayn vnto the College there at the end of the said worke.

The said John Wastell and Herry Semerk graunten also and bynde themselff by thies couenauntes that they shall perfourme and clerely fynyssh all the said vawte within the term and space of iii yeres next ensuyng after the tyme of their begynnyng vppon the same.

And for the good and suer perfourmyng of all the premysses as is afore specy-fyed the said provost and scolers couenaunte and graunte to pay vnto the said John Wastell and Herry Semerk. xij^C li. that is to say for euery seuerey in the seid church. C li. to be paid in fourme folowyng from tyme to tyme asmoche money as shall suffise to pay the masons and other rately after the numbre of workmen; And also for ston at suche tymes and in such fourme as the said John Wastell and Herry Semerk shall make their Bargeynes for ston so that they be evyn paid with C li at the perfourmyng of euery seuerey. And yff ther remayn ony parte of the said C li at the fynysshyng of the said seuerey, than the said M' provost and scolers to pay vnto them the surplusage of the said C li for the seuerey. And so from tyme to tyme vnto all the said xij seuereys be fully and perfithtly made and perfourmed.

(Willis and Clark, vol. 1, p. 608)

Contract B. *Agreement between John Wastell and Henry Semerk regarding the division of the work ; 7 June, 4 Henry VIII. 1512.*

This Indenture made the vij^te day of June in the iiij^th yere of our souerayn lord kyng Herry the viij^te bytwyn John Wastell M' Mason of the kynges workes within his College Royall at Cambryge on the oon partye; And Herry Semerk oon of the Wardeynes of the said workes on the other partye, witnesseth:

that wher the said John and Herry haue joyntly couenaunted and bargayned with M'provost and Bursers of the said College to make, set vpp and perfourme a vawte for the grete Churche there, as by indentures therof made more playnly dothe appere;

Neuerthelasse hyt is agreed and couenaunted betwyn the said John Wastell and Herry Semerk that the fornamed John Wastell shall occupye, vse, and haue the hole Bargayn of making the seid vawte, to his own profyght and advauntage. And to bere also almaner charges concernyng the same.

And the seid Herry Semerk to be no partyner with hym in the said bargayn As longe as hyt shall please almyghty god the said John Wastell shall lyve and haue his helth to rewle the werke.

And the said Herry Semerk is agreed that duryng the lyff and helth of the said John Wastell he shall dayly and hourely gyff his dylygent attendaunce to the said workes withoute he haue lycence of the said John Wastell to be absent for seasons as they shall both be content.

And the said John Wastell graunteth to gyff vnto the said Herry Semerk for his contynuall attendaunce in fourme aforesaid. xx markes. euery yere duryng the contynuaunce of the seid werkes and standyng the lyff and helth of the said John Wastell.

And yff hyt happen as god forbede the seid John Wastell to discece or elles to fall in suche syknesse that he can not be able to gyff attendaunce to perfourme the said workes; than the partyes aforesaid be agreed that the said Herry Semarke and Thomas Wastell sone vnto the said John Wastell shall joyntly be partyners in the said bargayn. And so they shall see the seid bargayn to be perfourmed, And shall parte aswell costes and charges as profytes and advauntages evynly betwyn them bothe in euery thyng concernyng the same bargayn.

(Willis and Clark, Vol. 1, p. 609)

Contract C. *Contract for the Finials of* 21 *Buttresses ; and for one Tower of the Chapel,* 4 *January,* 4 *Henry VIII.* 1512–13.

This Indenture made the iiijth. day of January in the iiijth. yere of the Regn of our souuerayn lord Kyng Henry the viijth. Betwene M' Robert Hacumblen provost of the kynges College Royall in Cambryge and the scolers of the same with the advise and agrement of M' Thomas Larke Surveyour of the kynges workes there on the oon partye; And John Wastell master Mason of the seid workes on the other partye, Witnesseth

that hyt is couenaunted, bargayned, and agreed betwene the partyes aforsaid that the seid John Wastell shall make . . . the fynyalles of all the Buttrasses of the grete church there which be xxi in number; The seid fynyalles to be wele and workmanly wrought, made, sett vpp after the best handelyng and fourme of good workmanship acordyng to the plattes conceyved and made for the same, and acordyng to the fynyall of oon buttrasse which is wrought and sett vpp: Except that all thies new fynyalles shalbe made sumwhat larger in certayn places acordyng to the mooldes for the same conceyvid and made.

Also hit is couenaunted . . . that the seid John Wastell shall make . . . the fynysshyng and perfourmyng of oon towre at on of the corners of the seid churche, as shalbe assigned vnto hym by the Surveyour of the seid werkes; All the seid fynysshyng . . . with Fynyalles, ryfant gablettes, Batelmentes, orbys, or Crosse quaters, and euery other thyng belongyng to the same to be wele and workmanly wrought, made, and sett vpp, after the best handelyng and fourme of good workmanshipp, acordyng to a platt therof made, remaynyng in the kepyng of the seid Surveyour.

The seid John Wastell to provide and fynde at his coste and charge asmoche good sufficyent and able ston of Weldon quarryes as shall suffyse [for the finials and tower] . . . Together with lyme, sand, scaffoldyng, mooldes, ordenaunces and euery other thyng concernyng the fynysshyng and perfourmyng of all the buttrasses and towre aforeseid, aswele workmen and laborers as all maner stuff and ordenaunces as shalbe required or necessary for perfourmaunce of the same:

Except the seid M' Provost, Scolers, and Surveyour graunten to lend vnto the seid John Wastell sum parte of old scaffoldyng tymbre, and the vse of certayn stuff and necessaryes there; as Gynnes, wheles, Cables, Robynattes, sawes and suche other as shalbe delyuered vnto hym by Indentures. And the seid John Wastell to delyuere the same agayn vnto the seid Surveyour assone as the seid Buttrasses and towre shalbe perfourmed.

The said John Wastell graunteth also, and byndeth hymself . . . to perfourme and clerely fynyssh all the seid buttrasses and towre on thisside the Feeste of the Annunciacon of our blessed lady next ensuyng after the date herof.

And for the good and sure perfourmyng of all thies premysses as is afore specyfyed the seid provost and scolers couenaunten and graunten to pay vnto the seid John Wastell for the perfourmyng of euery buttrasse vjli. xiijs. iiijd. whiche amownteth for all the seid buttrasses Cxl. li.; and for the perfourmyng of the said towre, C li. to be paid in fourme folowyng, That is to sey; from tyme to tyme asmoche money as shall suffyse to pay the Masons and other laborers rately after the numbre of workmen, And also for ston at suche tymes and in suche fourme as the seid John Wastell shall make his provisyon or receyte of the same ston from tyme to tyme as the case shall requyre;

Provided alwey that the seid John Wastell shall kepe contynually .lx. Fremasons werkyng vppon the same werkes assone as shalbe possible for hym to calle them in by vertu of suche Commissyon as the seid surveyour shall delyuer vnto the seid John Wastell for the same entent.

And in case ony Mason or other laborer shalbe founde vnprofytable or of ony suche ylle demeanour wherby the workes shuld be hyndred or the company mysordred not doyng their duties acordyngly as they ought to doo, than the seid Surveyour to indevour hymself to refourme them by such wayes as hath byn ther vsed before this tyme.

And also the fornamed M' Provost scolers and Surveyour shall fynde asmoch Iron werke for the fynyalles of the seid buttrasses as shall amownte to v. s for euery buttrasse, that is in all iiij li v. s. And what soeuer Iron werke shalbe ocupyed and spent abowte the seid werkes, and for suertie of the same above the seid v s. for a buttrasse, the seid John Wastell to bere hyt at his own cost and charge.

And for all the syngler couenaunts afor reherced of the partie of the seid John Wastell wele and truly to be perfourmed and kepte he byndeth hymself, his heires and exectours in CCC li of good and laufull money of Englond to be paid vnto the seid M' provost, scolers, and Surveyour at the Fest of Ester next commyng after the date of thies presentes. And in lyke wise for all and syngler couenaunts afor reherced of the partye of the seid provost, scolers and Surveyour wele and truly to be perfourmed and kepte they bynde them their Successours and executours in CCC li. . . . to be paid vnto the seid John Wastell at the seid fest of Ester. In witnesse wherof the partyes aforesaid to thies present indentures entrechaungeably haue sett their Seales the day and yere above wryten.

(Willis and Clark, vol. 1, pp. 609–611)

Contract D. *Agreement between Thomas Larke and John Wastell respecting a record to be kept of money and materials delivered to him, 24 January, 4 Henry VIII. 1512–13; with the memorandum of account to 12 May, 1514.*

This Indenture made the xxiiij[th] day of January, in the iiij[th] yer of our souereyn Lord Kyng Henry the viij[th] betwene M' Thomas Larke Surveyour of the Kings werks at Cambryge on the oon partye, and John Wastell M' mason of the seid werks on the other partye, witnesseth:

that wher as a bargayn is made and other bargaynes be in contemplacon betwene the parties aforesaid for perfourmyng certeyn masonry of the great church of the Kyngs College there as by Indenture therof made clerely doth appere, hyt is agreed and appointed betwene the parties aforeseid that specyal mencyon shalbe made in both parts of thies present Indentures shewyng particlerly from tyme to tyme all and singuler suche sumes of money and ston as the seid John Wastell hath receyued or shall receyue of the fornamed M' Thomas Larke for the accomplishment and perfourmyng of the said bargaynes made and of all other herafter to be made. In witnes wherof the parties aforeseid to thies presents have sett their Seals the day and yere above wryten.

Money and ston delyuered	The same xxiiijth day of January the aboue named John Wastell hath receyued of M' Thomas Larke vpon the bargayn for the fynyalls in money lxxi. *li* xij *s.* v*d.* Item the seid John Wastell has receyved at the same tyme for fynyshyng of the seid fynyalls Ciiij^{xx}. xij ton iij p. of Welldon ston at vj s. the ton Lvij *li.* xij *s.* x*d* summa	Cxxix *li.* v.*s.* iij *d.*
Yet ston delyuered	Item delyuered to the seid John Wastell x ton ij ped' of Weldon ston for the Corbel tables of the Chapells at vj s. the ton	lx *s.* ix *d.*
Ston remaynyng	Item the same day remayned in the place over and above the forsaid ij parcells of ston CCCxxxj ton v. ped' of Weldon ston. Item lxviij ton xiij ped' of Yorkshir ston. Item xxvij ton v. ped' of Clypsham ston. Item left in the place certeyn refuse ston and sawyngs of both Weldon Yorkshir and Clypsham and molded stones of sondry sorts not moten nor counted in the premisses	CCCC xxvij ton iij ped'
Money delyuered	Item betwene the xxviijth of January and the xxvth day of Marche in the same iiijth yere of the Kyng, the afornamed John Wastell hath receyued at sondry tymes of the forsaid M' Thomas Larke by the hands of M' John Ray	C lxiiij *li.*
Money delyuered	Item betwene the xxvth of March and the xiijth day of Aprylle in the same iiijth yere of the Kyng the afornamed John Wastell hath receyed at sondry tymes of the forsaid M' Thomas Larke	C *li.*
Money delyuered	Item betwene the above wryten xiijth day of Aprill anno iiij^{to} and the xxiiijth day of May A°. v^{to}. the afornamed John Wastell hath receyued at sondry tymes of the forsaid M' Thomas Larke by the hands of M' John Ray for the pay dayes and caryage of ston by land by water with xx li prest to Chikley and his felowes	C xxvi *li.* x *s.* x *d.*
Money delyuered	Item betwene the above wryten xxiiijth day Maii and the viijth day of July then next folowyng the afornamed John Wastell hath receyued of the forseid M' Thomas Larke at sundry tymes by the hands of M' John Ray for the pay dayes and caryage of ston by land and by water with certain prests delyuered to the Quarrymen as appereth in the fourtnyght Bokes	C xlvij *li.*

Money delyuered	Item betwene the said viij[th] day of July A°. v[to]. and the xvij[th] day of the same month than next fol-lowyng, the afornamed John Wastell hath receyued of the forseid Thomas Larke for pay-ments of ston, werkmanship prests and such other	lvj *li.* xviij *s.* iij *c*
Money delyuered	Item betwene the seid xvij[th] day of July A°. v[to]. and the xxvj day of Septembre than next folowing the afornamed M' Wastell hath receyued of the afornamed M' Thomas Larke by the hands of M' Ray at sondry tymes	C xiij *li.* x *s.*
Money delyuered	Item the seid xxvj day of Septembre the afornamed M' Thomas Larke hath paid vnto M' Kyrkeham for Cxlij ton iiij fote and a half of Weldon ston at ijs. iiij d the ton receyued by M' Wastell by land xviij li. xix s. ix d. and iiij ton xix p. by water xxiij s. iiij d. Summa of all by water and land	xx*li.* iij *s.* j*d*
Money delyuered	Item betwene the above wryten xxvj[th] day of Septembre A°. v[to]. and the xij[th] day of Maii than next folowyng A°. vi[to]. the afornamed M' Wastell has receyued of M' Thomas Larke by the hands of M' Ray at sondry tymes	xx CCCiiij *li.* lxxij *s.* vj *d*

Signed 'per me Johannem Wastell' and sealed. The original of this agreement is lost, and the document is only known through a copy in the Betham MSS. preserved in King's College Library.

(Willis and Clark, vol. 1, pp. 611–12)

Contract E. *Contract for building 3 Towers of the Chapel. 4 March, 4 Henry VIII. 1512–13.*

This Indenture made the iiij[th] day of Marche in the iiij[th]. yere of the reign of our souuerayn lord king henry the viij[th], betwene maister Robert Hacumblen Clerk provost of the kinges College Royall in Cambryge . . . and John Wastell maister Mason of the seid werkes on the other parte witnessith: that hit is cowenaunted . . . . . . that the seid John Wastell shall make . . . iij towres at iij Corners of the great new churche there: All the seid fynysshyng and per-fourmyng of the seid iij towres with fynyalls, ryfant Gablettes, batelmentes, orbis, crosse quaters, Badges, and euery other thyng belonging to the same to be wele and workmanly wrought, made and set vp after the best handelyng and fourme of good workmanship acordyng to oon towre at the iiij[th] corner that to sey at the North west ende of the seid Church which is now redy wrought.

[Then follow the covenants; which are exactly the same as in the former Indenture, except that the guarantee on both sides is £400, and the Towers are to be finished before Midsummer Day.]

(Willis and Clark, vol. 1, pp. 612–13)

Contract F. *Contract for the vaulting of two porches in the chapel, of seven chapels 'in the body of the same,' and of nine chapels 'behynd the quere' : together with the construction of all the battlements of the said porches and chapels. 4 August, 5 Henry VIII. 1513.*

This indenture made the iiij^th day of August in the vth yere of the regne of our souuerayn lord kyng Henry the viijth, Betwene Mr Robert Hacumblen provost of the kynges College Royall in Cambryge and the scolers of the same with the advise and agreement of M' Thomas Lark Surveyour of the kynges workes there on the oon party, and John Wastell M' Mason of the seid workes on the other party, witnesseth,

that hyt is couenaunted, bargayned, and agreed betwene the parties aforsaid, that the seid John Wastell shall make and sett vpp, or cause to be made and sett vpp, at his propre costes and charges, the vawtyng of ij porches of the new church of the kynges College aforseid with Yorkshier ston;

And also the vawtes of vij Chapelles in the body of the same Church with Weldon ston, acordyng to a platte made as wele for the same vij Chapelles as for the seid ij porches;

And ix other Chapelles behynd the quere of the seid churche with like Weldon ston to be made of a more course worke, as apperith by a platte for the same made:

And ouer that the seid John Wastell shall make and sett vp or cause to be made and sett vpp at his cost and charge the Batelmentes of all the seid porches and chapelles with Weldon ston acordyng to another platte made for the same remaynyng with al the other plattes afore reherced in the kepyng of the seid Surveyour signed with the handes of the lordes the kynges executours:

All the seid vawtes and batelmentes to be wele and workmanly wrought, made, and sett vp after the best handelyng and fourme of good workmanship, and acordyng to the plattes afore specifyed:

The forsaid John Wastell to provide and fynde at his cost and charge not only as moch good sufficient and hable ston of Hampole quarryes in Yorkshier as shall suffise for the perfourmaunce of the seid ij porches, but also as moch good sufficient and hable ston of Weldon quarryes as shall suffise for the perfourmyng of all the seid chapelles and batelmentes, Together with lyme, sand, scaffoldyng, mooldes, ordinaunces, and euery other thyng concernyng the fynysshyng and perfourmyng of al the seid vawtes and batelmentes, aswele workmen and laborers, as almaner stuff and ordinaunce as shalbe required or necessary for perfourmaunce of the same:

Provided alwey that the seid John Wastell shall kepe contynually lx fremasons workyng vppon the same.

The seid John Wastell graunteth also and byndeth hymself by thies presentes to perfourme and clerely fynysh al the seid vawtes and batelmentes on thisside the feest of the natiuite of Seynt John Baptiste next ensuying after the date herof;

And for the good and suer perfourmyng of al thies premisses, as is afore specifyed the said provost and scolers graunten to pay vn to the seid John Wastell for ston and workmanship of euery of the seid porches with all other charges as is afore reherced xxv li.

And for euery of the seid vij Chapelles in the body of the Church after the platt of the seid porches xx li.

And for vawtyng of euery of the other ix Chapelles behynd the quere to be made of more course worke xij li.

And for ston and workmanship of the lᴧtelmentes of al the seid chapelles and porches deuided in to xx seuereyes euery seuerey at C s. summa Cˡⁱ.

And for al and singler couenauntes afore reherced of the partye of the seid John Wastell wele and truly to be perfourmed and kept, he byndeth hym self, his heires and executours in ccccˡⁱ of good and lawfull money of England to be paid vnto the seid M' Provost, scolers and Surveyour at the Feest of the Purificacon of our Blessed Lady next commyng after the date of thies presentes; and in lyke wise for all and singler couenauntes afore reherced, of the partye of the seid M' Provost, scolers and Surveyour wele and truly to be perfourmed and kept, they bynde them self, their successours and executours in ccccˡⁱ of good and laufull money of England to be paid vnto the seid John Wastell at the seid feest of Purificacon of our blessed lady. In witnesse wherof the parties aforeseid to thies present Indentures entrechaungeably haue sett their Seales, the day and yere above wryten.

Signed 'per me Johannem Wastell' and sealed.

(Willis and Clark, vol. 1, pp. 613–14)

Contract G. *Note of expenditure from* 28 *May,* 1508, *to* 29 *July,* 1515.

Summa totalis anno primo	M¹CCCC.iij li. xix s. ob. q.	M¹CCCClviij li
Item pro feodis	liiij li. xv.s	xiiij s. ob. q.
Summa totalis anno ijᵈᵒ	M¹M¹ lviij li. ij d. ob. q.	M¹M¹C xxxix li.
Item pro feodis	iiijˣˣ.j li. viij s. iiij d.	viij s. vj d. ob. q.
Summa totalis anno iijᶜⁱᵒ	M¹DCCCC. iiijˣˣ. xij li. ix s. x.d	M¹M¹ lxxiij li.
Item pro feodis	iiijˣˣ. j li. viij s. iiij d.	xviij s. ij d.
Summa totalis anno iiijᵗᵒ	M¹DCCCC. xx li. vs. vd. q.	M¹M¹ xvj li. xiij s.
Item pro feodis	iiijˣˣ.xvj li: viijs. iiij d.	ix d. q.
Summa totalis anno vᵗᵒ	M¹iiijˣˣ.ij. li: j d.	M¹C.iiijˣˣ. iij li.
Item pro feodis	Cj li. viij s. iiij d.	viij s. v. d.
Summa totalis anno vjᵗᵒ	DCCC. iiijˣˣ.ij li. vij s. v d. q.	.DCCCC.iiijˣˣ.iij li.
Item pro feodis	Cj li. viij s. iiij d.	xv s. ix d. q.
Summa totalis anno vijᵐᵒ	C.xliiij li. xvij s. xj d.	Clxx li. v s.
Item pro feodis	xxv. li. vij s. j d.	
Summa totalis	Xᴹᴸ·xxvj. li. iij s. ix d.	
	M' Lark surveyour.	

M' Masons	John Wastell. John Alee
M' Carpenter	Richard Russell.
M' Plummer	John Burwell.
M' Carver	Thomas Stocton.

(Willis and Clark, vol. 1, p. 614)

EXTRACTS FROM THE BUILDING ACCOUNTS 1508–1515 [EASTER TO EASTER]

Individual Payments in fortnights

1509/10

to 8 July	£5 reward to Overseer
to 5 August	10s to John Alee, purveyor's costs
to 24 October	£5 3s 1d reward to Overseer
to 31 March	£1 2s to John Alee, purveyor's costs

1510/11

to 14 April	£5 reward to Overseer
to 12 May	£1 17s 4d to Henry Semark purveyor's costs
	£1 reward to John Worlyche
to 7 July	£6 17s reward shared by Overseer, Richard Russell, Thomas Stockton
to 13 October	£5 2s 8d paid to Overseer and 5 setters
to 8 December	13/2d to John Alee, purveyor's costs
to 22 December	£6 8s to Overseer for his costs
	£4 to Henry Semark, Robert Worlyche and Mr Py
to 19 January	£5 to the Surveyor of the works
to 16 February	7s to John Alee, purveyor's costs
to 16 March	£5 to Mr Surveyor and John Alee, purveyor's costs
to 13 April	£1 to John Alee, purveyor's costs

1511/12

to 11 May	£2 5s to John Alee, purveyor's costs
to 25 May	£5 16s Surveyor's costs
to 6 July	£7 reward shared by Mr Surveyor, Henry Semark and Robert Worlyche
to 12 October	£5 3s 2d reward to Mr Surveyor and others
to 26 October	£1 3s 4d to John Alee and Robert Motkyn, purveyor's costs
to 23 November	£2 16s reward to Mr Surveyor and others
to 7 December	£5 6s 8d and £1 reward shared by John Wastell, Thomas Wadlyngton and William Rowleston
to 4 January	£7 reward shared by Surveyor, Semarke and Worlyche
to 1 February	£2 2s 10d to Motkyn, William Buxston and Mr Lee, purveyor's costs

to 15 February	£1 to John Haynes and John Alee, purveyor's costs
to 29 February	17/4d to John Wastell and Motkyn, purveyor' costs
to 14 March	6s to Mr Lee purveyor's costs
to 29 March	£13 11s 4d reward to Mr Surveyor of the works and R. Russell

1512/13

to 25 April	£5 reward to Mr Surveyor
	£1 2s 8d to Perse, servant of Mr Surveyor and others as reward
to 9 May	£1 17s 4d to Mr Surveyor and others, purveyor's costs
to 23 May	£1 19s 10d to John Wastell and 3 others, purveyor's costs
to 4 July	£5 8s 6d reward to Semarke, Surveyor and others
to 1 August	17s to John Wastell, purveyor's costs
to 15 August	£1 17s 4d reward to Semarke, Worlyche and others
to 10 October	£5 reward to Mr Surveyor
to 21 November	7s to John Wastell, purveyor's costs
to 30 January	£3 9s 4d reward to Henry Semarke and others
to 27 March	£2 1s 8d reward to Henry Semarke and 1 other

1513/14

to 1 January	£1 reward to Semarke and Worlyche
to 26 February	£1 to John Wastell, John Haynes, Walter Flemynge, purveyor's costs

1514/15

to 23 April	£1 reward to Semarke and Worlyche
to 4 June	£2 3s 4d to Buxton, Haynes and Wastell, purveyor's costs
to 16 July	£1 reward to Semarke and Worlyche
to 30 July	8/6d to John Wastell and Thomas Wastell, purveyor's costs
to 24 September	£1 reward to Semarke and Worlyche
to 31 December	£1 reward to Semarke and Worlyche
to 8 April	£1 reward to Semarke and Worlyche

1515

to 1 July	£2 10s to Semarke, Worlyche, and 30 masons for 'styling'. A reward

Payments for stone: annual totals with high points in fortnights

Payments for Weldon only:

1509/10: £383 18s 1½d	HP to 17 March 1510: £59 18s 6½d
1510/11: £440 5s 3d	HP to 15 September 1510: £53 14s 4½d
1511/12: £367 13s 4½d	HP to 20 July 1511: £65 3s 8d
1512/13: £762 8s 7d	HP to 12 September 1512: £111 2s 5d
1513/14: £469 18s 3d	HP to 19 June 1513: £82 19s 3½d

1514/15: £363 3s 1d   HP to 2 July 1514: £90 14s 1d
1515:   £40 19s 5d   HP to 1 July 1515: £13 3s 7d

Tonnage of Clipsham and Weldon purchased with Weldon at 5/4d per ton

	Clipsham	Weldon
1509/10	1396	1439·6
1510/11	1601	1651
1511/12	—	1903·5
1512/13	—	2859
1513/14	—	1761·9
1514/15	—	1363·1
1515	—	153·6

Payments for brick

1511/12   £30 13s between 25 May and 31 August. High points to 25 May:
     £9 14s 8d and to 31 August: £8 18s 8d
1513/14   £1 1s 4d paid on 31 July

Carriage of brick from water to Chapel paid on:

8 June 1511
22 June
6 July
20 July
17 August
26 October
23 November

Payments for floor tiles:

1511/12: £1 6s 4d on 20 July, including some brick, paid to one tyler
1512/13: 8/8d paid on 13 March to 2 tylers:
     some 'rofe tyle'
     27 March: 2 tylers paid
     £2 11 8d paid to 2 tylers
1513/14: £2 4s 8d on 27 May for 7450 tiles
     £1 on 5 June for 5500 tiles
     £1 17s 6d on 19 June for 6250 tiles
     6/2d on 17 July for 1025 tiles
     2 tylers paid on 31 July

Ironwork payments in fortnights

1508/09

to 23 July   270 crossbars, 88 standards and 10 staybars for great
     windows

	4 great hooks for the great doors of the chapel. All paid to Robert Olyver, the Royal Smith
to 10 December	Iron for Chapel windows, 240 crossbars for great windows, 63 for low, and 96 standards for both and 6 staybars
to 21 January	From John Monday, smith, 80 great nails for scaffolding
to 18 March	Pair of hinges for a chapel door

1509/10

to 16 September	Iron for 4 great windows, £12 2s 4½d
to 23 December	Iron for 2 great windows, £34 10s 6d

1510/11

to 23 June	Iron for 6 great windows, £73 8s 8¾d

1511/12

to 27 April	Iron for 2 great windows, £51 10s 2¾d

Followed by odd payments March–August 1513, January–May 1515, May–July 1515

1512/13	Total costs £20 0s 11d
1513/14	Total costs (6 months) 14/2d
1514/15	Total costs (6 months) 14/10d
1515	Total costs (4 months) £2 7s 4d

Plumbers costs

Total
1509/10: to 16 September: £66 13s 4¾d
to 30 September: £13 18s 5½d

1510/11: to 1 September: solder bought
to 15 September: £318 9s 8¼d
to 27 October: £23 12s 11d

1511/12: to 3 August: £1 4s for firewood
to 9 November: £100
to 23 November: £10
to 4 January: £13 6s 8d
to 11 February: £20

1512/13: to 15 August: £7 6s 8d
9/6d for firewood
to 29 August: 6/- for firewood
to 12 September: £3 13s 4d
7/6d for firewood
to 10 October: £3 6s 8d

to 19 December: £11 18s
to 16 January £2
to 10 April: £67 7s 1d

1513/14: to 8 May: £20
to 3 July: 5/9d for firewood
        £5 17s reward to Sergeant
to 17 July: £1
to 25 September: £4 4s 8d

Lead totals

1509/10	£80 1s 10¼d
1510/11	£342 9s 8¼d
1511/12	£143 6s 8d
1512/13	£117 11s 9d
1513/14	£5 6s 8d
Total	£688 16s 7½d

Timber purchases

1508/09	to 18 February:	£1 9s 2d for 102 elms for scaffolding
	to 4 March	68 'loads' of elm
1509/10	to March	Estimated 1518 feet of timber bought
1513/14	to 25 September	Estimated 1418 feet of timber bought

Tracing House costs

1508/09	to 1 October	16/8d for paper and ink
		18/10d for elm board, 10/9d for poplar board. 2/8d for oak board plus paper and ink
	to 18 March	10/10d for elm board and paper
1509/10	to 5 August	Board purchased
	to 14 October.	Board purchased
	to 28 October	Board purchased
1510/11	to 21 July	Carriage of board
	to 4 August	Carriage of board
	to 15 September	£1 15s 2d for board
	to 27 October	12/3d for board
1511/12	to 28 September	£2 3s 2d for board followed by carriage

1512/13	to 29 August	£6 6s 8d for tracing costs
	to 30 January	Wainscot, parchment, paper and ink
	to 13 February	Wainscot purchased
1513/14	to 3 July	14/11d for board
		Wainscot purchased
	to 9 October	sawing of wainscot for moulds, and purchase of paper
	to 31 October	Elmboard purchased
	to 9 April	Elmboard purchased
1514/15	to 23 April	Elmboard purchased
	to 2 July	Board purchased
	to 16 July	Board purchased
	to 30 July	Board purchased
		Wainscot and paper purchased
	to 24 September	Elmboard purchased
	to 19 November	Board purchased

APPENDIX VI

THE PULPITUM AND STALLS

The most remarkable thing about the Tudor woodwork of King's College Chapel is that it survives. The pulpitum is by far the largest and most spectacular piece of early Renaissance woodcarving in England and perhaps, this has led to an exaggeration of both its stylistic significance and artistic quality. The only *182* date for the work is that suggested by the monograms of 'HR' and 'AR' and the quartered arms of Henry VIII and Anne Boleyn, who reigned as Queen from 14 November 1532 to 9 May 1536. The occurrence of the arms and the 'AR' monogram is limited only to the low relief panelled work beneath the coving of both facades of the screen. All the other monograms and ciphers on the lower sections are for Henry alone, while the upper panels of the loft have ciphers for Beaufort, Tudor and France. The pulpitum stands in Bay 7 and consists of a timber-framed east and west wall supporting a loft floor jettied on both sides. It is 14 feet deep from east to west at ground level, the depth specified in the Will and Intent of 1448. The space within the loft parapets incorporates

182 King's College Chapel, the pulpitum screen, west face

183 King's College Chapel, the pulpitum screen, cipher of Henry VIII

1 See p. Appendix VII.

184 King's College Chapel, the pulpitum screen, hanging pendant

2 For San Satiro see; L. Heydenreich and W. Lotz, *Architecture in Italy 1400–1600*, Harmondsworth 1974, pp. 103–6.

the complete width of the lateral windows of Bay 7 and had the Pulpitum been standing when these particular windows were glazed, (the north side after July 1540, the south between 1544–47 but see below), it would have inconvenienced the erection of the glazier's scaffolding. This is especially true on the north side where the pulpitum stairs are placed directly against the socle wall beneath the lateral window. Certainly the parapets of the loft are too weak to support any scaffold placed upon them.

The choir floor upon which the pulpitum and stalls stand was laid from approximately the January of 1535.[1] The stalls connected with the pulpitum are unlikely to have been in place prior to the glazing of Bays 5 N and 6 S, and as both these windows contain the arms of Queen Catherine Howard the glazing must date between July 1540 and January of 1542. Unless it was possible to scaffold over the stalls and pulpitum, the dating evidence for the glazing would suggest that the woodwork was not in place before July 1540. The window at the southern end of the Pulpitum, Bay 7 S, could have been glazed using scaffolding standing within the depth of the loft, for at that end there was no intervening internal structure. The 'AR' monograms and the quartered arms of Henry and Boleyn suggest that at least the coving beneath the loft was made prior to 1536 but possibly it was stored away to await the completion of the Chapel floor and glazing. Even so, the provision of the pulpitum and stalls would appear to pre-date the building of the High Altar in 1544 by some years.

The pulpitum is one of those curious English products of the reign of Henry VIII. It is dressed up in full Renaissance clothing, if a little quirky in design, yet it remains thoroughly medieval in structure. The screen is very solid and is conceived as a piece of traditional timber framed building. The lower section of the west facade consists of seven bays divided by antique pilasters with attic bases and inhabited Corinthianesque capitals. The pilasters have standard Renaissance decoration. The six bays flanking the central entry appear as a series of doors, firmly closed, with recessed panels in three tiers. The attic basement mouldings of the pilasters are carried across the 'doors' while the upper tiers are dressed with decorative bands and crowned monograms. The lunettes contain buckled shields with various supporters, all that is except the central southern bay which has a relief sculpture depicting the Fallen Angels – perhaps a pointed contemporary reference? The central entry consists of a two-leaved door with busts in roundels protruding from the spandrels above. *183*

The upper rood loft is jettied on both sides with panelled coving to conceal the joists. The imposition of the upper parapet beyond the vault supports VS 7/8 north and south has caused considerable damage to the Tudor stone ciphers and their crowns. The loft parapet design has elaborate cornices which define a middle zone containing double rounded headed panels coupled into pairs by projecting colonettes. The panels are decorated with foliate designs and Tudor Roses. The dividing colonettes combine a barbecue of antique confection. Their Ionic capitals are turned diagonally rather than being set square. The colonettes stand on bulges that project from the lower cornice, and these in turn excrete fantastic pendants. Possibly, the colonettes were intended to support figures on *184* the upper parapet, while the blank semi-circular panels of the loft may have been intended for panel paintings. The whole western face of the pulpitum shows a marked similarity to the interior elevations of the sacristy of S. Maria p. Satiro *185* in Milan, a work by Bramante of *c.* 1498.[2]

3 J. Gotch, *Early Renaissance Architecture in England*, London 1901, pp. 28–9.
4 N. Pevsner, *The Buildings of England, Cambridgeshire*, Harmondsworth 1970, pp. 108–9.
5 Summerson, p. 31.

185 Milan, Baptistry of S. Maria P. Satiro: interior

6 W. Ewing, Notices on the Norwich Merchants Marks, *Norfolk Archaeology* 3, 1852, p. 200.

7 The presence of terracotta objects in Norwich and environs *c.* 1507 might suggest that the city played a leading role in the early dissemination of the Renaissance style in eastern England i.e. the Pottergate figurine (see p. 210) and the terracotta works at St George Colegate Norwich, Wymondham, Oxborough, Bracon Ash, Barsham Suffolk and Layer Marney Essex. See also A. Baggs, Sixteenth century terracotta tombs in East Anglia *Archaeological Journal* CXXV 1968.

8 H. Wayment, King's College Chapel. *The Corpus Vitriearum Medii Aevi, Great Britain*, Supplementary Vol. I, Oxford 1972, p. 10.

A great deal has been written concerning the design of the Pulpitum at King's. It has been called 'completely Italian in treatment',[3] 'the style of the figurework is characteristic French Mannerism',[4] while a specific group of Italian artists has been suggested centred on Rovezzano and Majano.[5] Such judgments are coloured by the presumed precocity of the Renaissance details within the work, thus eliminating the possibility that it might be English. Therefore, the whole pulpitum and its decoration should be examined in detail in order to point up these 'innovations'. Firstly, the form of the structure with its coved and jettied loft is thoroughly English and has scores of parallels up and down the country. The solid aspect presented by the western face was probably as much determined by draftproofing and privacy as by any stylistic tradition, plus the fact that the antechapel had lost much of its liturgical usefulness by the late 1530s. An examination of the carving will reveal at least three hands at work, each of differing quality, while in general it might be said that the carving north of the door is superior to that to the south, with the notable exception of the Fallen Angels panel.

The decorative repertoire contains a number of motifs already well established in England by the 1530s. Antique pilasters first made their appearance on the Henry VII tomb at Westminster and were soon added to the design of the Christ Church Gate in Canterbury. Their popularity was immediate, particularly on tombs, and the 1520s saw a whole rash in southern and eastern England: the Layer Marney tomb of 1523, the Oxborough tombs and the Fisher monument at Cambridge of *c.* 1525, the Salisbury Chantry in Christchurch Hampshire of *c.* 1529 and so on. The more exotic free-standing pilasters of the rood loft parapet at King's were also current in the English 'Antik' style. They appear on the Jannis tomb in St George Colegate, Norwich, made some time before 1530.[6] This important terracotta tomb was clearly made to order for it contains the merchant's mark of the family, i.e. the whole tomb was not taken complete from a common, reusable mould. The Jannis tomb also contains egg and dart, angels supporting shields, flat antique pilasters with Ionic capitals and semi-circular headed panels. The whole design is a 'mini' pulpitum from King's Cambridge, but some years earlier.[7]

Another feature of the King's pulpitum is the series of heads in medallions and they too were becoming common in English woodwork, having been popularised in another medium by Majano, whose terracotta heads decorate Wolsey's Hampton Court. Woodwork examples can be seen at the west end of the hall of Magdalen College Oxford and on the hall screen of New College, both of *c.* 1525, and on the chancel screens at St Cross in Winchester of *c.* 1528, on the panelling of Cogan House in Canterbury of 1529, in Curat's House Norwich of *c.* 1535 and on the panelling brought from the Abbey of Benet Hulme to Norwich Cathedral in 1536. Yet more early Renaissance panelling of this type exists in the Norwich Guildhall and exceptionally fine medallion heads of *c.* 1525 can be seen at Scottow, Norfolk, incorporated into the organ case. This probably came from the ruined Paston mansion nearby. Of course, the nearest source for the medallion heads on the screen at King's would have been in the early glass just a few windows away, much of it made and in place before 1530.[8] The pendants that hang down from the loft parapet also have English prototypes – stone examples in the vault of the West Chantry at Ely completed by 1534 and wooden examples in the roof of the great hall of Hampton

186 Norwich, St George
Colegate, the Jannis Tomb

9 King's College Muniments
Kitchen Accounts and Oswald
p. 208.

10 Ibid.

11 When he assembled the Fisher
tomb. See Willis and Clark,
vol. II, pp. 282–3.

Court by Richard Rydge of London, 1534/5. The heraldry within the lunettes of the screen is modelled directly from the stone carving above the side closets of the antechapel, all except the northernmost, where a couple of fubsy angels have been pressganged to act as reluctant supporters. Similar heraldic schemes with angelic assistance can be seen at The Vyne, Hampshire, the Fisher Tomb from Cambridge and on the Jannis tomb in Norwich.   *186*

It would seem therefore that few of the motifs employed on the pulpitum of King's were new to the embryonic style of the English Renaissance. However, some of the work, most notably that of the highest quality, does hint of being foreign, though whether French, Flemish or Italian would seem impossible to say. Similar work, including the barbecue pilasters and hanging pendants, can be seen at St Pierre in Caen of *c.* 1520, there executed in stone, while the Cathedral at Evreux has very fine Renaissance screenwork of pre-1524 of considerable interest to the King's screen. But with so many English precedents for the decorative repertoire and the traditional nature of the structure, it would seem unnecessary to look outside this country for the overall designer and for at least some of the carvers.

The King's College Accounts are depressingly silent over the pulpitum save for a few references recorded in the dining lists. On 1 January 1535, 'Philip and another stranger' dined in King's in company with three local carpenters.[9] Five days later, 'Philippus sculptor' and 'five other strangers' were again entertained. A sculptor could of course be working at the college in any capacity, in stone, bronze or wood, and not necessarily on the Chapel.[10] The term 'stranger' was specifically applied in the reign of Elizabeth I to the French and Flemish Huguenots who sought refuge in England, though whether the term was so specifically applied to those nationals at this earlier date is unclear. The fact that Philip was singled out by name might suggest that, if he was working on the pulpitum, then he might have been at least the principal carver. If these references do apply to artists at work on the pulpitum then they would also help date the work more precisely – in progress in January 1535.

The pulpitum of King's College Chapel is clearly the work of many hands, as is the stained glass. Similarly, it may be that foreign carvers worked alongside their English counterparts who were, presumably, less adept at the new style. One hand must have had overall control, but this need not necessarily have been a carver – after all, Thomas Stockton may have been in charge of the great sculptural programme of the antechapel, but the sculpture was fitted into an overall framework designed by a master mason. The pulpitum is conceived in grand architectural terms, it is after all, a highly decorated timber frame building. As such it is possibly the work of a master mason. Cambridge already possessed a mason quite capable of the most advanced Renaissance work – John Lee, designer of the Fisher tomb in 1525. In its own way, this tomb was a far more remarkable piece than the pulpitum of King's. Lee was also chief mason of King's College and had been joint master mason of the Chapel project together with Wastell since 1509. He was certainly still active in Cambridge in 1532/3 long after Wastell's death.[11] Had Lee designed the pulpitum, then he might well have left the precise details of the carved work to a master carver, who employed a team of varying ability, and this might help to explain the wide variety within the work, even in repeated motifs such as the lunette heraldic ensembles.

87 King's College Chapel, the choir stalls north side

12 Ibid., vol. I, p. 523 and p. 521. It is not at all clear how the later canopies relate to the return stall canopies, i.e. are they all 1633?

13 Willis and Clark, vol. I, p. 522.

14 Ibid.

15 Ibid.

The central door of the pulpitum has pierced work panels topped by the arms of Charles I and a date of 1636. In that year 'Woodruffe, le Joyner' was paid £32 for the new doors to the choir.[12] They are a remarkable copy of the adjoining work of the 1530s. The seventeenth century also saw the transformation of the *187* stalls from low seats to tall canopied thrones.[13] The original Tudor work was more prosaic, and consists of the return stalls and two tiers of the side stalls with their throughly English carved misericords. Their later upward extensions are a rich mixture of balasters, cornices and coats of arms. The panelling dates from 1633 and was made by William Fells.[14] The canopies were built in 1675–78 to designs by Cornelius Austin at a cost of £305.[15] He also made the present doors in Bay 3.

THE CHAPEL FLOOR

The estimate for the paving of the Chapel envisaged that the whole building would be floored with marble or 'Ragge of Kent' – 12,947 feet at a shilling a foot. The twenty closets and two porches would require an additional 260 feet each, making a total of £907 7s, though the estimate totalled only £868 14s[1] Flooring already existed in at least some of the side closets, as in 1473 the pavement of one of the southern closets had to be repaired.[2] It is not altogether clear how much of the Chapel was paved after 1515, nor when the initial flooring was carried out. Two paviors were entertained in hall on a number of occasions on 1535, a time when the great bulk of the Chapel fittings were under way.[3]

The choir bays from the pulpitum door to Bay 2 is said to have had a floor of English grey marble,[4] while the antechapel had a brick floor flanking a central alley of marble stretching from the pulpitum door to Bay 11, from whence a marble processional path crossed from the north and south porches.[5] This central paved alley was extended to the west door in 1614/15 again in marble and Ragg.[6] Bay 1 was eventually paved or repaved in 1611, but in tile not marble.[7] This might suggest that in the original arrangement of the sanctuary area, the High altar stood in Bay 2 and not against the east wall. In 1643 a wooden screen was removed from Bay 3, evidently a post-Reformation fitting, and a new screen extended across Bay 2. This is another indication that the primitive arrangement featured an altar in Bay 2.[8] In 1702 a new black and white marble floor was laid throughout the choir bays and the old floor relaid in the antechapel.[9] About 1770, the college decided upon a replacement for the antechapel floor and in 1774 Lord Godolphin donated £400 for a pavement of Portland stone.[10] In the following year, Bay 1 and very probably Bays 2 and 3 were again refloored and the sanctuary walls panelled by James Essex 'in the Gothic manner'.[11] This work was associated with the building of a new High Altar in Bay 1 placed directly against the east wall of the Chapel. By this time, the altar was raised several steps above the choir floor: one step between Bays 4 and 3, three more between Bays 3 and 2 and another three within Bay 1. At least some of these steps existed in the sixteenth century.

In 1968 the Chapel floor was relaid to the present design. It was noted when the old floor was lifted that the flooring at the east end was supported by tiny brick arches while the west end of the antechapel stood upon 'Tudor' brick vaults some 1.5 m. high.[12] The choir floor pattern was returned to that of 1702 but relaid at one level. Wall benches were introduced in Bays 1 and 2 to conceal the scars left by the removal of the steps. The decision was highly questionable, especially as the original instructions of 1448 regarding the High Altar stipulated

1 Willis and Clark, vol. I, p. 482. The estimate is roughly three closet floors short, i.e. Bays 2 and 3 N and 2 S?

2 Ibid., p. 489.

3 King's College Muniments Kitchen Accounts and Oswald p. 68.
4 The original grey marble floor of the choir was relaid in the antechapel in 1702 and was in turn replaced in 1774. See Willis and Clark, vol. I, p. 529.
5 Ibid., p. 529.
6 Ibid.

7 Ibid., p. 528.

8 Ibid., p. 523.

9 Ibid., p. 529.

10 Ibid., p. 530.

11 J. Saltmarsh, *King's College*, Cambridge 1959, p. 41.

12 For the restorations of 1968 see R. Tibbs, *King's College Chapel*, Lavenham 1970.

that it should stand on a raised floor – see the relative height above the present floor of the eastern stair turret doors. The real reason behind the decision to reduce the choir floor to a single level seems to have been to enable the Rubens *Adoration of the Magi* to be squeezed under the cill of the east window, for it was too tall when placed above the previous altar raised upon the steps.

THE RUBENS *ADORATION OF THE MAGI*

The *Adoration of the Magi* by Sir Peter Paul Rubens has become an established fixture of King's College Chapel. The painting was commissioned by the Premonstratentions in Louvain in 1634 and was intended as an altarpiece. Rubens received 920 florins for his efforts. Sir Joshua Reynolds thought it a 'slight performance', but his view was not shared by the twentieth-century art-buying public. It fetched a world record price when it was auctioned in 1961. The painting was then donated to King's College on condition that it was displayed within the Chapel. This posed a number of problems, not least its size (3.30 by 2.50 m.) and the medium employed, oil on wooden boards, which requires a constant humidity.

While various schemes for housing the painting were proposed and abandoned, the College found itself in the centre of a heated national controversy regarding the style and content of the picture, its suitability and positioning. One of the strongest opponents of the placing of the Rubens against the east wall of the Chapel was Sir Nikolaus Pevsner: 'if any building in the whole country was not made for it, it was King's College Chapel'.[1] Liturgical questions were also posed by the decision to abandon the altar cross in order not to obscure the lower sections of the painting. The final solution, a simple altar on a three-step platform, ornate golden frontal, stark dark frame and 'tryptych' doors may not be to everyone's liking, but the overall low-key approach does provide the least distraction possible from the great architecture and glass that surrounds it.

1 N. Pevsner, *Cambridgeshire*, Harmondsworth 1970, pp. 106–7.

APPENDIX IX

THE STAINED GLASS

1 For a complete survey of the glass, historical, iconographic and stylistic see Wayment, King's College Chapel. *Corpus Vitriearum* 1972, from which all references are drawn unless stated otherwise.

The windows of King's College Chapel represent the finest collection of sixteenth-century glass in England and one of the best in Europe.[1] They are also wilfully out of sympathy with the architecture of the Chapel. The twenty-five completed windows were made in two campaigns: 1515–17 and from 1526 to *c.* 1547. The lateral window designs are divided into four scene areas, each spanning over two lights, and placed two scenes above two, with the central light of each tier occupied by a single figure composition. Hence, the major scenes cross the vertical stone mullions, cutting the events depicted, and sometimes even the figures, in half. Windows with such tall and comparatively narrow lights were designed for single figures and heraldic schemes such as can still be seen in the west window of Canterbury Cathedral and in the antechapel of All Souls Oxford. Something like this must have been the original intention for the glazing at King's, but by 1515 tastes and styles had changed. Evidently, the clerestory of the Henry VII Chapel at Westminster had already been filled with scenes similar to those at King's, possibly also in an early Renaissance style, and it was the Westminster windows that provided the model or at least the outline for Cambridge. The iconography, again taken from Westminster, was

188

188 King's College Chapel, the glass: detail of head, central lower light, Bay 7 N

2 Wayment numbers the windows of the Chapel from the westernmost on the north side, for him, I, but here Bay 12 N, and ending opposite, here Bay 12 S.

3 The west window received stained glass in 1879.

4 Willis and Clark, vol. I, pp. 474–5.

'The Old Law and the New', a familiar theme throughout the Middle Ages, in which parallels are drawn between events in the Old Testament and scenes from the Life of Christ i.e. The Triumph of David and Christ's entry into Jerusalem. The cycle begins in Bay 12N[2] and from there it moves east along the north side, crossing the east window at the Crucifixion, moving back along the south side to end in Bay 12 S. Thus the first and last windows face each other. As with most medieval stained glass cycles, the 'story' is told beginning to the left of the west door. The west window of King's though included in the original glass contracts, was not filled.[3]

The first contract for the existing glazing was signed on 30 November 1515, when £100 was paid on account to Barnard Flower, the royal glazier. There had been some glass in the Chapel since 1485 when panels containing heraldic beasts had been inserted.[4] In 1506, the College had paid Flower £30 out of the £100 given to them by Henry VII in order to complete the original glazing of the eastern bays of the Chapel, presumably with plain glass. The 1515 contract marks the start of a completely new glass cycle for the whole Chapel. By 1517, Flower was progressing on four of the existing windows, for which he was paid another £100 on 12 February. He died in the July or August of the same year, at which point work upon the glazing came to a standstill. Nothing more was done for nine years, due, it appears, to the reluctance of the executors of Henry VII to part with any more money. When work began again for the last time it was directly under the patronage of Henry VIII. A contract between the College and four glaziers, Galyon Hone, Richard Bond, Thomas Reve and James Nicholson, was drawn up on 30 April, 1526 under which the glaziers agreed to complete eighteen windows, including the east and west windows. Six were to be made during the first year and the twelve remaining over the next four years. A few days later, on 3 May 1526, Francis Williamson and Simon Symmondes undertook to glaze four windows, being two north and south. They had two years to complete the first pair, with a further three years for those remaining. According to these contracts, all the work should have been completed by May 1531. However, the glazing, like the rest of the fittings, dragged on into the late 1540s, with at least one window being finished only in *c.* 1547, while the west window appears never to have been begun. Henry VIII paid over a further £232 15s 9d to the College in June and July 1538, evidently to pay for the southern windows of the choir bays.

The College seems to have shown little sense of urgency about the work. By 1530, only about eight of the twenty-six windows needed had actually been inserted, all on the north side and spread erratically from Bays 1 to 12. But in 1537 the unexpected happened. The old College chapel fell down. Inconvenient though it had been, the old chapel had the virtue of being usable. Now the College had to act swifty in order to occupy the new Chapel as soon as possible. The choir bays from Bay 1 to Bay 7 had to be made ready with all speed. In the meantime, the College probably made use of the ill-prepared antechapel. The new altar in the choir was erected only in 1544, whilst the last of the windows of the choir bays dates from *c.* 1544–47. Once the choir bays were glazed and the scaffolding removed, work on the antechapel windows was taken up again, with the last window of all, Bay 11 S, inserted as late as *c.* 1547.

The random order in which the windows were made is somewhat surprising. It might be expected that the glass was inserted from Bay 12 eastwards both on the north and south, with the advantage that only one bay at a time would be encumbered with scaffolding. However, the dating currently proposed suggests that glass for at least six of the windows was in progress *c*. 1517, all on the north side and all from the early part of the iconographic cycle. There certainly appears to have been a northern bias during the early years – most of the glass on that side of the Chapel dates from before 1530 with only two windows containing some glass from the period 1535–40. The south side, by way of contrast, contains no work prior to 1535, while six of the windows on that side date from the 1540s. The situation is further confused by the reservation of finished scenes in the workshop, sometimes for many years, before being inserted in their correct iconographic sequence, e.g. Bay 7 N contains glass from 1517 whilst the tracery lights are of *c*. 1540.

The 'school' of glass painters has been identified as that of Southwark, which practised close to the great town house of Bishop Fox of Winchester, controller of the works at King's Cambridge on behalf of the executors of Henry VII. Barnard Flower, possibly a German, had worked for the English Crown since at least 1496 when he was employed at Woodstock. In addition, it is suspected that the glazier Galyon Hone was a Hollander, Nicholson and Williamson Netherlanders whilst the three others mentioned in the contracts were English, but with some continental training. It is accepted generally that the designs were based upon drawings by Dierick Vellert of Antwerp. The Renaissance character of the work has been closely examined and published elsewhere and is outside the scope of the architectural history of the building. However, attention should be paid to some of the architectural features occurring in the early, pre-1517 glass for any possible influence it may have exercised over the design of the pulpitum, for example, the busts in medallions.

The long glass campaign highlights the lax attitude of the College towards the use of the Chapel. After the completion of the fabric in the summer of 1515, only the most desultory effort was made to glaze and fit out the Chapel and to render the structure usable. Lack of money played its part, especially during the period 1517–26, but even when Henry VIII agreed to finance the glazing and fittings, the work still progressed only grudgingly and it took the collapse of the old chapel to instill any urgency. Despite even this, scaffolding still occupied the antechapel when Henry VIII lay on his deathbed. After his demise, no one was prepared to finance the completion of the glazing scheme and the west window stared vacantly for centuries.

The survival of the sixteenth-century glass is one of the most remarkable aspects in the entire history of King's College Chapel. The notorious John Dowsing visited the Chapel on 26 December 1643 on his tour of destruction. He noted in his diary on this occasion: 'Steps to be taken and 1 thousand Superstitious Pictures ye layder of Christ and theres to goe upon many crosses Jesus write on them'.[5] Despite this inchoate threat, the glass survived and was even repaired by the College on no less that eight occasions between 1643 and 1650.

No additions to the glass were made before 1827, when the College ordered that the half window in Bay 1 S should be extended as the rest and the scars of the Henry VI east range removed. While the work on the removal of the jagged scars was carried out, the extension of the window and the subsequent addition to the glazing cycle had to wait until 1845. The west window was finally filled with stained glass in 1879.

5 Ibid., p. 511.

189 King's College Chapel,
lectern with revolving
bookrest. The Tudor
Roses and the inscription
'Robertus' and
'Hacumblen' provide a
date of 1509–28
(Hacumblen as Provost)

BIBLIOGRAPHY

ALLINE, M., La Facade occidentale de la Cathedrale de Rouen. *Bulletin des Amis des Monuments rouennais* 1912.

ANDERSON, W., *The Architecture of the Renaissance in Italy*, London 1901.

AUBERT, M., Rouen, La Cathedrale. *Congres Archaeologique* LXXXIX 1926.

BAGGS, A., Sixteenth century terracotta tombs in East Anglia, *Archaeological Journal* CXXV 1968.

BAUCHAL, C.H., *Nouveau Dictionnaire des Architectes Français*, Paris 1887.

BONY, J., *The English Decorated Style*, Oxford 1979.

BRANNER, R., Paris and the origins of Rayonnant Gothic Architecture down to 1240, *Art Bulletin*, 44 1962.

BRANNER, R., *St Louis and the Court Style*, London 1965.

BRAYBROOKE, LORD, *The History of Audley End*, 1836.

BRITTON, J., *The Architectural Antiquities of Great Britain*, London 1807–1826.

BUSHELL, W.D., *The Church of St Mary the Great*, Cambridge 1947.

CAIUS, J., *Historiae Cantabrigiensis Academiae*, 1574.

CALEY, J. ed., *Valor Ecclesiasticus tempo Henry VIII auctoritate regia institutus*, London 1810–34.

CARTER, A., Excavations in Norwich 1973, *Norfolk Archaeology* 36 1973.

CARTER, T., *Notes on King's College Chapel Cambridge*, 1867.

COLVIN, H.M. et al., *The History of the King's Works*, London, vols I and II, 1963; vol. III, 1975.

COOK, G.H., *English Collegiate Churches*, London 1959.

COOK, G.H., *Medieval Chantries and Chantry Chapels*, London 1963.

ELTON, G., *Reform and Renewal*, Cambridge 1977.

ENLART, C., *Architecture Religieuse*, Paris 1902.

EVANS, J., *English Art 1307–1461*, Oxford 1949.

EWING, W., Notices of the Norwich Merchant's Marks, *Norfolk Archaeology* 3 1852.

FITCHEN, J., *The Construction of Gothic Cathedrals*, Chicago 1961.

FOSTER, J., *The Churchwardens Accounts of St Mary the Great, Cambridge*, Cambridge 1905.

FOWLER, K., *The Age of Plantagenet and Valois*, London 1967.

FREW, J., The Destroyer Vindicated? James Wyatt and the Restoration of the Henry VII Chapel at Westminster, *Journal of the British Archaeological Association* CXXIV 1981.

GOTCH, J., *Early Renaissance Architecture in England*, London 1901.

HARTWRIGHT, H., *The Story of the House of Lancaster*, London 1897.

HARVEY, J., OSWALD, A. et al., *English Medieval Architects, a Biographical Dictionary down to 1550*, London 1954.

HARVEY, J., The Origins of the Perpendicular Style, *Studies in Building History*, ed. Jope, London 1961.

HARVEY, J., *The Perpendicular Style*, London 1978.

HASTINGS, M., *St Stephen's Chapel Westminster*, Cambridge, 1956.

HEWETT, C., *English Medieval Carpentry*, Chichester, 1980.

HEYDENREICH, L. and LOTZ, W., *Architecture in Italy 1400–1600*, Harmondsworth 1974.

HEYMEN, J., Spires and Fan vaults, *International Journal of Solids and Structures*, 3 1967.

HOPE, W. ST. JOHN, *Windsor Castle*, London 1913.

HOWARD, F., Fan Vaults, *Archaeological Journal*, 68 1911.

INNES, A., *England under the Tudors*, London 1905.

JACOB, E.F., *The Fifteenth Century, Oxford History of England*, Oxford 1961.

JAMES, M.R., The Abbey of St Edmund's Bury, *Cambridge Antiquarian Society, Octavo Publications* XXVIII 1895.

KIDSON, P., The Architecture of St George's Chapel, *The St George's Chapel Quincentenary Handbook*, ed. M. Bond, Windsor 1975.

KNOOP, D. and JONES, G., The Building of Eton College, *Ars Quatuor Coronatorum* XLVI 1933.

KNOOP, D. and JONES, G., *The Medieval Mason*, Manchester 1949.

LANCE, J., *Dictionnaire des Architects Français*, Paris 1872.

LEEDY, W., *Fan Vaulting, A Study of Form, Technology and Meaning*, London 1980.

LEHMBERG, J., *The Reformation Parliament*, Cambridge 1970.

LETHABY, W., *Westminster Abbey Reexamined*, London 1925.

LOGGAN, D., *Cantabrigia Illustrata*, 1690.

LYTE, M., *History of Eton College*, 1889.

MACKENZIE, F., *The Architectural Antiquities of the Collegiate Chapel of St Stephen's Westminster*, London 1844.

MACKENZIE, F., *Observations of the Construction of the Roofs of King's College Chapel Cambridge*, London 1840.

MACKIE, J., *The Earlier Tudors, Oxford History of England*, Oxford 1952.

MARKS, R., The Patronage of Sir Reginald Bray, *Friends of St George's Windsor*, 5 1973.

MATHEW, D., *The Courtiers of Henry VIII*, London 1970.

MORRIS, R., *Cathedrals and Abbeys of England and Wales*, London 1979.

OSWALD, A., Andrew Doket and his Architect, *Cambridge Antiquarian Society Proceedings* XLII 1949.

PEVSNER, N., *Cambridgeshire, The Buildings of England*, Harmondsworth 1970.

PURCELL, D., *Cambridge Stone*, London 1962.

RACKHAM, H., *Christ's College in Former Days*, Cambridge 1939.

REYNOLDS, S., *English Medieval Towns*, Oxford 1972.

ROYAL COMMISSION ON HISTORICAL MONUMENTS, *Oxford*, London 1939; *Cambridge*, London 1959.

SALET, F., La Madalaine Troyes, *Dictionnaire des Eglise de France*, 5 1968.

SALTMARSH, J., *King's College*, Cambridge 1959.

See also *Cambridgeshire, Victoria County History*, 3 1959.

SALZMAN, L., *Building in England down to 1540*, Oxford 1952.

SANDARS, S., *Historical and Architectural notes on Great St Mary's Church, Cambridge*, Cambridge 1869.

SANFACON, R., *L'Architecture Flamboyant en France*, Quebec 1971.

SCOTT, G.G., *Essay on the History of English Gothic Architecture*, London 1881.

SIGNORET, P., Mortagne au Perche, *Dictionnaire des Eglise de France*, 4 1968.

SOMERVILLE, R.: *The Duchy of Lancaster*, London 1953.

STEIN, H., *Les Architectes des Cathedrales Gothique*, Paris 1929.

SUMMERSON, J., *Architecture in Britain 1530–1830*, Harmondsworth 1953.

SUTERMEISTER, H., *The Norwich Blackfriars*, Norwich 1977.

THOMPSON, P., *Boston*, 1856.

TIBBS, R., *King's College Chapel Cambridge*, Lavenham 1970.

TYMMS, S., *The Church of St Mary, Bury St Edmunds*, 1854.

VICKERS, H., *England in the later Middle Ages*, London 1913.

WATKINS, D., The Virtue of Magnificence, *Architectural Review* CXLV 1969.

WAYMENT H., King's College Chapel, *Corpus Vitriearum Medii Aevi. Great Britain Supplementary Volume I*, Oxford 1972.

WEBB, G., *Architecture in Britain in the Middle Ages*, Harmondsworth 1956.

WHITTINGHAM, A., St Gregory's Church, Charing Cross Norwich, *Archaeological Journal* 137 1981.

WILLIS, R., On the Construction of the vaults of the Middle Ages, *Transactions of the Royal Institute of British Architects* I Pt II 1842.

WILLIS, R. and CLARK, J., *The Architectural History of the University of Cambridge*, Cambridge 1886.

WILSON, C., The Original Design of the City of London Guildhall, *Journal of the British Archaeological Association* CXXIX 1976.

WOODMAN, F., Great St Mary's, a Quincentenary, *Cambridge Review* C 1978.

WOODMAN, F., The Blackfriar's Norwich, *Archaeological Journal* 137 1981.

WOODMAN, F., *The Architectural History of Canterbury Cathedral*, London 1981.

WOODMAN, F., The Vault of the Ely Lady Chapel, *Gesta*, 23 Pt 2 New York 1984.

INDEX